Good Book

THE ASPEN ACCOUNT

—————⊷⊱※⊰⊶—————

BRYAN DEVORE

Printed in the United States of America.

ISBN-10: 0-9852413-0-6
ISBN-13: 978-0-9852413-0-8

Also available as an e-book.

Those who wish to acquire favor with a ruler most often approach him with those among their possessions that are most valuable in their eyes, or that they are confident will give him pleasure.
—Niccolò Machiavelli, *The Prince,* 1527

Virtue alone is for real; all else is sham. Talent and greatness depend on virtue, not on fortune. Only virtue is sufficient unto herself. She makes us love the living and remember the dead.
—Baltasar Gracian, *The Art of Worldly Wisdom,* 1647

Prologue

———— ❋ ————

Vail Mountain, Colorado

KURT MATTHEWS FELT as though he had just made a deal with the devil—a deal he had no intention of keeping. As he sat gazing over the forty-foot drop, a cold gust brushed across his face and nearly blew the lit joint out of his gloved hand. He looked out over the tops of the evergreens and aspens sloping down below him. Hearing a rustle behind him, he swore at how easily he had let himself be lured into the secluded woods in the ski resort's back bowls. He fought to appear relaxed.

"You're doing the right thing, Kurt," said the voice behind him. "Just do what you're told for the next month and everything'll work out fine."

Right. Something sarcastic in that tone—he was just being toyed with. To his right, through the trees, the trail ran past like a white, frozen river, a group of four skiers working their way down the far edge of its challenging terrain. How hard would it be to get off this ledge and escape through the woods? He was a good skier, and he would have a fair chance of racing to safety if he could just get out of the trees and onto the open trail.

"A month is a long time," Kurt said without turning around. "I don't see how you can keep it a secret." If he wanted to make it out of these snowy woods alive, he had to sound convincing, as if he would help keep it all under wraps.

"My God," the voice said. "You really don't know what you've stumbled on, do you?"

There was a brief silence, then a sudden hiss behind him— the sound of a fast movement in ski clothes. He must have made a mistake, said something wrong. He spun around just as something hard *thwacked* across the side of his head. Though the heavy ski boots slowed him, he still managed to get one hand on the front of his attacker's red ski coat. Looking into his attacker's eyes, Kurt felt rage explode inside him as the man cocked the metal baton for another strike. Kurt lowered his head and tried to lunge, but the baton arced again, knocking his hand from the coat and sending him reeling backward. He felt himself slide on the snow, toward the drop-off.

Frantically, Kurt scrabbled in the snow with his hands, then tried to dig in with his elbows as he slid backward. A second later, he felt the snow disappear underneath him. Falling over the ledge, he fell through the air, his speed gaining. His left thigh hit something hard, but he kept falling. Then, with a thudding jolt, he was lying in the snow, looking at the rocky ledge above.

Pain shrieked through his back. His legs felt as if they were someone else's, and raising his head, he saw a bright red stain in the snow. Rolling sluggishly onto his stomach, he glimpsed a skier gliding by not fifty yards away, through the trees. Stabbing his gloved hands deep, he struggled to haul himself a few feet forward through the loose powder, ski boots dragging behind him like useless clubs. A group of three snowboarders floated past, weaving in and out of the outermost trees with barely a sound. He cried out, knowing he was too far back in the trees to be heard. As another bolt of pain shot through his head, he dragged himself forward another few feet.

A swooshing sound came from above—his attacker was skiing around the rocky ledge to get down to him. Adrenaline fired, pulsing through his body as he hauled himself forward, toward the open trail, still a hundred feet away.

You can do this, Kurt told himself. *Stay focused. You can make it . . .*

Pulling himself through the stand of pale aspen trunks, half blinded by the pain, he heard the swooshing above him grow louder.

1

---※---

MICHAEL CHAPMAN KNEW that he had just made the biggest mistake of his young life. Sitting in the small cubicle padded with puncture-friendly walls, he rubbed his temple to ward off a looming headache. He had gotten a little too careless during the past few months, taking too many chances, and now some of them had caught up with him. He looked at his watch: almost three—the conference meeting would begin in a few minutes. Rising from his ergonomically designed chair, he straightened his tie, took a deep breath, and walked toward the corner conference room at the end of the long hallway.

"It's just a game," he whispered nervously to himself, walking through the offices of the largest international accounting firm in Denver. "Stay focused—it's just a game."

The Pike's Peak conference room was one of eight gravitas boardrooms spread throughout Cooley and White, in its towering office building downtown. A smooth white marble conference table stretching the length of the room was surrounded by twenty black leather chairs. As Michael entered the room, he glanced out the window. Seeing the snow-capped Rockies rising in the distance behind the Front Range, he recalled his job interview with Cooley and White, nearly two years ago in this very room. So much had changed during those two years that he only vaguely remembered the excitement he had felt on joining the firm. Now, with his career on the line, he just needed to keep his anxiety at bay long enough to survive the meeting.

The other three audit associates, already seated, were avoiding eye contact with him. Michael was their supervisor on the current audit for Pipco Industries, one of the Denver office's twenty biggest clients. The engagement had gone like clockwork for the first two months, but as pressure for the work deadline mounted this past month, things had suddenly turned disastrous. Now he and his three subordinates waited for the emergency meeting called by his boss, John Falcon.

The door to the conference room opened, and Falcon strode into the room. For a senior audit partner working an average of a hundred hours a week, the man still found time to stay remarkably fit. Rumor had it that he slept only four hours a night. His jet-black hair and trim, tanned physique belied his fifty years, and his nonstop energy had made him one of the most successful of the firm's forty partners. Falcon stood stiffly across the table, staring at the four auditors and making no attempt to hide his ire.

With over seven hundred offices across the globe, Cooley and White was one of the biggest international accounting firms in the world, and its Denver office was more than twice the size of the next largest firm in the city. And Michael well knew one of the main reasons for the firm's dominance: mistakes were not tolerated.

"This is a complete disaster!" Falcon said, pressing his palms to the conference table and leaning forward. He stared a hole in each of them. "I can't believe you've upset a client that pays us over a million dollars a year! Do you realize that the CFO personally called me to complain?"

The young auditors squirmed in silence. Michael suddenly realized that they were all in much more trouble than even he had thought.

Falcon turned from the table and moved to the window. Thirty-seven floors below, the city awaited a winter storm that was already swallowing up the mountains before their eyes.

Michael focused on keeping his composure. Half an hour ago, he could almost taste the strong lime margaritas at the Rio in LoDo's bar district, where he was to meet two coworkers, Kurt Matthews and Todd Osgood, for an early happy hour. Now all he wanted was to keep his job.

Falcon turned from the window, rubbing his forehead. "Look," he said evenly, "I just spent thirty minutes in a meeting discussing how we're going to respond. Do you guys realize how serious this is? We lost original invoice documents that belonged to the client. How the hell could that have happened? Michael, you're the senior on the engagement—it's your job to supervise the team in the field. Care to explain what happened?"

Despite his effort to relax, Michael could already feel the sweat beading on his forehead. "This was a big misunderstanding," he said. "No one knew what happened to the documents. The client thought they had given them to us, but we thought *they* still had them."

"Well, which is it?" Falcon demanded.

It was me, *damn it,* Michael thought to himself. *I broke firm policy—took the original documents from the client's premises and hid them in the trunk of my car for two days. There was no other way.* "We don't know," he said. "The documents turned up a few days after we noticed they were missing."

"They just 'turned up'?" Falcon said, raising his eyebrows in mock astonishment.

"I found them," said the young blonde woman sitting next to Michael. Her fingers fidgeted on the table without her knowing it as she withered under his gaze. "They were buried under some of the workpapers in the audit room."

"They were with our papers the whole time?" Falcon asked. "So the client was right—we did have them."

"No," she replied. "We had already looked through everything when they went missing. I searched everything—we all did. I swear they weren't there before."

"But they *were* there, Amanda," Falcon insisted. "If you had found them the first time you looked, we would have avoided all this."

Leave her alone, Michael wanted to say. *It's me you want. After two days I put them in a pile of work papers where I knew someone would find them. She's innocent.* But all he said was, "It's not her fault, John. We all stacked workpapers around the area, and the client kept bringing things in and out. These just got misplaced in the shuffle."

"You're missing the point here," Falcon said. "Misplacing the documents for a few days wouldn't have been the end of the world. It's what happened next that really upset the client."

"The accusation," Michael said.

Falcon nodded. "It was way out of line. Do you realize how bad it looks that you guys accused the client of misplacing these docs, only to find out that you had them the whole time? Do you know how serious that is? The client's procurement manager was terrified she would get fired over this, and the controller was taking heat from the CFO. Then the documents turn up in *our files,* and everyone realizes the whole thing was really our fault. Christ, people thought they were going to lose their *jobs.* This has struck a real nerve with the client—I'm doing everything I can to keep us from losing their business."

"John," Michael said, "I'm sorry this got so out of control, but I've apologized to the CFO and everyone else involved. We had a long talk, so hopefully things will calm down at Pipco."

"Well, that's something, at least, but it may be too little, too late. I was also appalled that you didn't properly document the sales transaction of the discontinued operations. You should know better than to blow past an issue that important. You were careless."

"I'm sorry about the problems on the engagement," Michael said, "and I take full responsibility for what happened, but I think we can still—"

Falcon's upraised hand cut him off, and Falcon shook his head as if to say there was no point in continuing the discussion. "It doesn't matter anymore. All of you have been pulled off the engagement. It was the client's request, and to be honest, I agree with them. We can't afford to lose them. You will transfer all your files to me, and I'll forward them to the *new* team that will be out there next week."

Falcon strode toward the door and opened it while motioning for everyone to leave the room. "I still need to decide what we're going to do with the four of you, but for the time being I think you all need to give some serious thought to everything that went wrong on this engagement."

The mortified staff auditors rose from the conference table and left the room with eyes lowered, unable to look at the senior partner as they walked past. Michael put himself last in the procession so he could offer one final apology, but before he could open his mouth, Falcon shut the door so that they were the only two in the room.

"This is your third project in a row where something has gone seriously wrong," he said.

"Yeah, I know," Michael replied. But he offered no explanation, no rehearsed defense, nothing to counter the grave indictment. He knew he had been pressing his luck for the past few months, and for the first time, he considered the terrifying possibility that he had finally pushed it too far.

Seeing that Michael had nothing to say in his own defense, Falcon shook his head. "The others will all get negative evaluations in their employee files for their part in the project, but for you this is a little more serious." He looked at his watch. "I'd like to take a moment to cool down, but then I want to see you in my office in fifteen minutes."

When Michael finally walked out of the room, he looked at his watch and made a quick note of the time. *Fifteen minutes.* That might give him just enough time to leave the building and make an urgent call in case this proved to be the end of his career at Cooley and White. Walking down the hallway as fast as he could without drawing attention, he grabbed his coat from his cubicle and moved past glass-walled offices and more cubicles to the marble-floored elevator bay. Hitting the button, he stepped back and looked again at his watch. *Fourteen minutes.* He would need to hurry.

2

---✺---

MICHAEL WALKED OUT the revolving glass doors to the Wynkoop Courtyard, where fat clumps of snow drifted like goose down on the faint breeze. On sunny days, the courtyard had a lunch crowd of three hundred, but today's storm had left it under a foot of snow, and empty. To make sure he couldn't be overheard by anyone coming or going from the building, he walked into the center of the plaza. He stepped out into the open, lowered his head, and punched in a number on his cell phone as wet snow fell down the back of his jacket collar.

"Glazier," a crisp voice answered.

"It's Chapman."

"Michael? What the . . . ! You can't just call me like this. We're scheduled to talk next week."

"I wish it could wait, but there's something you need to know right away."

"Make it brief."

"Something happened today," he began. "There were some mistakes made on a project."

"Any trouble for you?"

Michael swiped the snow off a concrete bench with his arm and sat in the center of the desolate courtyard. "I didn't think there would be. I've been in this situation before, so I assumed I would still have a little breathing room with the firm."

"You *assumed*?"

"Damn it, Glazier. It's right before busy season. The firm can't afford to let anyone go this time of year. A slap on the wrist—that's all I expected. It's the only way this'll work, and you know it."

"Not if you get fired. You can't let that happen, no matter what. It would ruin everything."

Michael squeezed the phone tight. His fingers were getting cold. He looked at his watch: six minutes.

"I've been pulled from my current project. My entire team's being reassigned. And now I have to meet privately with Falcon."

"Shit! What did you *do*?" After a brief pause, the voice known as Glazier said, "Look, too much is riding on the line. I don't care what you have to do—just make sure you still have your job at the end of the day. I don't have to tell you what'll happen if you get fired—too many people are depending on you."

"I've gotta go, Glazier. I just wanted to update you. I'll touch base later."

Michael snapped the phone shut and turned to look up at the dark monolith that housed Cooley and White. Even in the muted light of snowfall, the building's black windowed surface had a slick sheen that earned it the nickname of the "Darth Vader building." It was an image of power, but also of gloom and despair. Walking back across the snowy courtyard, toward the revolving doors and the inviting warmth inside, he felt as if he were heading back into the lion's den. Glazier's words lingered in his mind: . . . *just make sure you still have your job at the end of the day.* His contact was right, of course. Everything they had done together for the past three years could be destroyed in the next twenty minutes of his life.

*   *   *

"Michael. Please, come in." Falcon's demeanor had softened in the short time since their last meeting, and Michael was terrified that the man was taking the polite, respectful attitude often extended to someone before they got the sack.

He glanced around Falcon's office, taking in his surroundings, as if he might somehow save his career by understanding the man who now held it in his hands. On the shelf sat a family photo, a black-and-white that reminded him of one of those old Austrian films set in the Alps. There were professional certificates from various states and universities, and a watercolor of aspen groves in a hanging valley.

"Well, Michael," Falcon began, "I want to get right to the point. I know you've already had some meetings about your problems on your past few engagements. Because of these new problems, there has now been a great deal of discussion between the partners regarding your future at the firm."

He paused to let this last comment sink in before continuing. "It has been suggested that we let you go from the firm. Michael, I don't know if you realize this, but after we conclude our work this year for Pipco, there's a very good chance they will begin shopping around for another accounting firm. We could be losing a client that generated substantial revenue for our firm last year. That is not a mistake many people in your position would survive."

Michael didn't say anything. He sat in silence, maintained eye contact with the partner, and nodded his head, looking appropriately concerned, aware that the wrong word or gesture could spell the end for him at the firm. *You can't get fired.*

"When you joined our firm two years ago, you had scored in the top one percent in the country on the CPA exam. You were one of our most promising young professionals. But over the past six months you seem to have lost interest in your career. Your performance evaluations have gone from 'exceeded expectations' to 'met expectations' to 'needs improvement.' Michael, I don't understand this. Is this really the profession that you want to be in? You need to tell me what's going on."

For what seemed an eternity, Michael looked down at the desk. What would his father think of him if he could hear this? Ernest Chapman, one of the most respected accounting professors in the Midwest, had written textbooks, won national awards, and was practically a deity at Kansas State. It horrified Michael to think of how his father would feel if he knew his son was on the verge of getting fired from this prestigious firm.

He could see the bright image of snow, rising in reflection on the polished desktop as it drifted downward outside the window. Falcon had a point, though—Michael *was* growing tired of his life in the firm. All he really wanted right now was to go have a margarita with Kurt and Todd. Why should he put himself through this torture? *No, just a little longer,* he told himself. *Just last a little longer and you'll be free.*

He could feel Falcon's eyes on him. "I've been having some personal problems lately," he lied.

"Michael, we all have problems, but in this kind of environment we need to handle those problems, or we won't succeed."

"I know, I know," he said apologetically.

"Look, we want you to be able to succeed here, but this situation has become so severe that we need to formally place you on our 'action plan' program. You need to come up with a detailed plan specifying exactly what areas you need to improve on and how you plan to achieve each of your goals. I need to see some immediate improvements. Traditionally, the time frame for the action plan is thirty days, but because we're in our second week of busy season, I've decided to extend it to sixty days. That should give you the entire busy season to show us if you're ready to continue your career at Cooley and White."

A swarm of thoughts surged through his mind, the most prominent being that he still had his job. After everything he had done in the past few months, he had somehow been able to diminish his reputation within the firm without being fired. This last incident had nearly been the end to everything he had worked so hard to achieve, but somehow, after the dust had settled, he was still standing. Glazier was right: he had been way too careless. There would be no more room for mistakes.

"Thank you for this second chance," he said. "I will get my personal life together and will focus one hundred percent of my energy on improving my performance."

The partner smiled. "I know you will. Let's get the plan on paper in the next few days so we can see how we're going to tackle this. Unfortunately, I've had to take you off the Pipco engagement. But we'll get you scheduled on another client by next week, and then we could . . ." Falcon broke off his sentence as his phone rang. He looked at the number and then back at Michael. "Well, let's circle back on this tomorrow morning." He turned and picked up the phone.

Michael flipped open his portfolio and made a quick note. Then, closing the folder, he stood up to leave the office.

"Oh, my God," Falcon said into the phone. "No, no, Patti. Thank you, but I should be the one to send an announcement to everyone . . . No, I'm okay . . . I'll take care of it."

Michael turned back to look at the senior partner after the call ended. Falcon was looking with a bemused face at the receiver.

"Is everything all right?"

Falcon shook his head. "That was my admin. She just received a phone call from Kurt Matthews's parents. There was some kind of skiing accident. This morning his body was found, frozen in the woods at Vail."

All his life, Michael had never been good at handling death. He tried to take a deep breath, but the air felt shallow and insufficient in his lungs. He felt as if he were suffocating. The horrible realization was settling into his mind. Not Kurt . . . It wasn't possible. His eyes focused again on the impressionistic painting of aspen trees—shimmering yellow leaves and a dusting of new snow. His head felt light; the painting seemed to give off a sense of violent chaos. He had to leave Falcon's office, had to quit the firm. He had to get out. But no matter how badly he wanted to start a new life, he knew that he couldn't leave Cooley and White . . . not yet—not until the game was over.

3

⸺⋅⊩✳⊪⋅⸺

THE SILVER ELEVATOR doors opened on the eighth floor
of the Commerce Building, headquarters of the *Denver
Post*. The young woman with flaming red hair stepped into a
hive of activity as various staff reporters and seasoned journalists
pounded away on their laptops, scrambling to file their stories
before deadline. A small cluster of employees hovered around a
mounted television, making snide remarks as a politician spoke
into a dozen microphones. But the redheaded woman kept her
head low and largely ignored the activity around her.

"Oh, my God, Sarah, you poor thing! What are you doing
here?" a veteran copyeditor said, getting up from her desk and
rushing toward her.

"Mrs. Adams," the young woman said, "is Jack around?"

The copyeditor reached forward and gently grabbed the
woman's shoulders as if she had just returned unharmed from
some perilous journey. "Oh, Sarah, I'm so sorry. Come here,
child." She pulled the woman close and hugged her. "You
shouldn't have come in. You know you don't have to be here—
everyone would understand."

"Is Jack around?" Sarah Matthews asked again in a quiet voice.

The copyeditor gently released her. "Honey, he's in his office."

Sarah nodded. "I'm okay. Really. I just need to ask Jack a question." And taking a deep breath, she nodded briefly before sidling around the woman and heading to the senior editor's office.

Her knuckles made a hollow dinging sound on the glass door. Jack Bayman looked up from his phone and waved her in. He sat hunched over his desk, tie loosened, sleeves up. Barking some final words into the receiver, he hung up.

"Sarah, you shouldn't be here," he said, standing up and sending his chair rolling backward. "I want you to take the week off."

"Jack, I have a story I want you to put me on."

"A *story*? Jesus, what are you trying to do to yourself! You're in no condition to investigate anything right now." He shook his head in bewilderment. "Go home, Sarah. Please, take some time off. That's not a suggestion; it's an order."

She stood her ground. "Jack, after I broke the McCleery story, you said I could pursue anything I wanted for my next major piece—you promised."

"And you can. But you oughta give yourself some time off right now? I don't know of *any* journalist who would be back at work after what you've been through. Take a week off, and we'll discuss any story you want once you come back."

Sarah was getting frustrated now. She hadn't expected this resistance from her editor. She knew he was just trying to help, but she also knew she didn't have a choice.

"This story can't wait," she said with a crackle of frustration in her voice. "I've already started on it. If you don't support me, I'll just quit and freelance it to the *Tribune* or the *Times* when I'm finished."

"Come on, Sarah . . ." Her boss stepped around from behind the desk, studying her determined expression. "You're the best rookie reporter I've seen in years. I'm not going to lose you. You know this paper's behind you all the way. I just think it's too early for you to be back here. I've seen too many good journalists burn out in this job just as their careers were reaching their prime. It's a tough business. You'll learn that in time, but meanwhile you should learn to take it easy when your editor tells you to."

"Jack, this story's a hell of a lot bigger than a slimy city manager." She walked forward and grabbed the copy of the *Post*'s morning edition on his desk. Picking up a red pen, she scrawled something in the margin of the front page.

Jack leaned in to read it, and his eyes shot up to her. "That's crazy."

She shook her head.

"I don't believe you," he said. "What could you possibly have?"

"I can't tell you—not yet."

Jack turned and walked to the outside window. He stared out at the vast lawn, turning brown in the early winter weather, that stretched between City Hall and the Capitol. Pedestrians moved between the two buildings, past park benches where a few homeless people lounged in the sunshine.

"Okay," he said. "I'll let you look into it. But you sure as hell better keep me informed on this one. No more of that cloak-and-dagger crap like with the McCleery story. If you really do find something, we'll discuss running it. But it better be airtight, understand?"

When he turned around to look at Sarah, he saw only the glass door swinging to and a flash of red hair bobbing around the corner.

*   *   *

Michael walked into Falcon's empty office Thursday morning. The partner's laptop sat on the other side of the desk, and its whisper fan told him the man couldn't be far away.

"Morning, Michael," Falcon said as he walked into the office. "Glad you could make it."

"Morning."

"Michael, this is regarding Kurt Mathews. I know the two of you were good friends. Kurt was also one of my five senior associates, just like you are. He was supervising one of my biggest clients."

"X-Tronic," Michael said, referring to the largest software company in Colorado and the fourth largest in the country. They specialized in large-scale business application software that rivaled Oracle, Microsoft, and Cygnus International.

"Yes. Well, as difficult and shocking as his death is, we still have business in the firm that needs to be done. We're right in the middle of our three-month scheduled work for their year-end financial audit. My team's been working at X-Tronic for the past six weeks, and Kurt was running the engagement in the field. We're in a real bind with scheduling, so you've been assigned to replace him until we complete the engagement. I know it must seem awkward to take over for a coworker and friend so soon after his death, but we have to get this done. Now, despite the terrible circumstances that brought it about, you should recognize this as the golden opportunity it is: you can get off the probation you've been placed on."

Michael was speechless. Yesterday his neck was on the block, and today he was being handed the lead of the X-Tronic audit team. He could scarcely believe his luck. During graduate school at Kansas State, he had written extensively about X-Tronic and its ambitious founder, Don Seaton, in his thesis examining the correlation between ambitious corporate leadership and innovative financial growth strategies. Mr. Seaton had become a legend in the world of high-tech executives, rising from a humble upbringing in New York City to become a self-made billionaire through the success of X-Tronic. There was no businessman in the world whom Michael respected more.

But Michael's excitement was soon eclipsed by the reality of his situation. He felt a twinge of guilt at the thought of finishing the project Kurt had begun. It had been less than twenty-four hours since he first heard of his friend's death, and now he would have to sift and scavenge through his friend's computer files and work papers, searching for any information relevant to the audit engagement. He felt ashamed. How could he just start working on X-Tronic as if nothing had happened? How could he just brush aside his friend's death?

"When do you want me to go out to X-Tronic?" Michael asked, hoping he would be given some time to digest the news.

"Right away," Falcon said without emotion. "I'm e-mailing you the contact information and directions now. Kurt's work papers are in the audit room they set up at the company, and I'm having the IT department scrub the files from his laptop for anything related to X-Tronic. You should have those by this afternoon."

Michael stood and turned to leave the room, but Falcon stopped him. "Oh, one more thing—I'm afraid I'm going to have to keep a close eye on you during this engagement. I don't have to tell you this is your last chance to succeed at this firm. If you do exactly what I ask, we won't have any problems. We just need to get through the next month; then the project will be done."

Michael nodded, but he had concerns. There weren't a lot of good reasons for Falcon to put him on an audit of one of the firm's largest clients. Sure it was possible that the scheduling committee had found no better options because of Kurt's sudden death. But getting assigned to a large client after repeated mistakes was a scenario Glazier had warned him about. His instincts were now on high alert.

4

⸺⸻•◦✻◦•⸻⸺

FORTY-FIVE MINUTES AFTER leaving Falcon's office, Michael arrived at the Denver Tech Center high-rise that would be his workplace for the next two months. Stepping out of his silver Audi, he slung his computer bag over his shoulder and looked up at the impressive twenty-story glass building in the center of the corporate suburbs. So this was the headquarters of X-Tronic. The software company had acquired fame fifteen years ago when it bought up three smaller companies and beat a hostile takeover bid from a larger competitor during the same twelve-month period.

Over the past four years, he had kept up with developments at X-Tronic. On the front page of the *Wall Street Journal,* the company had continuously beaten analysts' earnings expectations, just as it had been one of the few stocks whose price continued to rise even during the sluggish financial markets of the dot-com collapse many years earlier. He found it hard to believe that he was now in charge of auditing their financial statements—the same statements that would have the attention of the financial wizards of Wall Street.

The lobby, floored with a harlequin pattern of elegant red and black marble slabs, was the size of a basketball court. A few expensive couches in the center divided the entrance from the security desk at the far end. He walked across the marble floor toward the security officer, who was already eyeing him.

"I'm here to see Jerry Diamond," Michael said. "I'm one of the auditors from Cooley and White."

"Is this your first time at X-Tronic?" the guard asked in a bored monotone.

"Yes."

"One moment, please." The guard flipped around to his computer. "Your name, please?"

"Michael Chapman."

"Yes, here it is. Looks like you'll need an extended pass."

"I plan to be here for two months."

"Follow this corridor down to the elevators. You'll need a security pass to go up into the building, but you don't need anything to go down. Just go to the basement and follow the yellow line on the floor. It leads from the elevator to the main security office. They'll check your identification and issue you a pass. Then come back to me, and I'll tell Mr. Diamond you're ready."

Michael wasn't surprised at the tight security; after all, programming codes and other intellectual property were any software company's lifeblood. If the wrong person ever got access to sensitive information in the building, it could cost the company its competitive advantage and billions of dollars in future revenues.

Michael spent the next fifteen minutes getting his security pass. Afterward, waiting in the lobby for Mr. Diamond, he gazed up at the eighteenth-century French painting that covered much of one wall. An ancient Roman in a red cloak offered swords to the extended arms of three warriors while, at the far right side, a small group of women huddled in an archway, weeping in each other's arms.

"It's very powerful, isn't it?"

Hearing the friendly baritone voice behind him, Michael turned to find a man in his mid-forties, wearing a tailored suit. He was big: six-four and 250, most of it muscle. And his square jaw and shaved head made him look like a battle-hardened field general transposed into a life requiring tailored business suits instead of razor-creased uniforms.

"Have you seen it before?"

"*The Oath of the Horatii,*" Michael answered, "but not the original."

"How can you tell?"

"Because I saw it in the Louvre three years ago."

The man smiled. "Do you know what is happening in the painting, or did you just memorize the name in Paris?"

Michael realized he was being tested, and saw little reason to hold back now that the challenge had been extended.

"The three brothers, the Horatii"—he gestured with his eyes at the three men receiving the proffered swords—"were chosen by Rome to challenge the Curiatii, champions of the town of Alba. In this scene, as they receive their weapons from their father, they are taking an oath that they will either win or die."

"Win or die?"

"Yes. It symbolizes courage in the face of risk—and the desire for dominance."

"And the women?"

"Weeping for the men, whom they may never see again."

"Very good. Michael Chapman, I presume?"

"Yes," Michael said, extending his arm in the same direction as the Horatii in the painting. "Jerry Diamond?"

The man nodded. "Please follow me and I'll introduce you around."

They walked to the elevators, and Diamond pushed the button, then turned to look back at the corridor. "One more question, Mr. Chapman: why do you think X-Tronic has that painting in its lobby?"

Michael looked at the man's dark eyes. "I thought it was X-Tronic's way of saying this is an extremely competitive software company."

Diamond smiled. "Good, Mr. Chapman. Very good indeed. By the way, that painting *is* the original. Mr. Seaton purchased it from the Louvre for fifteen million dollars when he was in Paris last year, and insisted that it be placed in the front lobby so that everyone would see it when they first enter the building." He stepped aside and gestured for Michael to take the first step into the elevator. "Welcome to X-Tronic, Mr. Chapman."

5

————————◦✳◦————————

THE TWENTIETH FLOOR of X-Tronic was a warren of cubicles surrounding large, open work areas in what was essentially a very high-end sweatshop. Diamond showed Michael through the main accounting department before they moved around the corner wing of the top floor. An immense glass-walled conference room stretched twenty feet along the hallway, looking isolated from the rest of the corporation's activities. Piles of documents two feet high lined the inside wall and covered much of the long cherrywood conference table.

"This conference room has been reserved for external auditors," Diamond said. He glanced at his watch. "As you meet with people today, please keep in mind that everyone's pretty swamped right now. Tensions are high because of the visit from the board of the directors."

"They're having a board meeting today?" Michael said, shifting the heavy computer bag's strap on his shoulder.

"Mm-hm. They all jumped on flights to Denver for an emergency session as soon as we got word of Cygnus's takeover bid."

Seeing Michael's astonished look, he said, "Ah, you haven't heard yet? I guess the public only got this information a few hours ago. Yesterday Cygnus International made an informal takeover bid for X-Tronic. The potential merger would create the third-largest software company in the U.S., just behind Microsoft and Oracle. Some members of management and the board are in favor of the offer; others aren't. I'm afraid things are starting to heat up around here."

"I'll keep that in mind," Michael said. He wondered why Falcon hadn't mentioned anything to him—surely the partner would have been privy to the information before it was announced to the public.

"Well, if you want to just throw your things in here, we can continue our tour."

Michael set his computer bag next to the conference table, and the two proceeded down the hallway. He had never seen such extravagant corporate offices. The rounded metal cubicles looked straight out of the latest science fiction film, and the break rooms felt like eclectic bars.

Having circled most of the floor, they entered the final corridor. To Michael's surprise, the environment here was even more lavish. The carpet was finer, and the chestnut-paneled hallway was hung with enormous scenic photographs capturing the isolated beauty of deep mountain ranges covered in snow.

"This is the executive wing," Diamond said, anticipating Michael's question. "My office is at the end of the hallway. That's Don Seaton's office." He pointed to a large corner suite.

Inside the glass walls, Michael could see a classic mahogany desk worthy of the Oval Office. Two chairs sat facing the desk for the occasional business formalities, but in the other half of the office were two leather sofas, implying that at least some of Mr. Seaton's meetings took place in a more leisurely setting.

"Mr. Seaton won't be here until tomorrow," Diamond continued. "He's usually here only one or two days a week.

Sometime he's traveling for business, but he works pretty light hours these days."

"What does he do when he's not here?"

Diamond stopped and turned to look at him. "The mountains got some good snow earlier this week, so he's probably out heli-skiing today."

"He *heli-skis*?" Michael didn't try to conceal his astonishment. "But he must be, what, seventy?"

"I know—crazy, isn't it?" Diamond said. "But then, Mr. Seaton isn't your average seventy-year-old. His helicopter flies him to the summits of the most remote mountains. There are no other people around, and he and his friends are free to ski down fresh, untouched powder." As they stood in the middle of the executive hallway, he leaned in toward Michael, then tensed for just a beat, as if realizing that he was revealing more about the billionaire than was prudent. "He also has a mansion in Aspen, where he spends most of his time. Since it's three hours into the mountains, he often just stays there for the entire week."

"It's good to be king," Michael said. "But . . . who's in charge of running things if he's gone so much?"

Diamond nodded toward an office a few doors down. "Mr. Seaton has twin sons: Lance and Lucas. They both finished their MBAs at Harvard Business School four years ago, and Mr. Seaton has been priming them for the top executive jobs ever since. As copresidents, they're mostly responsible for X-Tronic's day-to-day operations, but they also play the role of CEO when Mr. Seaton is unavailable."

Suddenly, a wave of shouting exploded from a nearby doorway. Neither of them could make out what was being said, but it was clear that an argument had just erupted. Diamond tried to get Michael to move back the other direction, but Michael easily sidestepped him to get a better view of the office. He could see two men arguing. One, obviously enraged, was flailing his arms in a way that suggested physical threat. The other man stood with arms crossed, shaking his head from side to side.

"Come on, we should go," Diamond said forcefully, putting his hand on Michael's shoulder.

"Those are the twins?"

"Right." He patted Michael's shoulder with his palm, all but shooing him away from the office.

"They're not identical."

"I never said they were. Come on. We're leaving."

Michael ignored him for a few seconds, eyes riveted on the two brothers. Finally, the one who had been waving his arms and shouting looked over and saw him gaping at them. Taking two quick steps to the window, the man stabbed a button on the wall and stared at him as the glass fogged with translucent white crystals. Though Michael could no longer see inside the office, he could still hear the argument raging on.

Diamond stepped in front of him. "They are obviously discussing a sensitive matter. Now, please, come with me back to the audit room."

Michael forced a weak smile and nodded, and they turned and walked back the way they had come.

"Well, I'll let you get set up," said Diamond. "The stacks of papers over there are the last things Kurt was working on earlier this week." He started away, then turned in the doorway. "Oh! When do you expect the rest of your people?"

"There will be two more staff coming out tomorrow. They'll be here four weeks. I believe Falcon is planning to come out next week to review some of the workpapers."

Diamond nodded. "Well, just let me know if you need anything." And he left.

Michael pulled out his laptop, plugged it into the network connection, and booted it up. He looked around the silent room, and an eerie feeling sank in as he faced the reality that he was his dead friend's successor. He looked over at the stack of papers that had occupied his friend's thoughts only a day before his death. Perhaps he was even sitting in Kurt's chair.

Taking a deep breath and letting it out slowly, he opened an e-mail from Falcon. It had all the files for X-Tronic that the IT department had taken from Kurt's computer. He tried to rein his thoughts in. This was a big audit engagement, and he needed to focus if he was going to get it completed with no delays. But even as he began opening the various files on his screen, his thoughts kept wandering back to the Seaton twins. What had them arguing so violently? But more important, why was the legendary Don Seaton off heli-skiing in the mountains instead of attending the emergency board meeting to discuss the threatened takeover of X-Tronic, the company he had built over the past thirty years?

6

WALKING INTO THE Red Room Tavern, Sarah Matthews stood against the wall and searched for a few seconds until her eyes found a familiar face at a table in the back. The bar, only a block from the State Capitol Building, was a favorite watering hole for seasoned and aspiring politicians alike. She moved through the tightly packed tables in her long, leather coat and bouncing red tresses. Her emerald eyes seemed to smile, but her mouth had a serious set. She reached the back booth and slid in across from the man seated there.

"I thought we were never going to do this again," he said to her. He leaned forward, raising his shoulders as if trying to hide.

"What made you think that?"

"You told me we wouldn't."

"And you believed me?" She gave him a disarming smile.

He sighed. "No, I guess not. But I didn't think we'd be doing it again so soon."

"You're just too good, Andy—a girl can't live without you."

He laughed. "Apparently not." He glanced over his left shoulder at a group of senate pages gossiping over their beers a few tables away. "Well, all right, I'm here. What do you need this time?"

"You have any friends at Cooley and White?"

"Cooley? Sure, I know some people. But you don't need me for that. Hell, you have as good a contact in there as anyone. If you need something about Cooley, just ask Kurt—he can't say no to you . . . unless you're afraid it could hurt his career."

Her eyes fell to the table. "Then you haven't heard," she said with a fading whisper that was almost lost to the chatter from the four pages drinking behind them.

"Heard what? Sarah, you okay?"

"Kurt died," she said. She slouched back in the booth and stared at her feet under the table. Every time she said those two words, she got a little more used to the idea that seemed so alien to her. And she hated herself for that. She hated herself for accepting the facts that everyone had given her, for giving up on Kurt without screaming out that everyone was lying. She wanted to pretend that he was just pulling another prank and was probably drinking a beer in a Breckenridge hot tub, surrounded by girls. But she *did* believe them—believed every damn thing they had told her. Kurt was dead.

"*What!*" Andy asked. "How?"

"Skiing."

"Oh, my God, Sarah. Are you serious? Kurt . . . ? I'm so sorry."

She sat up and wiped away a welling tear before it could escape and betray her vulnerability. "Thanks, Andy. I appreciate it, I really do, but I didn't come here for that. Now, can you help me out at Cooley and White?"

"Sure, of course, I'll do what I can. Just tell me what you need."

"Here," she said, pulling a folded piece of lined yellow notepaper from her purse. "I wrote it all down on this. That's what I'll need to start with."

Andy reached out for the paper without taking his piercing blue eyes off her face. His fingers drummed on the table, as if he sensed that she wasn't telling him everything.

"To start what? What kind of story could you possibly be doing on this?" he asked, unfolding the sheet of paper. "This isn't some corrupt project manager stealing from Public Works. I had access to those files directly—a fringe benefit of working for the attorney general. But now you're talking about *outside* the government. I'll talk with the people I know at Cooley, but I can't promise anything."

Sarah looked at him with deep, sad eyes. "You were the best law student at Columbia, Andy. And some day you're going to be a great U.S. senator for Colorado. I know you'll do your best to help me—you know I wouldn't ask if it wasn't important."

"Just tell me it's not something personal, okay? Just tell me it has nothing to do with Kurt."

She didn't respond. Getting up from the table, she leaned in and gave him a quick kiss on the cheek. "Thanks, Andy, you're a sweetie. I'll talk to you soon." Then she turned and walked back to the double doors and the glaring sun outside.

7

————————————◦✳◦————————————

A T SIX O'CLOCK Friday morning, Michael walked through the eerie shadows of X-Tronic's twentieth floor. Automatic motion sensors turned on a flood of lights in small sections ahead of him, twenty feet at a time, as if the building itself were an ominous life form watching his every move. He glanced at one of the many security cameras peering out of small black spheres in the ceiling and wondered if, somewhere in a gloomy security room, human eyes were even now watching him.

After only one day of work with his new client, he had already read through most of the documentation in the audit file. So far, he hadn't noticed anything unusual with X-Tronic's numbers other than the impressive increase in revenue over the past few years. Cooley and White had kept clean workpapers, so he found no red flags in the audit files. It appeared that Kurt was performing the audit tests in an unusual order. It probably meant nothing, but Michael made a mental note to look into it further.

He went in the closest break room. Filling the coffeemaker, he heard a quiet shuffling behind him. He couldn't believe that someone else had shown up for work this early. He had always prided himself on being the first to arrive in the morning and the last to leave in the evening, but here was this old guy across the room, getting a tea bag out of the cabinet.

"Good morning," the man said, half glancing over his shoulder. He was in his sixties perhaps, but with an athlete's strong posture. His silver hair was cropped close, and his impeccably tailored suit and gold cufflinks made a statement of quiet elegance.

"Good morning," Michael replied.

"Not many people in this early," the old man said with a warm smile. "In fact, I think it may be just us."

"I'm sure others will be in before long," Michael said, turning back to the coffeepot. He was still thinking about the unusual nature of Kurt's work and wasn't really looking for small talk.

"Mm," the man mumbled to Michael's back. "Don't believe I've seen you around. Are you new?"

"I'm one of the auditors. Yesterday was my first day here."

"Oh, you're with Cooley and White. What's your name?"

"Michael Chapman," he said, finally turning from the coffeemaker to face the older man.

"Welcome to X-Tronic, Michael. My name's Don Seaton. I hope everyone is being helpful in getting you what you need."

"Yes, everyone's been great," Michael said, mentally kicking himself for not recognizing the man. Looking more closely at the famous billionaire, he now noticed the same features he had seen in so many press photos: the youthful sparkle, the serious intelligence, the glow of confidence.

"Good. Well, we've got some terrific people working here, so I'm sure they'll help you however they can."

Seaton finished brewing his green tea and left, no doubt already wrapping that brilliant mind around the many weighty problems he must juggle today.

Returning to the conference room with his coffee, Michael was soon immersed in a pile of work. He had been at it for more than an hour when he heard two voices approaching. His two young audit staffers walked into the conference room. "Morning," he said.

"Morning," they replied in unison.

Dustin had thick, dark hair and even thicker, darker eyebrows. Shorter than his female coworker, he had a quizzical look on his face, as if he were perpetually contemplating a problem he would never solve.

Andrea's long dirty-blond hair hung straight as wet string. She looked as if she had just stepped out of the shower, and Michael realized that she probably had. He smiled wryly to himself. Only a few weeks into the firm's busy season, and already the perky college grads were feeling the grind.

He thought about asking them if they had any idea why Kurt was testing things out of order, but he decided instead to keep it to himself for now.

Andy Ferguson left the senate subcommittee meeting and hustled down the marble staircase that circled the rotunda of the State Capitol Building. Ever since he took the job of assistant attorney general six months ago, his life had become a constant, harrying race against time. The cold hallway on the first floor echoed with the click of heels on the marble floor as a steady flow of buttoned-down professionals moved quickly past.

Andy saw the familiar face coming down the legislative hallway. He ambled toward the staircase under the white glow of the rotunda. Glancing around and seeing no one suspicious, he approached the short, wide man with a flat nose, now standing at the base of the stairs.

"Any trouble?" he asked quietly, reaching out to shake hands. Feeling the data storage thumb drive in the man's palm,

Andy curled his fingers around it and slipped it into his pocket while his free hand idly patted the brass banister.

"So, any trouble?" Andy asked again. Something in the man's expression bothered him—something he wasn't saying.

"Come on, Wes," he persisted. "What is it?"

The question seemed to make the guy more nervous than ever. He lowered his eyebrows and glanced nervously at the two men and a woman moving past them, and leaned in a little.

"You know I don't like doing this," Wes Garland finally said, the barest quaver in his voice. "Doesn't feel right."

"But it *is* right," Andy replied. "You know I wouldn't have asked you if it wasn't important."

"Important for *what*?" Garland said. "What could you possibly need that information for?"

"It's not for me . . . Listen, Wes, how long have we known each other—twelve, thirteen years? I think by now you know you can trust me. If I tell you it's for something important, that's all you need to know. You haven't done anything illegal."

"Legal, maybe, but not ethical," Wes whispered. "That's confidential information."

"You're a journalist's protected source, relaying confidential information," he said. "I can protect you from any fallout from that. The attorney general can protect you. And if we're right about this, it would have been unethical of you *not* to help us."

Wes crossed his arms, pressing the breast of his charcoal suit jacket against his tie. "You and I both know the attorney general doesn't know anything about this. And even if he wanted to, he couldn't save my job. It could ruin my career."

Andy shook his head. "I can even protect you from that." He slapped his friend on the shoulder. "Now, you'd better get. We'll talk again soon—I promise."

As the two went their separate ways, Andy flipped open his cell phone and scrolled through the directory to "Sarah Matthews." But after selecting it, he paused and glanced around the rotunda as if looking for a tardy colleague. Too many people coming and going for him to see if anyone was watching him. He moved from "Dial" to "View Contact" on the menu and noted her work number. Then, snapping the phone back on his belt, he moved across the cavernous room to the bank of wooden call boxes straight out of the 1930s. Stepping inside one, he pulled the folding door closed, plunked a few coins in the slot, and dialed Sarah's number on the pay phone.

"This is Sarah." A busy newsroom clamored in the background.

"It's me," he said. "I have what you asked for. Meet me at the Union Station light rail in thirty minutes. South platform. Buy a ticket for the E line all the way down to Arapahoe."

"Moscow rules?" she said jokingly.

"Yes, actually. This time it has to be. Someone could be watching me. Be on time." He hung up the phone.

*   *   *

Sarah slung her purse over her shoulder and crossed the floor of the newsroom to the elevator bay. Outside the *Denver Post* building, she looked over to the Capitol, where a man was hurrying down the long flight of steps that stretched down the hill to the street. She could tell it was Andy by the way he scampered along: two steps at a time, one hand sliding along the metal rail, head lowered, tie flapping behind him in the wind.

She had to make it to the Sixteenth Street Mall bus station before Andy. It was the quickest way to Union Station, but she couldn't ride the same bus as he—*Moscow rules.* They had joked about it when investigating Bruce McCleery, the crooked Denver Public Works manager, but now he was deadly serious about the precautions. Tucking her purse under her arm, she picked up her pace as fast as she could without attracting attention.

She stepped inside the first bus in line, just before its doors closed. As it pulled away from the station, she looked out the back window in time to see Andy hit the sidewalk at a trot and jump into the next one.

She leaned her head against the window and looked up at the wall of glass skyscrapers going past. When her bus got held up at a stoplight, she could hear Andy's bus catching up, and as the light turned green, she glanced back and made eye contact with him through the window before they both looked away. Moscow rules? Who were they kidding? She was a first-year staff reporter for the *Post,* and he was an assistant attorney general with less than three years' legal experience. Yet they thought they could track down and expose every corrupt element in the system, one crook at a time. It was something they had often talked excitedly about in Manhattan coffeehouses and bars when they were studying at Columbia. It had seemed such a perfect combination at the time: a young prosecutor and a young journalist working together in secret. He would give her sources and information she couldn't otherwise obtain; she would ruffle some feathers in the press and help raise the public outcry for investigations he couldn't start on his own. Then he could prosecute the slimeballs she exposed. A divine collaboration—in theory, anyway— though they had always allowed for the possibility that they might be biting off more than they could chew. But it *had* worked, and a crooked bureaucrat had fallen. Now they were really getting ambitious—leaping from a smalltime government graft case to a potentially enormous scandal involving what could be an extensive network of corporate executives at one of Kurt's clients. But, understandably, Andy was getting nervous. She only hoped she could convince him to trust her a little longer.

The moment the shuttle bus stopped at the end of the line, she was on the street, and walked a few blocks without looking back. At Union Station, she navigated through the crowded terminal, bought her ticket as Andy had instructed, went out the back of the enormous building, and proceeded along the concrete pedestrian bridge to the light rail platform.

The 2:35 train arrived just as she reached the end of the walkway. She took the steps up the empty car and waited. She had been there half a minute when she heard pounding footsteps and looked up to see Andy practically leap through the open doors. Panting from his run, he didn't look at her, watching instead the concrete bridge he had just walked over. Nostrils flaring and chest heaving, he watched with the intent gaze of a hunter—or was it prey? After a few seconds, Sarah, too, grew worried enough to raise her head and look down the bridge. On the far side, a heavyset man lumbered toward the train as fast as he could, one hand holding on to a dark brimmed hat, the other holding his side. But before he could make it halfway across the bridge, the electronic ding sounded, and the doors slid shut. The three-car train pulled away from the station and was soon gliding at speed toward the south end of Denver.

"Who was that?" Sarah asked as the little train hurtled along its elevated track. The cars on the freeway below them moved at practically the same speed, giving her the eerie sensation of standing still while the world rolled past.

"I don't know," Andy replied. "Maybe nobody, but he was with me since I got on the Mall Ride. He see you? Get a look at your face?"

"I don't think so. What's going on?"

He handed her the thumb drive. "Here's some of what you asked for."

"Some?"

"I had to take some things off the list."

"Why?"

As the car gently rocked through a curve, Andy grabbed the plastic handgrip attached to the metal bar above him. "We have to be careful about this, Sarah," he said.

His eyes were fixed on the two plastic seats next to an open space reserved for wheelchairs. Sarah had seen that look enough times to know that his legal mind was whirring along, working through a problem.

"There's a fine line between what's legal and what's not," he said at last. "I had my man pull the list of client names that match with employee assignments at the firm. I also had him match employees with their supervisors. It's an internal document distributed within Cooley and White. It's considered confidential information by legal standards, but I can defend our actions in obtaining it under the whistle-blower provision of the code. I just need to make the argument that my man came to me with concerns about the firm's management activities. But that's as far as I can go without crossing the line—absolutely no employee files or firm workpapers relating to client records. Under the right circumstances I could subpoena that information, but I just don't have any reasonable suspicion right now to authorize an action like that."

Sarah knew he was right. She had been so eager to get information about Cooley and White and Kurt's clients, she had just bulled her way forward, requesting everything without considering the legal ramifications. "But you at least got me the names of all employees and how they match with the managers and client assignments?" She was leaning against the Plexiglas divider near the door, wondering whether the little thumb drive contained enough information to identify who at Cooley and White was working with Kurt.

"Yeah. It should be current."

The light rail began to slow for the next stop, and the freeway traffic, which had been keeping speed alongside them, overtook them and rocketed past.

"Now, what's this all about?" he asked.

She turned away to look out the window. Outside, an old woman had risen with great effort from a bench on the rail platform and was inching her way toward the train's open doors. The conductor waited patiently, watching her in his side mirror.

"Kurt spoke to me about Cooley and White a few weeks before his death," she said, still looking west. "He was suspicious—said he had found something he might need me to write about. He thought he might have some kind of story. Said he couldn't tell me anything until he looked into it more . . . Now he's dead. I have to find out what he was looking for. I just know he'd want me to be doing this."

Andy had moved toward the door. "Be careful what you look for," he muttered. "You might not like what you find."

"You think I'll find something?"

He shook his head. "I meant, be careful about *expecting* to find something. I just don't want you creating a story in your head because of Kurt—convincing yourself of something that may not be there at all."

"He was onto something," she replied. "I just know it. And he knew it, too. You didn't see the look in his eyes—I did." She looked down at the thumb drive as if it were a long-sought treasure. "He was scared of someone at Cooley and White— someone he worked with . . . someone who's on this disk." She slipped the thumb drive in her purse and looked up at him, her eyes ablaze with cold green fire. "This could be the big one, Andy—the one we always dreamed about. Remember Columbia? Wanting to change the world? This could be it. My brother was as smart as anyone in that firm. If he thought something was wrong, then we have to look for it—we have to finish whatever he started."

8

MICHAEL STOOD IN line outside the Church nightclub. After two busy days at X-Tronic, his colleagues from Cooley and White hadn't had much trouble persuading him to join them for Friday happy hour at a sports bar downtown. After a few hours, they had dispersed, but he wasn't ready to call it a night. The Church was only four blocks from his apartment, so it had felt like an easy detour during his cab ride home. Standing in the cold air, he watched a white Hummer limousine stop in front to deposit a dozen well-dressed VIPs, who were whisked past the bouncers and into the club. Turning up his coat collar for warmth, he shrugged his shoulders in playful flirtation and tried out his smile on the girl in front of him.

The line crept forward a few steps. Michael looked up at the old stone church, which had been converted into a dance club. The sidewalk where families once promenaded after Sunday worship was now crowded with pale-skinned, black-clad goths, techno enthusiasts, and other, less easily categorized members of the local underground music scene.

Twenty minutes and twenty dollars later, he was finally inside the club. The house music's amplified bass line came thumping through the floor as he headed toward the old church's main sanctuary, where the action was in full swing. Here was just the temporary escape he needed.

Michael stopped to take in the scene. There must be three hundred people in the main room alone, where four separate bars surrounded the dance floor. The high, vaulted ceiling, shot through with flashing lasers, gave the room a cavernous feel, with eerie qualities of echo and reverberation. Just as he was marveling at the visual effects, a burst of dry-ice "smoke" shot up from the floor, rising slowly into the air as a cloud consumed the vanishing dancers. The smoke climbed a few feet above his head before drifting into a barrage of blue lasers that momentarily formed an eight-foot ceiling, a tightly packed blue grid that hovered low over the dance floor. Michael reached his hand into the air and watched it turn blue as it penetrated the ceiling of lights.

He closed his eyes and focused on the intoxicating energy of the music. His mind drifted back into a memory of warmth and adventure: a time in his life that he had all but forgotten—nights spent in the maze of underground clubs of Berlin, Prague, Krakow, and Budapest. He danced alone, eyes closed, envisioning himself back in Eastern Europe. A blissful smile broke across his face.

After a few minutes, he opened his eyes and saw that he had subconsciously gravitated toward the center of the dance floor. He pushed himself through the thick crowds to one of the side bars, got a drink, and went through an arched vestibule into another room. It seemed a perfect haunt for party vampires. A dozen false windows along the stone wall were illuminated with red backlighting that flushed the space with a darkroom crimson glow.

A young woman sitting alone on a couch near the wall caught Michael's eye. Long jet-black hair veiled her face. She leaned back into the couch with a confidence that told him she was not searching for anything in life—that what she wanted, she took. He watched her for a moment, then swallowed the last of his drink and went to the bar for another.

Waiting for his second drink, he turned back to face the crowd, just visible over a low banister. As he watched the ebb and flow of people amid the loud techno beat and flashing lasers, thoughts of his father came unbidden to his mind: the boy, the small-town hero, the college prodigy and eventually the brilliant professor. Michael turned back to the bar and grabbed his drink. He had lost so much when he moved to Denver. He had strayed far from the path that his father and grandfather might have imagined for him. He was haunted by what he had become, by the thought that the great and worthy father would no longer recognize the son, that even his grandfather might question his motives from the grave. His job kept him so busy that he rarely found time to reflect on the chain of decisions that had brought him to Denver in the first place, or the hidden agenda that had brought him to Cooley and White. But the alcohol and the solitude, even here amid the noise and movement of the club, gave him too much time to think about his past decisions and the risk he was willing to take because of his family's past. He just had never imagined that there would be such a high price to pay for his self-determined mission to revive his family's lost legacy.

As he leaned back against the bar, he again caught sight of the young woman as she rose and walked toward the stairs to the club's basement rooms. Turning at the stairs, she looked at him and gave a little grin as she beckoned him with two slow curls of her index finger. Then she turned and disappeared down the stairs.

He finished his drink, grabbed another, and went down the stone staircase into the enormous dungeon below the main dance floor. The only illumination came from the spinning strobe lights mounted on the ceiling. Through the darkness, he saw her in the middle of the small dance floor, flanked by a hundred silhouettes. As he approached shyly from the side, he watched her dance with a slow seductiveness that was as aloof as when she had been sitting by herself. Her head was lowered so that her hair continued to veil her face.

She stopped dancing when she saw him. Lights flashed, illuminating their faces at random intervals, allowing their eyes to meet between intervals of darkness. Smiling playfully, she moved in closer and began dancing against him until one of his legs rubbed between her thighs. He couldn't always see her in the moving shadows, but he could feel her. He wrapped an arm around her lower back and pulled her close, and they moved together in a lazy dance.

Her scent intoxicated him, as if she existed solely to seduce him. Something about the blend of isolated strength and solitary vulnerability reminded him of himself. The idle thought came to him that he was feeling pretty drunk. He leaned in and kissed her before she had a chance to resist. But the moment his lips touched hers, their tongues entwined. She pulled him off to a small brick alcove.

"What's your name?" he managed to yell over the music.

"Alaska."

"I'm Michael." He paused, bemused. "What's your *real* name?"

She had a mysterious smile and a sly look in her eye—a gamer.

"Nice to meet you, Michael, but now I have to go."

"Wait. Can I at least get your number?"

"No, but you can tell me yours and maybe I'll remember it."

"I'll write it down," he said.

"No, just tell me. If I can't remember it, then I must not have been that interested."

After he told her his number, she leaned up on her toes and kissed him one last time. Then, as she pulled away, she bit his lower lip, hard enough to hurt, before running up the staircase.

He watched her disappear around the corner of the passageway. Reaching a finger up to his lip, he brought it back down to see a trace of blood. He shook his head. Definitely a gamer.

Making his way back to the main dance floor, Michael grabbed his jacket from the coatroom. Outside, he found the city's outlines pleasantly blurred by the alcohol and a pale blanket of snow, with more drifting down in great, feathery clumps from the dark orange clouds that reflected the city lights. He was surprised at the sudden metamorphosis. Only three hours ago, the skies had been empty and the cold ground gray in the moonlight. How quickly the world could change the moment he looked away.

Shuffling through the snow, he quickly covered the four blocks to his apartment building. He went straight to his balcony, where he looked out at the hazy skyline through the storm. A smile crept onto his face, and he started to laugh—laughed because he had met a beautiful woman tonight and because he had gotten drunk in a church.

And then, just as suddenly as it had come, his laughter turned to despair, like the laughter of a prisoner overcome by solitude. He didn't know how much longer he could continue to work for the firm, but Glazier had made it clear that he couldn't leave. He had come too far in the past few years. He had found himself an opportunity to atone for his grandfather's failures. How proud the old man would be if he could see him right now. Michael prayed that he was doing the right thing. How would he ever salvage his career and his father's respect if he was wrong. Even Glazier, his own handler, might crucify him if he couldn't pull this off. Gazing out at the snowy night, he realized that he had never been more terrified of what the future held.

9

———————❊———————

AS SARAH PULLED her jeep into the two-car parking area behind Kurt's house, the headlights shot through the low chain-link fence, casting a prisonlike shadow that moved across the back of the small white house. The dark neighborhood was quiet, especially in this snowy back alley she had just driven down. She held a big metal flashlight but didn't turn it on for fear of being seen. It hardly mattered, though, for anyone within earshot would have heard the metallic shriek as she pushed the gate open. Using the spare key that Kurt had given her at Christmas only a month ago, she opened the back door and entered her dead brother's house.

The inside looked different somehow, as if someone had been here since Kurt's death. Moving through the darkness, she used her cell phone's display to cast a low blue light across the kitchen. She still wasn't comfortable using the heavy flashlight or turning on the house lights. Her pupils had adjusted to the sparse lighting, and using anything brighter would make it impossible for her to see out the windows, and very easy for anyone outside to see her. In the darkness, she felt safe.

She wasn't sure exactly what she was looking for, but it was clear that Kurt had recently found something while working at the accounting firm. He had only one computer—the one assigned to him by the accounting firm—so anything he had kept on it would be out of reach because the firm had reclaimed it. Her only hope was that any information he may have found was hidden somewhere in this house.

As she moved through the dark house, the cell phone's soft blue light captured the outlines of objects tied to her memories. On the wall was a triumphant shot of her and Kurt with five friends at the snowy summit of Kilimanjaro, taken two years ago. On the coffee table was a small plastic Statue of Liberty she had given him as a joke during her first year at Columbia, to remind him that he *still* had never been to New York City. She wanted to take these things with her, for they were now remnants, mementos, of who her brother was to her.

Her brother and she had always shared a sense of responsibility to be at the top of whatever careers they chose—in light of their parents' professional successes, how could they do less? And they had been well on their way. She had felt a balance in her life as her journalism career progressed almost as she had imagined. But now, with Kurt's death shaking her beliefs, her life felt off balance and out of her control for the first time.

She forced herself to push aside the pain and anger and disbelief so she could get on with the search for answers. She checked his desk first. Holding her phone an inch away, she scanned each paper in the desk but found nothing relating to his work. Then she moved to the bookshelves, passing the phone's light across the spines. As a kid, Kurt had sometimes taped things inside books, so she pulled every one from the shelf and flipped through it, searching with fingers as well as eyes for any little thing. It took her fifteen minutes, and she found nothing.

Outside, a dog started barking. A car passed, flooding the room with light, and dropping instinctively, she felt a stab of fear when a human silhouette filled in the window, distorted by the moving light. But once the car had passed, the object seemed to vanish.

She remained motionless, crouched on the floor in the dark and staring with wide eyes at the window across the room for thirty seconds before telling herself it was nothing more than an illusion, a trick of the eye and her own fears.

When she moved back through the dark living room and into the back half of the house, it hit her. She couldn't believe she hadn't thought of it until now. The little house had a one-room cellar beneath the kitchen, accessible only through a hidden staircase under a floor hatch that Kurt covered with a rug. If he had wanted to hide anything in the house, it would be the perfect place.

She went to the kitchen and pulled the rug aside, revealing the four slits in the floor that outlined the entrance to the little tornado shelter beneath the house. She grabbed the recessed ring handle and pulled the trapdoor up. As it opened, the two-by-four hinged to the bottom of the door banged against the side of the entrance. It seemed as loud as a gunshot.

After the fright passed, she put a hand on either side of the open square in the kitchen floor and carefully stepped down onto the steps into the pitch-black void below. The open-tread wooden stairs creaked and bent with every step until, at last, she touched the hard concrete floor at bottom. She had left the heavy trapdoor propped open above her for fear that closing it might somehow trap her under the house. Now, down here, she could use the heavy four-cell Mag flashlight. She found herself in a six-by-ten concrete cubicle, something like a prison cell, containing the water heater for the house, and a rickety unsanded wooden shelf along one wall. The concrete walls reached only five feet up before opening to a large crawl space that ran beneath the rest of the house. Pointing the flashlight beam onto the bookshelf, she saw a dozen finance and accounting books with hundreds of colored legal flags sticking out between the pages. Bingo.

She reached for the nearest three-ring binder on the shelf, but before her fingers touched it she heard a sudden creak from somewhere above in the house. The jolt of fear made her bobble the flashlight, nearly dropping it in her haste to flip it off. She crouched in the darkness under the stairs, listening and waiting. A heavy creak came from the wooden floor above her . . . then another. There was definitely someone else in the house with her.

She had never checked the bedroom. She had been so anxious to check this storage space, she had made the terrible mistake of not checking every room in the house before cornering herself in the cellar.

The creaking stopped at the top of the stairs. Whoever it was now stood at the open trapdoor directly above her. She could feel eyes peering down into the darkness. She froze, terrified that her slightest move would give her away.

A dark boot lowered gently onto the top step. Then the other boot took the next step. And there they stopped. Wellingtons— suede, maybe—with jeans stacked low over the instep. How many blows would she get in with the Maglite before the guy overpowered her? She fitted her right hand around the lens section, designed to double as a club handle. On the next step, slip out right and swing the heavier, battery-weighted end into his shin—catch him above the boot top. If the blow sent him tumbling to the concrete floor, find the head and knock him senseless or worse. And if he didn't fall, the pain reaction would bring his head down close enough for a piñata swing to smash his nose, blinding him with his tears. Then yank the bottom foot to send him sprawling, clamber up onto the steps from the side, get the hell out, drop the trapdoor, and pray he came alone . . . Shaking from the adrenaline, she felt the immediate reality of mortal danger—something she hadn't experienced in a long time.

The live threat took the next two steps, then hesitated. This was it. She couldn't believe this was really going to happen.

"Sarah?" a voice whispered. "You down here?"

"Andy?"

"Yeah."

"Oh, fuck, man!" She stepped out from under the stairs and flipped the flashlight beam onto his face. He looked as terrified as she felt. "Holy crap, Andy! I almost beat your head in with this! In fact, I think I just might, God damn it!"

Andy stuck his hands out. "What? You called and asked me to come over here."

She shook her head. "I asked you to park on the street and watch for anything as I came in the back. Neighbors, police—anything. You were supposed to be like a lookout, a backup, while I entered the house."

"I thought I was supposed to come in when I got here."

"No," she said, the tension falling off her in great waves of relief.

"This is a cool room," he said, taking the rest of the stairs. "Little creepy at night, though."

"Christ, my heart's still racing!" she said, taking a deep breath. She pointed the beam of light toward the bookshelf. "Well, since you're here, you can help me carry this stuff up to my car. I don't want to be here any longer than necessary."

"What is it?" he asked.

"A bunch of accounting books Kurt flagged. Those look like they're about fraud. And it looks like he's put some stuff in those three-ring binders. He must have spent a lot of time on it, and he obviously wanted to keep it hidden."

"Well let's get it and go," Andy said. "This place is creeping me out."

They carried everything up the wooden steps and made three stacks on the kitchen floor, then lugged it all out to the car. All the while, Sarah felt like a grave robber, stealing from the dead.

But as Andy dropped the last stack on the backseat, her guilt morphed into anger at her brother for not being careful enough to avoid whatever killed him. Then her rage seemed to feel around until it found its true object: Kurt's killer. And somewhere in this pile of neatly flagged financial documents lay a clue to just who that was.

10

————————⊶✵⊷————————

SATURDAY NIGHT, MICHAEL was sitting on his balcony drinking a beer. The city lights below him expanded toward the dark horizon, like a luminescent reef in an otherwise dark ocean. He had been thinking about the information on Cooley and White he was compiling for Glazier, and also Kurt's unorthodox testing order at X-Tronic. He had just gotten back from Kurt's funeral in Boulder only hours ago, and he just couldn't shake the feeling that his friend had been doing some strange things at X-Tronic.

Taking a long swig of beer, he felt the vibration of his cell phone and answered. He could hear loud electronic music in the background.

"Hey! Remember me?"

His pulse quickened as he recognized Alaska's voice. "Hi! Of course!"

"I'm at a club called the Rise. Come try to find me." Then the phone went dead.

The Rise was by Coors Field in lower downtown, only a couple of miles from his apartment. He needed to get his mind off everything that was stressing him out, and this mysterious, quirky, gorgeous woman was a godsend.

Twenty minutes later, Michael was standing in the growing line outside the Rise. The three-story building's exterior was smooth concrete, with huge panes of dark glass outlined by blue neon lights. The faint, thumping techno bass beat blared suddenly louder every time one of the three burly bouncers opened the doors to let someone in.

Inside, he checked his jacket and made his way out to the main dance floor without even stopping at the bar. He searched the bobbing, swaying strobe-lit faces in the dark, then walked through both levels of the club, but she was gone—left before he could arrive, or perhaps was lying the whole time.

Feeling like a sap, he made his way to the bar and got a vodka tonic. Then, drink in hand, he walked past a wall of distorting mirrors toward the main dance floor. Though miffed that she had suckered him with a false tryst, he was still determined to get his twenty dollars' worth. He stepped into the crowd, wending his way to the center of the floor.

He felt a hand on his shoulder. Turning around, he found himself staring into her eyes. She had been here all along, watching him.

"I couldn't find you!" he yelled over the music, as if they were a hundred miles apart.

She reached up, cupped the back of his neck, and pulled his lips to her. Then she slid her mouth past his cheek until he felt her warm breath just below his ear. "You told me you have an amazing view of the city from your apartment."

He nodded as his eyes gazed out at the dark shadows and silhouettes pulsing under the strobe light behind her.

"Show me."

Michael's hands moved across Alaska's pale-silk skin. He would let her moan softly for a moment before kissing her lips, silencing her again. In the dim glow of city lights through the window, her soft breasts shrank as she stretched her arms above her head to grab the headboard.

Kissing her, he forgot what she looked like and who she was; he could think only of how her body felt. Her aggressiveness excited him. She had come on to him so quickly . . . everything happening so fast. He loved it, and the consequences be damned.

Afterward, she turned away from him. They were exhausted and satisfied, but with the heated excitement over, they found they had nothing left; they were strangers again. Michael tried to be sensitive, gently stroking her back, but she didn't respond, ignoring him even when he asked her a question. She pretended to be asleep. *Warm women sleep close to a new lover; cold women turn away.* He wondered what secrets she was keeping, and this made him think of his own. At last, she turned and rolled toward him to nestle in his arms. It was as if she had read his mind, as if she knew him better than he knew himself.

11

———━◦╫❋╫◦━———

S UNDAY MORNING, AND it felt strange to have someone
  sleeping beside him in his apartment. He had been so buried
in work, it had been a while since he brought a woman here.

Standing in the doorway to his bedroom, he watched the slow
rise and fall of Alaska's naked back. Now, with the fevered
urgency of first sex behind them, he found himself wanting to
learn everything he could about her. He hoped he could convince
her to spend at least part of the day with him.

Leaving the doorway to step out on the apartment's sunlit
balcony, he couldn't help feeling impatient for Alaska to wake
up and join him in the cool air outside.

Michael watched as Alaska wielded the brush over the big
canvas in bold, waving strokes. They had spent much of the day
together, rambling in the city and learning about each other. She
had brought him to a friend's small gallery on Santa Fe, in
Denver's art district, to show him the space upstairs where she
was allowed to work. She repeated the movement over and over
until he saw the developing outline of a weeping willow on an

otherwise desolate snow-swept mountainside. The scene was unrealistic, of course—not even a bristlecone could survive in such a harsh environment. But he loved the image.

"Where's that supposed to be?" he asked.

"Near Aspen. North of my dad's house."

"You said he was a folk singer, right?" Michael asked, grinning.

"Careful," she said, her eyes still on the painting. "He's not, and he'd kill you for saying such a thing. In fact, I might do it for him. I said he was in a metal band in the late seventies and early eighties."

"Did they have any success?"

"Moderate success. A few albums that sold okay. Had some groupies, did some U.S. tours, but nothing huge. That's how he met my mother. Made some good cake back then, but my parents went through money pretty fast. They were young—I think a lot of people would have made the same mistakes in their situation."

Michael was silent. Considering his family's own past, he didn't have a lot of room to criticize someone else's fall from grace. Looking at that graceful willow gamely sticking it out on a freezing, snow-covered crag, he found himself imagining the source of her inspiration.

"Your pop seen any of these paintings?"

She turned away from the canvas. "He hasn't seen any of my paintings in years—lost his sight when I was fifteen."

"Aw, Jesus . . . I'm sorry. What happened?"

"He used to love working on cars. He was under the hood of his 'seventy-seven Firebird one afternoon when the battery exploded. Sprayed battery acid in his face and blinded both eyes."

"That's horrible . . . I can't begin to imagine it."

"Yeah, it's been really tough on him," she said.

"Hard on everyone, I'd think. You, your mother."

"Actually, my mom divorced him before the accident. I was ten when she left us. The band had all but vanished by then, and so had most of the money. She's remarried now with two kids and lives with her new family in France. So she's basically out of the picture. I've only seen her once in the past ten years. I think she's embarrassed of her old life. And now it's been too long since she was part of our life. Seeing her again would be difficult for everyone."

She had grown up witnessing her father's continual decline. Michael got it, knowing what he did of his own grandfather's downward arc.

"How about you?" she said. "You've heard my depressing life history; now it's your turn."

Michael smiled. "How about I tell you over dinner?"

"Only if it's sushi," she said, lifting the brush and dabbing it in the palette.

"I know a place," he replied.

Watching her so quickly reabsorbed in her work, he was captivated. Alaska was the antithesis of all the hard-edged, business- and career-obsessed women Michael met every day. She lived outside the world that most people were happy to strap themselves into. She was alive, exotic, free.

With everything he was trying to do for Glazier, Michael knew that one of the stupidest things he could do right now was fall into a serious relationship. *It's just for a day,* he told himself. But he was tired of waiting for the happiness that ought to be in his life by now. He was ready to fall in love with someone— really ready, for the first time, to open up his life and make room in it for someone. Few people could imagine how crazy things had been these past four years, and it would take a special woman indeed to accept him for the life he had chosen after all was revealed. And Alaska just might be that woman in a million who could accept what he really was.

"Like it?" she asked, putting the brush down on the palette.

"No . . . I love it. You're amazing."

Be smart, he told himself. *Just one day.*

12

———————————————

SARAH MATTHEWS SAT in her cubicle, staring blankly into her computer. It was early Sunday evening at the *Post*. There hadn't been many people on the newsroom floor all day as she finished scanning through the accounting books and binders from Kurt's house. She had been reviewing them all weekend, pausing only Saturday afternoon to go to Boulder for the funeral. Seeing the pale, lifeless face in the casket had been the bucket of cold water waking her up to a world without her brother in it. She had hated being exposed to everyone at the funeral. She wanted only privacy to deal with the loss she still could not comprehend. After a few hours with extended family at her parents' house after the funeral, she had excused herself—"not feeling well"—and driven directly back to the *Post* to continue her work.

Now she had finished going through everything. She wasn't exactly sure what Kurt had been working on, but she had identified two main topics he had flagged or highlighted the most: revenue accounting and fraud. She could tell by his notes that he had discovered something suspicious through his work.

Next to one highlighted paragraph in an accounting book about fraud was written in red ink, "*Ways to inflate profit margins!*" A few pages later was the note "*Motivation for fraud.*" And the note that had really caught her eye was in another book where he had written, "*Ways to manipulate revenue recognition! Must look at original software revenue contracts!!!*"

She looked through the Cooley and White work schedule Andy had gotten her. Kurt had worked on the *X-Tronic* audit for the six weeks before his death. Her blood boiled as she connected his numerous notes of suspicion to the fact that he had been working on the software company's audit before dying in the "ski accident." Her journalist's instincts had kicked into high gear, and at this point she had all but convinced herself that Kurt got murdered because he had found something wrong at X-Tronic.

She now looked at the Cooley and White schedule to see who else was on the X-Tronic job. The first thing she noticed was that a Michael Chapman had been placed at X-Tronic just after Kurt's death, apparently as his replacement. The name seemed somehow familiar, but from where? On a hunch, she opened her e-mail account and found the last mass mailing Kurt had sent out—about a hut snowshoeing trip he had been trying to organize. Scanning down the list of recipients, she nodded when she saw "michael.chapman@cw.com." Kurt rarely hung out with people from the firm outside of work, so he wouldn't have included this Chapman guy on the e-mail unless they were good friends. And now Chapman was Kurt's replacement on X-Tronic.

Her cell phone rang.

"Sarah, are you at home?" her mother asked.

"No, at work."

"Can you talk?"

Sarah took a deep breath and let it out. "For a minute . . . I have a lot of work to do."

"I'm worried about you, honey. Are you all right?"

Sarah felt the tears well up at the sadness and worry she could hear. "I'm okay." She didn't want to say much more—just hearing her mother's voice was threatening to break her composure.

"We'd like to see you sometime. It'd be nice if you could come up to Boulder when you have a chance. Your father and I would really love it if you could stop by for dinner some night this week."

"I know, Mom. I'll try, but I'm just really busy right now. I'll come up to see you guys as soon as I can."

"Honey, you'll give us a call if you need anything, okay? Anything at all."

"Yeah, sure."

Silence weighed heavily between them as they both considered anything else they wanted to say. Kurt, as her older brother and her parents' firstborn, had always been the energetic jokester and lighthearted charmer of the family. He had played the vital role of connector, pulling the family together whenever they had problems. And his death had left a void, separating the rest of the family with a sadness they each refused to share.

"We love you," her mother said in a tone that sounded more like a reminder than anything else.

"I love you guys, too."

The call ended. She dropped the phone back in her purse and thought about her mother's concerns. Why was it so hard to go home after Kurt's death? She knew that a family was supposed to come together after a tragedy, but her brother's death had split her from her parents. She used to believe that her life was being directed by fate, that because of her parents' career successes, she, too, was destined for great professional achievement. She had once dreamed she would write an article or book that might somehow change the world, but now it seemed that fate had destroyed those ambitions forever. She didn't want to go home, and she no longer cared about changing the world. She just wanted to work on discovering whatever story Kurt thought he had stumbled upon—it was the only thing that made her feel better.

The newsroom was too open and desolate for her to work in any longer. She packed up her laptop, shoved all her hard-copy files into a weathered valise, and sent a text message to her editor saying she would be working from her apartment for the next few days, that she needed to avoid any distractions from work.

She needed answers on what was wrong at X-Tronic—what Kurt had found. She had gone down this path as far as she could on her own, and she needed help if she wanted to keep going. As a journalist, she was no stranger to the *need* to unravel a mystery once it was introduced to her, but finding the real reason her brother had died was now an obsession she was willing to risk her future for. And she planned to start by e-mailing this *Michael Chapman* tomorrow morning.

13

---✦---

M ICHAEL PRESSED THE call button at the front door of
the Victorian apartment building in Denver's Upper
Heights district. After getting the mysterious e-mail Monday
morning, he had replied immediately to set up a meeting for this
evening. Now he had just gotten off the phone with Glazier, and
they both were eager to see what he might learn.

"Hello?" a voice asked through the speaker.

"Sarah Matthews? It's Michael Chapman. You e-mailed me."

"Yes, please come up."

Hearing the buzzer, he opened the door. He was surprised at
how nervous he felt about seeing Kurt's sister. He knew from
Kurt that she was a reporter for the *Post,* and though he had seen
her at the funeral a few days ago, they had never met.

Just as he reached her apartment door, it opened. Her emerald
eyes sparkled in the dim doorway, yet she seemed hesitant to
invite him in. It was not the greeting he had expected. He could
tell something was wrong by the way she took slow, gingerly
steps backward into her apartment without ever taking her eyes
off him.

Inside, the floor was strewn with pages of notes and news clippings, scattered books, and open three-ring binders. Maybe she was busy researching another story for the *Post*.

"You worked with my brother," she said.

"Yes, I did."

"And you were also his friend."

"I was," he confirmed. "He spoke of you often . . . Sarah, I can't tell you how sorry I am."

She nodded, but he could tell she didn't want to talk with a stranger about her brother's death. Yet she must have had a reason for asking to meet. He reminded himself to be careful what he said—after all, she was a journalist.

"You're his replacement on the X-Tronic audit."

"How do you know that?" he asked. He could feel it—something was very wrong.

"You've been looking at the audit documentation he was working on before he died?"

"Yes."

"The firm gave you access to his computer files related to X-Tronic?"

"Yes. Why are asking me this?"

"Have you noticed anything unusual or suspicious?"

"Sarah, what is this? What you are doing?"

She seemed distracted by something scribbled on a whiteboard against the far wall—a list, perhaps, though he couldn't make it out in the low light. "You know, he used to hardly ever talk to me about his work," she said, looking toward the wall. "But a few weeks ago he started talking about it a little bit, telling me exactly how his job worked, how he would audit the details of various accounting activities that all rolled up into the hundred-plus pages of financial information issued to Wall Street. I thought he was just trying to tell me how important his job was—we've always been competitive. Then, over a week ago, he told me he might have a story for me to report on."

"What story?" Michael said, his eyes locked on hers with a sudden intensity.

"How much do you know about revenue accounting?" she asked.

"A lot."

"How much do you know about financial statement frauds?"

"Sarah, stop playing games. What's this about?"

"Kurt found something he shouldn't have—something illegal about X-Tronic." She looked up at him, pleading for him to understand. "Something that got him killed."

He couldn't believe his ears. She had gone nuts, locked up in her apartment researching God knew what. "What are you talking about? Nobody killed Kurt. He died skiing."

"He was an expert skier. He could never have died that way."

"Come on, Sarah. You and I both know he was a daredevil. Even expert skiers have bad accidents in the mountains. Anything can happen up there."

"Yeah, anything . . . even murder."

"Sarah, listen to yourself. Do you know how *crazy* that sounds? Kurt's gone. Don't torture yourself."

"He never skied in the trees." She blinked, and the tears spilled down her cheeks.

"What?"

"He fell in the trees when he was ten years old—lost control and fell sideways against a tree. It broke his leg." She seemed to be pleading for him to understand her. "He was just a little boy. It was my first time skiing on the big slopes, and he tried to impress me. I waited with him for twenty minutes while our dad went for help. A ski patroller finally came with a toboggan to take him down the mountain. It was the only time in my life I ever saw my brother cry. After that day, he never skied in the trees again."

Torn between Sarah's suffering and the confusing new details surrounding Kurt's death, Michael couldn't speak.

"Something led him into the trees," she said. "Kurt was terrified—phobic—about skiing in the trees. He wouldn't have gone in unless he had a good reason. Are you even *listening* to me? Someone was with my brother when he died!"

"All right, look. I'm sorry about what happened to Kurt, but let's just settle down for a second and think about this. What makes you think he found something illegal at X-Tronic?"

Sarah gestured at all the books and documents spread over the floor of her apartment. "I found these things hidden in Kurt's house. He thought he had found something, but I'm not sure he had time to work it all out. Something about revenue, maybe. I'm not an accountant. You were his friend, and now you're his replacement at X-Tronic. Maybe you can figure out what he was doing."

Michael looked at Sarah in disbelief before moving his gaze across the items on the floor. He couldn't even process the possibility that Kurt had been murdered, but he definitely wanted to look through anything Kurt had left behind regarding suspicions about X-Tronic. He agreed to help Sarah understand the documents, and for the next three hours she walked him through all the items she had flagged that she thought Kurt seemed most concerned about. When they were finished, there was no question in Michael's mind: Kurt had believed there was fraud in the revenue accounting at X-Tronic. But there was no proof.

After reviewing everything with Sarah, Michael told her it looked as though Kurt was preparing to examine the revenue contracts at X-Tronic even though this was an area that the partner, John Falcon, had insisted on examining himself. Michael wasn't even sure where the contracts were kept at X-Tronic, but he promised Sarah he would find them tomorrow.

14

WHEN MICHAEL ARRIVED in the audit room the next morning, he figured he had perhaps an hour before Andrea and Dustin showed up—enough time to track down the revenue contracts. He grabbed his leather portfolio, left the room, and went to Diamond's office. "Jerry," he said, peeking in the open doorway, "quick question. I'm trying to locate the revenue contracts so they're ready for Falcon when he comes out next week. Can you help me track them down?"

"Oh, that won't be necessary," Diamond said, eyeing him coldly. "Falcon has insisted we keep them filed away so as not to clutter up your work room. He said he'd be testing them himself, so he'd rather I just let Mr. Laidlaw maintain them until he comes out." Then, looking suddenly worried, he said, "Oh, I do hope that's all right, Michael. Maybe you should give Falcon a ring to discuss it."

Michael held back a grimace. Falcon had been adamant about his leaving the contracts alone. "No, that's fine. I . . . didn't realize you had spoken with him."

"Oh, no worries—anything else, then?"

"No, I guess that's it. Thanks."

Heading back to the audit room, Michael couldn't shake the feeling that both Falcon and Diamond were trying hard to keep him in the dark about something with the contracts. At the end of the hallway, he stopped and looked back over his shoulder, then glanced at his watch—seven thirty, and no one was around. He still had some time before most of the employees started filtering back in to work.

Leaning into the staircase door, he pushed it open and pelted down the steps two at a time, two flights to the eighteenth floor. All the lights were still off, and as the sensor picked up his motion in the doorway, they flickered on. He must be the only one on the floor. He still had time, but early birds could start showing up for work at any moment.

He jogged along the outer wall of the office, reading all the names until he found a Russell F. Laidlaw. He turned the handle; it was unlocked. But instead of going right in, he took a step back. The next step, once taken, was irreversible. His stomach felt tight, and he could feel his heart quicken. Looking both directions down the corridor, he stepped into the office.

Russell Laidlaw pulled his powder blue Acura into the sublevel of X-Tronic's west parking garage. Following the painted traffic lanes, he turned into his spot, got out, and headed toward the orange elevator doors surrounded by gray concrete. The elevator started up and, a few seconds later, deposited him on the first floor of the campus complex, where he switched to the central elevator bank to get to the upper floors of X-Tronic's main building. As he stepped out onto the first floor, his cell phone vibrated in his pocket.

"Morning, Jerry," he said.

"Russell, I need to see you first thing this morning. Are you in the office yet?"

He wondered at the urgent tone of the CFO's voice. "I just got here," he replied.

"Good. Please come to my office as soon as you can. And bring the documents we discussed yesterday."

"I'm on my way—just need to grab them from my office."

The call ended, and he headed down the long hallway through the main complex of corporate headquarters. In the lobby, he saw his energetic young assistant, Danny Rossingh, approaching from the opposite direction.

"I think we're going to have another busy one today, Danny," Laidlaw remarked as they entered the elevator.

"Why's that?" the young man asked.

"I've already gotten a call from Diamond. I need to grab something from my office, and then I'm to head straight up to see him. Christ, I wouldn't be surprised if some of these guys stayed here *all night*. I think something's going on with the acquisition bid—something they're not telling us."

The elevator doors closed, and they started upward.

Michael went straight to the four stainless steel file cabinets against the far wall of Laidlaw's office. Starting on the nearest cabinet, he pulled the top drawer open and started flipping through the labeled files. His eyes glided across the various contract names. The documents were organized by client type, some of them going back several years. No good—what he needed was current.

A sudden change in his peripheral vision made him jump, banging his elbow on the edge of the open file drawer. The lights he had activated by walking down the hallway were now turning off. He watched as the darkness rushed toward him in twenty-foot jumps, until all the lights were out and he found himself standing exposed in the only lit office in the department. Then he realized with horror that if the revenue manager arrived to find his lights on, he would know at once that someone had been in his office. And since all rooms and offices had motion sensor lights, there was no way for Michael to turn them off from inside. Only time could cover his tracks, and time was in short supply.

He flipped frantically to the end of the alphabet, to a customer's name he recognized from the new-contracts schedule he had seen last week. So the new contracts were here, he thought to himself—stored out of reach, waiting for Falcon to do his worst with them. But as Michael returned the contract to the folder, his forearm brushed it, smearing a thin streak of blood along the right margin—the file drawer edge had cut him just below the elbow. Knowing he could do nothing about it, he pushed the paper back into the folder and closed the cabinet. But just as the latch snapped shut on the shiny metallic doors, he saw a glimmer of light reflected in the metal. The light grew brighter, and he turned around to see a wall of illumination approaching steadily down the hallway, just as the wave of darkness had done a few minutes earlier. Someone was coming to work.

Shutting the drawer, he left the office and closed the door behind him. The corridor lights were still moving toward him in the distance, but no one was visible yet above the cubicle walls. His own motion triggered the lights above him as he hurried toward a cubicle across the hallway and grabbed an interoffice envelope from the side of the person's desk. Making sure it was empty, he snatched a pen and scribbled "Russell Laidlaw" on it before darting back to the revenue manager's office and shoving it under the doorway. Then he turned, tucked his hands in his pockets, and, with his head discreetly lowered, walked away from the two approaching men who were now visible in the distance.

As Michael moved down the far end of the corridor, Laidlaw and Danny, his assistant, rounded the corner and went to Laidlaw's office. In the assistant's hand were the revenue carve-out schedules they had taken from the assistant's desk on the way. Both men stopped as they reached the window to the office.

"Why are your lights on?" Danny asked.

"I don't know," Laidlaw confessed.

But the answer became clear when they opened the door and saw, in the center of the room, an interoffice envelope addressed to Mr. Laidlaw. Clearly an overzealous employee from the mailroom had shoved it under the door just minutes ago, so quickly that it had triggered the motion sensors in the ceiling. But curiously, the envelope was empty, and Laidlaw shook his head at the mailroom personnel's sloppy performance of late. Then, remembering the urgency in Diamond's voice, he rushed to the filing cabinet and grabbed the documents needed for the meeting. Closing his office door, they moved back down the hallway at a brisk walk to the elevator.

As they waited to be taken to the twentieth floor, he noticed a strange red smear on the edge of the last file.

*   *   *

At eight o'clock that night, Michael told Andrea and Dustin they could go home. He was comfortable with the progress they had made, but the real reason he was excusing them was so he could get back to the revenue contracts.

"How late are you staying?" Andrea asked him.

"Oh, just a bit longer. I want to wrap up this testing memo before I go home."

"Well, don't stay too late."

They packed up their computers and left the room, and he waited fifteen minutes before walking around the floor. Everyone had gone home; entire sections of the building were now dark. The only trace of life was from the distant sound of vacuum cleaners as a cleaning crew moved slowly through the other half of the floor. Looking across to the corridor leading to

the executive wing, he was relieved to see it also in darkness—
the twins were gone, along with Mr. Seaton, too, and all the other
executives. Michael would have all the freedom and privacy he
needed to move throughout the building undisturbed and
undiscovered.

He scanned his security badge to enter the inside stairway
and bounded down the steps to the floor where the revenue
manager worked. As he entered the eighteenth floor, the dim area
lit up once again.

Even when it was empty, the corporate headquarters seemed
to have its own life force, reacting to various stimuli like a living
thing. He looked up at one of the small black spheres on the
ceiling, wondering which direction the masked security camera
was pointing. Praying it was watching only the exits, he moved
down the hallway toward the revenue manager's office.

He was relieved to find that the revenue manager had not
locked his door. However, when he tried to open the top drawer
of one file cabinet, it wouldn't open. Michael had been a
notorious amateur lock-picker in college—impressing his friends
and occasionally leading to minor trouble with local sororities.
His abilities were limited to simple locks, of course, but the lax
tumbler design for these cabinets shouldn't present much of a
problem. Using two paperclips from the desk, he had unlocked
all four cabinets in five minutes.

Happily, the files were well organized. As he found the
various contracts, he checked each off the list he had printed,
until he had pulled what looked to be all the new contracts for
the year. Once he had amassed a sixteen-inch pile, he lifted them
in his arms and headed back to the staircase. He had to scan his
security badge going in and out of the stairwell, and to his horror,
he almost dropped the files while balancing them on his knee to
work the badge across the door's scanner.

Then, opening the door to the twentieth floor, he felt a fresh
stab of fear. All the lights in the corridor running toward the

executive wing were now lit, meaning that someone had triggered the sensors in the past few minutes. He set the contracts under the desk of a vacant cubicle and walked slowly toward the executive wing. It was possible that someone from the cleaning crew had triggered the lights, but he needed to know for sure whether anyone else was working in the executive wing. If someone was still around, he would need to be very careful indeed.

His instincts warned him that he was not alone, and he found himself peeking around each corner down the long corridor. His eyes widened as he peeked around the third turn and saw both twins in Don Seaton's office. Lucas was working at the computer; Lance stood behind him. Michael pulled his head back. It was now after nine o'clock—he had thought surely they were gone by now. Peeking around the corner again, he watched them at a distance until he was convinced they hadn't seen or heard him. Then he backtracked to the cubicle where he had hidden the contracts.

Back in the audit room, he started digging through the details, verifying the legal language and figures with the findings in the firm's audit. Everything appeared fine until he got to the twenty-third page of the fifth contract. Here was language that didn't belong. He had seen nothing in the company's records to account for this language. In fact, the only place he had seen such a scenario was in his fraud identification training. If this one short paragraph, which completely changed the terms of the business deal, was repeated in enough contracts, it would overestimate the company's income by millions, artificially inflating the stock price. The results could be disastrous.

He tensed, now on full alert. Slapping a sticky note next to the paragraph, he moved on to the next contract. He flipped back to the same section and felt a tingle as he saw the same wording again. Then he looked at the remaining contracts and found the same words in most of them. He reread the paragraph. It was verbatim every time: the same blatant accounting misstatement, the same inflation of earned revenue during the period. The consistency left no doubt in his mind: it was intentional, which meant it was fraud.

It was impossible to tell how the fraud had happened or how many people might be involved, but the truth was inescapable: the accounting records were reporting two to three times the actual revenue for these contracts. It was too early to know how much the company's total revenue was overstated, because he still needed to work through some calculations to determine how much revenue *should be* reported for the contracts, then compare that with the inflated figure being reported. By three in the morning he had read through every contract and calculated the proper revenue amounts, and what he had found was precisely the conspiracy that he and Glazier had spent the past eighteen months searching for. And apparently—he realized with a sudden sense of danger—Kurt Matthews must have found it, too.

He made copies of the contracts before returning them to Laidlaw's office. As he left the building, he sensed an unusual calm in the air. The parking lot was quiet as a graveyard. He went to his car, a leather case of copied documents in each hand. Putting them in the back of the Audi, he noticed a newish-looking Ford Mustang in the far corner of the lot. Its black exterior had rendered it all but invisible in the night, but he could see that it had parked diagonally across the rows, as if to give it a clear view of the front of the building.

Turning back to his Audi, he got in and drove out of the parking lot. But as he entered the main boulevard that snaked back toward the interstate, he kept his eyes on the rearview mirror, watching the Mustang for as long as the fading image remained in sight.

Nearing the edge of the Tech Center, he abandoned the interstate, cut through a sleeping neighborhood, and circled back to the corporate park—he had to know if he was just being skittish.

He was back at X-Tronic only ten minutes after leaving. Scanning the parking lot, he felt a deep sense of foreboding. The Mustang was gone.

15

———✴———

MICHAEL THREW THE Audi into third gear, punched the accelerator, and pulled through another tight turn overhanging a steep drop-off deep in the Rocky Mountains. With a racer's aggressiveness, he pushed the car along the winding road. In his rearview mirror, the morning sun had set the snowcapped peaks ablaze. The cool air was reviving him after a sleepless night.

He hadn't bothered calling in sick for work. He had merely woken up, sent a quick e-mail from home telling Falcon, Andrea, and Dustin that he had a stomach flu, and then thrown on his warmest casual clothes before dashing to the mountains to find a certain retired physician from the Parks and Wildlife Department.

After pulling through the next turn, he held third gear for two seconds, waiting until the needle passed six thousand rpm, then slapped it down-and-up into fifth gear. He was the only driver not respecting the electronic signs flashing "7% GRADE FOR THE NEXT 2 MILES."

As he reached 90 mph, he tapped the button on the car's Bluetooth twice, triggering the redial on his cell phone. He got a raspy recording—he would have to leave another message. He waited impatiently for the message to end before he began yelling into the phone.

"Glazier! Where the hell are you! I need to talk to you about Aspen—now! Something's happened out here, and . . ." He tightened his grip around the wheel and pulled through another overhanging turn. "Look, this is going way beyond money now, so you'd better get ready to rethink this whole thing. I don't know if I can do this much longer. I don't care what you have to do to make it happen, but it's time for you to take a trip to Denver." Disgusted, he pressed the button again to end the call. Glazier was supposed to answer his calls immediately—no excuses. "Where the *fuck* are you, Glazier?" he asked again, this time to himself.

* * *

Michael followed the instructions he had printed from the Internet. When he turned onto a quiet snow-covered road, he realized he had entered the secluded high country. Tall, snow-covered firs and spruces canopied the road, enveloping him in a long, white tunnel. A half mile in, he came upon a scattering of cabins, built away from the road at regular intervals and half hidden in the trees. A husky stuck its head above the snow and watched with keen interest as he passed.

A few hundred yards farther, Michael saw what he was looking for: 475 Maple Road. As he turned the car into the rough driveway and killed the engine, the cabin's front door squeaked open, and an old man stepped onto the cold porch. Under a heavy wool balaclava, pale blue eyes glittered from a face weathered by many winters in the thin mountain air.

"Don't tell me—you're Michael Chapman," the man's voice announced calmly. "You're thirty minutes late."

Michael caught the fresh scent of pine needles as he approached the cabin. "Dr. Speer. I'm sorry. I didn't expect so much snow on the roads off the highway."

The old man swatted the air in front of his face, as if to dismiss Michael's miscalculation. "Welcome to the highlands. This isn't Denver, you know. The snow sticks a little longer up here." He turned to make sure his door had latched, then returned his gaze to Michael. "Anyway, I gave up on you. I'm on my way to take my two grandchildren ice-skating."

"Dr. Speer, please—it's very important that I speak with you."

"It's very important that I take my grandchildren ice-skating," Dr. Speer corrected him. "They are my future, you know."

"I'm here about your *past*," Michael said, tucking his hands into his jacket after stopping in the crusty snow at the base of the front steps. "You met a friend of mine a week ago. I'd like to speak with you about that."

"I meet a lot of people," the old man replied as he came down the snowy steps toward Michael.

"Yes, I'm sure that's true. But this one would have left a strong impression—he was dead when you met him, up on Vail Mountain."

The doctor stiffened halfway down the steps. His gaze had locked on to the snow, and his lips tensed, as if he were struggling with something. Then, after a few seconds, the doctor's eyes cut sideways at him with a stern expression, and Michael realized the man was judging him. *He knows something,* Michael thought. *And he's trying to decide if he should tell me.*

"Come with me," the man finally said.

The hard, dry snow crunched underfoot as the doctor moved past him, toward an old red truck parked next to the cabin. There was no other sound from the snowy woods surrounding them. And the stillness of this beautiful, solitary place only seemed to heighten the sense that behind those kind gray eyes lay information that would forever change Michael's life.

*   *   *

"If you see enough death, you begin to see patterns," the doctor began. "A businessman's heart exploding because he lived life too fast. When you first find the corpse, you can almost see the fear he felt when he realized he was going to die, that the party was over. Or an old woman, withered with age, with a.long life in the distant past—perhaps she lost her husband twenty years ago and now longs for the promised reunion. But you can almost see the peace in her face when she went to sleep for the last time. Or a victim of a car accident, astonished, even in death, that such a thing could happen to them. But it never seemed right, you know, the way I found your friend. His face was not like any of the others. I had only seen that look once before, nearly thirty years ago."

They were walking along the outer edge of the frozen lake outside Dillon, watching while Dr. Speer's two grandchildren glided over the ice amid a few dozen other skaters of all sizes and ages.

"What look?" Michael asked.

Dr. Speer stopped and pulled his gloved hands from his coat pockets to snug the checkered scarf around his neck. "I must warn you that you could be hearing the intuition of an experienced doctor, or the delusions of a crazy old man."

The muscles in the back of Michael's neck were tight from the long hours he had worked the past few weeks. He rolled his head in a circle to ease the stiffness, then said, "Please, tell me what you saw."

"Thirty years ago, a Summit County Search and Rescue team found a victim of a bear attack near the Arapahoe National Wildlife Refuge, a few hours from here. He was a nature photographer that was reported missing. I was called in once they found the body." Dr. Speer paused to watch the two small girls skating in endless circles, blissful in their small world. "The way his body had shriveled, his widened jaw, torn with claw marks, but above all, the horror in his eyes—they were open so wide, we were afraid they'd fall out if we moved him."

"I can't imagine such pain," Michael said.

Dr. Speer's lips pressed tight together, almost as if he felt the pain he was trying to describe. He continued, "It wasn't that; it was something else: anger. He died with an anger that most never know."

"Anger at the bear?"

"Mm-m, maybe. At the time, that's what I thought. But I could never forget his face, and years later, after my wife was killed, another idea occurred to me." He paused a second, arms dangling at his side, looking as if the words were hard to say. "What if he was angry at God?"

"I'm not sure I follow."

Dr. Speer's lip curled as if he were trying to smile. But then he gave up the attempt, and his eyes grew sad. "Well, think about it. Anger towards fate. Anger at an injustice. That kind of anger, in the end, can only be directed at God." He sat down in a patch of snow that had formed along the rim of the frozen lake, as if his memories were making him tired.

"If it's not too presumptuous of me, how was your wife killed?" Michael asked, feeling a pang of sympathy at the painful solitude revealed in the old man's face.

Dr. Speer looked down, seeing a preserved memory before glancing back at Michael with apologetic eyes. "I wasn't angry with God for long, you know. A place like that . . . no, a person can't stay there very long."

"I'm sorry; it has to be a terrible loss."

"It was a long time ago, I'm afraid. But back to your friend—I had every instinct that he was not killed in surprise. When we found his body, it didn't seem full of shock or sorrow—it was anger."

Hearing a sharp clatter, Michael turned toward the ice in time to see a young man whose skates had slipped out from under him, sending him sprawling on the hard ice. The man grunted and rolled onto all fours, and Michael was surprised at how sharp and clear the sound was. Looking over his shoulder to make sure no one was in earshot, he saw the skate rental hut, the cold parking lot lined with six-foot snowbanks, and the vast frozen lake that stretched far beyond the orange-coned perimeter of the polished skating rink. Seeing no one near them, he felt safe again about speaking to Dr. Speer.

"Do you think he died from hitting a tree? Do you think it was an accident?" he said, impatient to get to the real question he had been wanting to ask.

"Injustices don't come out of accidents. Bad luck does, of course, but true injustice has both a victim and a perpetrator. For my wife, it was a drunk driver. For the photographer, it was a bear. And for your friend, I'm not sure what it was, but I don't think it was a tree."

"Did you perform an autopsy?"

Dr. Speer frowned. "It wasn't required. Besides my unfounded gut impression, there was nothing to lead the authorities to perform one. To them, it was no different from a tragic car accident, with all the answers lying in the obvious circumstances of the setting. And also, I was retired—just meeting with an old colleague in Vail—so I informally joined the Vail Mountain Rescue team."

"Do you think it's possible that someone murdered him on the slopes?"

The older man thought about the question for a second. "How could anything like that happen? It's almost impossible to contemplate. But I hesitate, because in all my reluctance to allow for the possibility of murder, I have to concede that your friend looked as if he was taking a horrible secret to the grave. I'm not certain what happened to him on the slopes that day, but I've never been convinced it was a tree that killed him."

Michael looked across the sun-spangled ice as the breeze whipped up a plume of fine snow and carried it over the skaters' heads and into the silent woods. "I'm trying to believe your instincts, but you have to admit, it's not the most scientific evidence."

"There's something else," the older man added. "You're not the first person to ask me about your friend's death."

"What?" Michael stared at the doctor.

"A few days after your friend's body was discovered, a man in his late thirties came to my cabin asking the same questions as you."

His thoughts awhirl, Michael tried on every combination of possibilities. Sarah and he weren't alone in their search for answers. He thought about his findings at X-Tronic, Glazier's warning about the twins, Falcon's suspicious behavior. He thought about Sarah, the files strung across the floor of her apartment, her plea for help. He thought about Kurt's notes. Then there were Dr. Speer's suspicions, his impressions from the "accident," his revelation that someone else was inquiring about Kurt's death. Michael took deep, slow breaths, feeling his anger as the realization sank in that Kurt had been murdered.

"What else?" he asked the doctor, his voice tense. "This man who visited you—what did he look like? Tell me everything!"

"His face was very ordinary, no outstanding features—as if he were an actor who could make himself look like anyone." The doctor paused to raise his index finger. "But there was one thing he couldn't hide. He had a terrible twitch in his left eye that would come and go. A severe case of blepharospasm, I'd say. If you met him, I don't think you could miss it."

Another sharp gust whipped across the frozen lake, buffeting Michael's face with tiny, sharp spicules of ice. And for a moment, his anger was pushed out by fear that much more was going on at X-Tronic than he had imagined. Sarah must be right: Kurt had discovered something, and it got him killed. And now Michael had to wonder whether he was stepping in and launching blindly off down the same ill-fated run as his friend.

16

———⊷✹⊶———

"I'M AFRAID WE have a problem," Jerry Diamond said, leaning over his draft beer so that Falcon could hear him over the cheers. They were sitting at a corner table, apart from the crowd that had gathered to watch the Nuggets game.

"With things in Portland?" Falcon asked as the Nuggets sank a three-pointer on the huge projection screen. His eyes turned from the game and casually scanned the digital scoreboard that made the front wall look like a Las Vegas sports bookie's headquarters. "You said things were going fine up there," he said, frowning.

"I'm told things in Portland are fine. I'm going there in a few days to make sure. What I'm talking about has to do with *your* responsibilities."

"I don't understand," Falcon said to the man sitting across from him. He suddenly felt put on the defensive. Well, he would stand his ground. Just because the guy outweighed him by sixty pounds of muscle and had a head like a battering ram didn't mean he could intimidate him.

"Is it always customary for you auditors to work at the client's office late at night?"

"Part of the job," Falcon replied. "That's why they call it 'busy season.'"

"So you often work at the client's until three a.m.? I'm just curious, because that's what your boy Michael Chapman's been doing."

The game forgotten, Falcon turned to Diamond with a confused stare, not even glancing back at the screen when the entire bar erupted in cheers.

"You know," Diamond continued in his deep baritone, "he's beginning to remind me of another auditor of yours that used to work late at our house."

"He's not like Kurt Matthews—trust me!" Falcon said, leaning forward again to be heard over the ambient racket of the bar. "I've done my research on Chapman. He's been with us almost two years. Before that, he was with a small firm in Kansas City. I've personally phoned his references and past supervisors. They all say the same thing: he's loyal, hardworking, gets the job done, but can sometimes use a little motivating, so he does his best work when he has a lot of manager oversight and direction." Falcon paused to let Diamond digest the words before continuing. "I got the sense he's a good soldier but not much of a leader. He'll do only what he's told. That's why I handpicked him for this engagement. Trust me, Chapman's the last person in the world that would discover what's going on at X-Tronic."

Diamond's eyes narrowed. "You told me he got one of the highest scores in the country on the CPA exam."

Falcon laughed as if the man had somehow missed the whole point. "Oh, he used to be brilliant, all right, but now he's just burnt out. The last client he was on ended in a total disaster. Now his career's on the line. He doesn't have the motivation to pose any threat to us."

"Then why the hell does our security log have his badge moving throughout our building—elevators *and* staircases—at three a.m.? I've seen a printout of all badge activity after regular business hours—your boy's all over the place. There's something going on here. And the twins agree."

"You told this to the twins?" Falcon asked in surprise. Tension returned to his face. He didn't know which to worry about more: Michael's unusual behavior or Diamond getting the twins involved.

"I tell them everything—that's my job!"

Falcon muttered something under his breath. An overstressed waitress, maneuvering through the dense crowd, finally broke through the opening and arrived at their table. She asked if they wanted another round. Falcon nodded with a lackluster expression. She couldn't help noticing that these were the only two people in the whole bar not jubilant over the Nuggets' sudden lead.

"What exactly did the twins say?" Falcon asked after she left.

"Well, it seems they think it's time for them to become more involved. They plan to get more familiar with your Mr. Chapman." Diamond sat back with a coy grin on his face, as if the twins' interest in Michael vindicated him of Falcon's apparent disapproval.

"Christ! They can't keep getting involved like this."

"They're the ones running this show."

"No, they're not!" Falcon said, clinching his fist on the tabletop and flexing his arm muscles instinctively. "We all have risks here! They need to respect that. Now, I made sure we wouldn't have to worry about anything like Kurt's situation again. And that's exactly why I picked Michael. He's not capable of exceeding anyone's expectations anymore—Christ, even today he called in sick. Does that sound to you like he's looking for something?"

Diamond shook his head briefly without looking at Falcon, looking as if *he* was now the one disappointed. "Michael wasn't sick. He spent the day in the mountains near Breckenridge. He met with a doctor who was apparently involved in finding Kurt's body."

Falcon's mouth dropped. "What! How do you know that?"

Diamond looked down at his beer, seemingly hypnotized by the bubbles rising to the inside edge of his glass. As if his thoughts were elsewhere, he said, "We're already having him watched, John. I'm telling you, your boy is definitely something we have to worry about."

17

———————✳———————

THE NIGHT WIND whipped a thin layer of snow off the three-foot base in the woods, rearranging the powder like desert sand dunes. Only a few miles outside the glimmering lights of Aspen's village center, the wooded mountainside lay in white-blanketed silence. A gray Siberian husky raced through the snow and jumped up against the base of the tree, barking excitedly.

"What's you got there, boy?" Marcus Graham yelled. In a red-and-black flannel coat, jeans, and heavy boots, he moved comfortably through the shin-deep snow. He slapped the dog playfully with his big hands, and its barking grew more excited, its tail beating a tattoo against his legs.

Marcus left the dog and ran back toward the house—a stately replica of a Tudor country manor. The three-story mansion had an exterior mostly of pale stone that seemed to blend naturally with the surrounding snow. Stopping at the glass double doors to the courtyard, Marcus turned again toward the trees lining the back of the yard. He bent down, hands against his thighs, and called to the husky. "Thurgin! You stubborn brute, come!"

The only sound to be heard inside the mansion's den was the crackling of the fireplace. Don Seaton sat in his high-backed leather chair, immersed in a file of documents. Behind the walnut burl desk where he sat, bookshelves covered the entire back wall from floor to ceiling. Near the rolling ladder at the far end stood an outdated globe that still showed the vast empire of the USSR—a gift from an old colleague.

He scanned through the documentation his lawyers had obtained from Harvard Business School—campus records for Lance and Lucas during their university days. Also, there were transcripts of various interviews his lawyers had conducted with former professors and acquaintances of the twins.

As he read the pages, he became more and more concerned that his sons had inherited too many of the traits he could remember from his own youth. Their grades were outstanding, and their professors reconfirmed their quick grasp of even the most complicated economic and financial theory models. But Seaton knew all this. What captured his attention more were the stories of reckless pranks and insubordinate disrespect.

Hearing a light rap at the double doors, he looked up from the folder. One of the solid oak doors opened as Marcus stepped into the den.

"Yes?" Seaton asked in the tone of a sea captain receiving a report from an officer.

"Sir, the jet is ready at the airport, and the car is warming."

"Thank you, Marcus," Seaton replied to his bodyguard. "Oh, Marcus?"

"Yes sir."

"I've read most of the information you had compiled about the twins, but despite your concerns, I still don't think they are a threat to me."

"Sir, I know this isn't easy for you to accept, but their behavior at Harvard is consistent with the other inquiries we made at Westington and Dover-Scheffler."

"So they got a little restless at a couple of boarding schools and an Ivy League university. A lot of kids act the same way when pushed into an environment like that. It's my fault—I shouldn't have sent them away so soon after their mother's death." Seaton was silent for a few seconds as his thoughts darted back through time to the day his wife died. "Thank you, Marcus," he finally said, returning to the present and looking back down at the papers. "I'll be out in a few minutes."

"Yes sir," Marcus replied, and left the room.

Seaton set his glass on the mantel, picked up the folders on his desk, glanced once more at the familiar documents, and stuffed them into the remaining space in his soft briefcase.

As he left his den, his suede shoes padded quietly along the corridor to the grand staircase that wrapped the wall of the front entryway. Just as Seaton descended the staircase, Marcus walked into the anteroom from a side door and took his briefcase, then handed him a cashmere overcoat and a gray wool flat cap.

"Where's Thurgin?" Seaton asked.

"Resting in the game room. He's a little tired—had a nice frolic in the woods earlier."

Seaton smiled. "Besides you, Marcus, that dog is the best security money can buy. I don't think much could slip past him."

A short, plump man in black livery appeared in the anteroom doorway. "Excuse me, sir," he said.

"Yes, Hopkins?" Seaton replied.

"I'm sorry, sir, but I wanted to remind you that the boys are having their party here this weekend."

"Ah, that's right—I'd nearly forgotten. Do you think we should have someone keep an eye on them?" Seaton said, turning to Marcus. "I'd like to continue monitoring them."

"I've already made arrangements," Marcus replied.

The billionaire nodded as if he had almost assumed that his head of security would anticipate such things. They both walked out of the mansion toward a red Hummer that idled in the driveway.

Marcus drove them along the packed snow of the mountain roads for twenty minutes before they had weaved their way around enough of the mountain to reach the open land next to the river gorge, which housed Aspen's small commercial airport. The Hummer was waved through the security gate, and they drove along the edge of the single runway toward a Learjet 60 XR that had emerged from a cluster of private hangars. As the Hummer neared the aircraft, they could hear the droning of the jet engines.

Seaton stepped out onto the runway and was immediately greeted by a tall man in uniform. "Good evening, Mr. Seaton," he said, smiling.

"Evening, Captain Steiner," Seaton said to his pilot. "How does the weather look tonight?"

"Clear skies from here to New York."

"Good—I'm glad there's at least one thing on this trip that I can count on going smoothly."

"I'm sorry, sir?"

"Oh, nothing. The people I'm meeting in New York . . . Let's just say I'd rather be vacationing in Siberia. Here's a little free advice: don't ever try to prevent a multibillion-dollar corporate takeover—you wouldn't believe the number of enemies you can make."

Seaton had planned to read more of the background material on the Cygnus proposal once they got in the air. But as the jet accelerated across the runway and took off with the red sunset backlighting the mountainous horizon, he felt suddenly small and alone amid such majesty. And he wondered whether he still had enough fight in him for one last battle.

18

FRIDAY MORNING, MICHAEL went to work at X-Tronic feeling an overwhelming languor that seemed to slow and diffuse his concentration. He was already a half hour late, but he didn't care. Yesterday's trip to the mountains had only added to the weight on him, which he felt almost as a physical burden. Both Andrea and Dustin were busy working. Everything seemed loud and busy in his ears. He was tired and desperately ready for the weekend to begin.

The morning passed with a slow dreaminess. Managing to gather a little energy by lunchtime, he threw himself back into his work. Even Andrea and Dustin noticed that his energy had returned. They even had to take down his order for lunch because he didn't want to take a few minutes to run down to the corporate deli.

Once the two staffers left the room with his order for a turkey and Swiss on pumpernickel, his work so completely consumed him that he missed the first knock on the conference room door.

"Mr. Chapman?" a voice asked.

Michael looked up to find the Seaton twins in the doorway. He wondered how long they had been there watching him.

"Lance and Lucas Seaton," he replied. "Pleased to meet you. I've seen you around the office but haven't had the pleasure. I'm Michael Chapman, the new senior on the engagement."

"Yes," said Lucas. "It's terrible what happened to Kurt. I hope things are coming along well."

"Isn't it a bit . . . I don't know . . . *awkward* to come into the middle of an engagement on such short notice?" Lance asked.

"Yeah, how does something like this affect the quality of the audit?" Lucas added. "I can't imagine it's all that efficient to change the engagement team in the middle of the job."

Michael held his tongue. He had heard stories about the cold superiority the twins could lord over people, but he still had to resist the urge to confront them. He had wanted to say, *Next time we'll try to do a better job of scheduling our audit personnel on jobs that don't conflict with their deaths.* But he was speaking to the client, so he kept his response more politic. "No need to worry. In fact, we're ahead of schedule."

"Have you noticed any problems? Any issues we should know about?" Lance asked.

"Nothing major," Michael lied. "We have about forty small audit adjustments so far, but that's not unusual for a corporation this large."

The twins separated and moved around the sides of the conference table, exuding the confident patience of predators that had cornered their quarry. Casually Michael minimized his computer window before they reached his side, to hide the document he was preparing. He had been warned not to let them know what he was working on. *Speak to them only in generalities,* Glazier had told him. *Never specifics. Keep them curious, and they'll be forced to bring you into their circle.*

Lance's eyes scanned the room as if looking for something specific. "We just stopped by to see how everything's going. We're glad things seem to be coming along."

"At this point, as well as they can be," Michael assured them.

"What are you working on now?" said Lance.

"Oh, just reviewing some workpapers, getting things organized. You know how it is."

Lucas grinned. "I'm glad we caught you before the weekend."

"Yes," Lance continued. "We're having a bit of a party this Saturday at our father's estate in Aspen. A group of people will be up for the weekend, and we wanted to invite you as well."

"You're inviting me to your father's house for the weekend?" Michael asked, unable to hide his astonishment.

"It's a party. There's going to be about four hundred people there. Most are from Aspen, but we're inviting a few dozen up from Denver as well."

"Yes," said Lance, picking up the conversation from his brother, "but we only have room to board those from Denver. The Aspen crowd is on its own, but we'll have room on the property for you to stay."

"A party in Aspen *this* weekend?" He was still befuddled.

"Saturday night," Lance said.

"Well, yes, of course—I'd love to," he confessed, trying to keep some modicum of composure. He was thinking as much of Glazier as of himself. The party could be just the thing for getting answers to some of his questions. And Glazier had wanted him to get closer to the twins in case they might put him onto the money trail he was trying to follow.

"And please, feel free to bring a friend if you'd like," Lucas added.

The comment sparked another idea in Michael's head—another opportunity. "I think I will," he replied.

"Well, we won't keep you any longer," said Lucas. "We know you're busy."

"Yes, well, thanks very much for the invitation. I'm really looking forward to it."

"We'll have someone e-mail you the invitation this evening."

Michael thanked the twins, and they left the room as suddenly as they had appeared. The heavy glass door closed slowly behind them. Once they were out of sight, he stepped toward the corner window, as far as possible from the door, and speed-dialed Sarah Matthews.

19

————•▪❈▪•————

D ON SEATON TAPPED his index finger on the large rosewood conference table on the second floor of the New York Stock Exchange. Expansive windows looked out on New York's financial district in lower Manhattan, while those opposite looked down on the vacant trading floor of the exchange. Seaton looked out at the financial district, the seat of an endless cycle of transferring wealth, run by ambitious men and women. It was a world determined to change faster than society could control it, so that the masses had little choice but to react to the decisions of the few. It was a world with a short attention span, quickly bored, always hungry for more—a world that couldn't have been further from the reclusive lifestyle Seaton had chosen more than two decades ago when he built the huge chalet on his isolated estate outside Aspen. But as with so many men who retired to the mountains, his ambitions had been formed by an earlier life in the energetic, chaotic city. New York had been his first home, and it had taught him most of the lessons that he carried with him still.

The masters of finance sat around the table: Randle Cuttingham, the NYSE chairman; Todd Farrell, the U.S. trade commissioner; Richard Donnelly, economic adviser for the Securities and Exchange Commission; and Fredrick Kavanaugh, CEO and Chairman of Cygnus International. Both Kavanaugh and Seaton were accompanied by legal counsel from their corporations. The meeting had been called to discuss preliminary responses to Cygnus's acquisition bid for X-Tronic's common stock and to thresh out any antitrust issues that were likely to result from a merger. The meeting was being held one month before the highly anticipated X-Tronic annual shareholders' meeting in Denver.

"Mr. Seaton? Excuse me, Mr. Seaton?"

He looked up from the table to find the trade commissioner looking at him. "I'm sorry, Todd. Could you please repeat the question?"

"Mr. Seaton, I was hoping to get your initial reaction to the proposed acquisition."

"There isn't going to be any acquisition," Seaton proclaimed.

"Come on, Don," Kavanaugh interposed. "If the shareholders of X-Tronic vote to accept the generous offer my company is making, we will all walk away rich."

"I'm already rich."

"*Richer,* then," Kavanaugh corrected himself. "X-Tonic's software products would compliment Cygnus's products. It will strengthen our competitive position in the market and expand our customer base. Everyone wins with the acquisition, Don."

Seaton shook his head. "What you're trying to create is dangerously close to a monopoly. Research and development in the industry will suffer because of decreased competition. Innovation will lag. Massive layoffs at X-Tronic will be inevitable. The results of Cygnus's previous acquisitions are well documented, Fred. You assimilate your target acquisitions into Cygnus, destroying every shred of independence in their entrepreneurial spirit. This is something I'm not going to let you do to X-Tronic."

Kavanaugh's wide mouth puckered, as if he had just tasted something sour. His dark, shifty eyes scanned the other faces at the table almost as if he expected someone else to protest in his defense. No one did.

"You're missing the big picture," Kavanaugh said, returning his gaze to Seaton. "We're talking about massive international expansion of our companies' operations."

Richard Donnelly leaned forward and cleared his throat. "Technological innovation and ongoing deregulation have driven the globalization process by tearing down barriers. A merger of this size would have a dramatically positive effect on the economy."

"Dr. Donnelly," Seaton said with a sigh, "I respect your understanding of economic theories, but with all due respect, the merger would have a dramatically *negative* effect on X-Tronic's workforce."

Donnelly shook his head. "A key element of the U.S. economy is a flexible labor market. Short-term layoffs from inefficient or obsolete jobs are good for the economy in the long term. In other words, your employees will find new jobs."

"That is not acceptable," Seaton replied. "I have a responsibility to all fifty thousand employees at X-Tronic."

"You have a responsibility to the X-Tronic *shareholders*," Kavanaugh retorted. "In any event, I don't think your shareholders will join in your efforts to prevent the merger."

Seaton stood up from the table and shuffled some analyst reports into his leather portfolio. "Fred, you're forgetting that even though I'm not a majority shareholder of X-Tronic any longer, I still have thirty percent ownership in the company—and a great deal of influence with both our board of directors and our shareholders. I built X-Tronic from the ground up, and I'm not going to let you take control of it. Now, please excuse me, gentlemen. It's obvious to me that this meeting is over."

Taking one last look to survey the disappointed faces around the table, his eyes met Kavanaugh's. The man's arrogance made Seaton dislike him more now than ever before in their long, adversarial history. Even as Seaton left the table, he knew he was taking a risk walking away from the meeting. He had much to do if he wanted to save his company.

He found Marcus waiting for him in the hallway, and together they walked toward the grand marble staircase and the looming chaos waiting below.

Lance and Lucas Seaton sat drinking their Singha beers in the Gold Room of the Geiberstein ski lodge, overlooking the base of Aspen Mountain. The VIP dining room was the premiere place for intermission luncheons amid the day's skiing and snowboarding. It was one of the many places in Aspen where the rich and famous could be seen.

The region hadn't had a decent snowfall in over a week, but the high altitude and low temperatures had maintained the slopes' sixty-inch base. The flow of skiers and snowboarders riding up in the chair lifts and flying down the mountain created an endless bustle of activity in and out of the lodge.

The waiter returned to the twins' table with their papaya salad with crab, tiger prawns, and grilled squid encircled with tangy limes, sweet coconut, and lemongrass. They ordered another round of Thai beers.

"You know Dad's going to try to stop the merger," Lucas said after inspecting his salad.

"He won't succeed," Lance replied.

"He doesn't usually fail at things?"

"He's doing it for all the wrong reasons—everyone will be against him."

"Everyone's been against him before, and he's still prevailed."

Lance chewed thoughtfully and swallowed. "This time will be different. He's getting old—he's not the man he used to be."

But Lucas didn't feel as he imagined Lance did. For Lucas, it felt as if events were accelerating out of his control. He was surprised at the suddenly nostalgic turn his thoughts had taken in recent weeks. He had recalled that last happy summer in their youth, only months before their mother's death, when they all learned to ride horseback. Their father had been so excited with the idea at first, he had a large stable built on the Aspen property. Their parents had even flown to Wyoming for a weekend to pick out the four horses they eventually bought from a top breeder. Lucas could remember with perfect detail the day the horses were delivered, when Lance and he had practiced posting and cantering under the trainer's watchful eye while their beautiful mother and proud father looked on. Even their butler, Hopkins, whom he and Lance had always loved growing up, had stood at the back porch rail, applauding and calling, "Bravo!" and "Good show, lads!"

Lucas dipped a prawn in the saucer of coconut broth. He was silent for a moment. "Do you think he'll be proud of us? When everything's finished, do you think he'll look back and be proud of what we're about to accomplish?"

"How would I know what he thinks?"

"Aw, come on, Lance, you must have thought about it."

"All right, then. No, I don't think he'll be proud. But fuck 'im. We both know he would have done the same thing when he was our age. Hell, he practically *did.* He ran out all his business partners to gain control of X-Tronic. Then he abandoned us after Mom died. He's not the saint people think he is."

"So it's *his* fault?" Lucas asked, as if looking for confirmation that they were doing the right thing.

"It's his fault," Lance confirmed. "Everything that's about to happen is his fault. Don't ever forget that."

Hearing this surprised Lucas. Seeing how easily Lance waited for the denouement to all they had worked toward over the years, it occurred to Lucas—perhaps for the first time—that he and his brother were not so alike as they had once been. The idea of a weakening bond with his brother made him suddenly uneasy, and a certain lightheadedness enveloped him. Perhaps they were about to make a horrible mistake. For the first time, he wondered if there might be another way, another option to consider. But he knew better than to mention any such thought to Lance.

"And the guys'll be there tonight?" Lucas asked after refocusing. He needed to be sure the plan hadn't changed.

"Yes," Lance replied, "but not till real late—almost dawn." He took the last sip of his beer and tried to flag the waiter down from across the room.

"And Michael Chapman?" Lucas asked. His survival instinct kicked in at the very thought of the new auditor at X-Tronic. He knew a threat when he saw one. "He'll be there tonight."

"Has he left Denver yet?"

"No, but he's being watched. We'll get a call once he hits the road. What do we do when he gets here?"

Lance smiled as if amused by the slight challenge they both sensed from Michael's mysterious actions. "We let him come and have fun. We get to know him socially. And then we see what happens."

"I think he's trouble."

"Maybe, but we don't know for sure. Falcon says he won't cause any problems."

"I don't trust Falcon anymore." Lucas's expression had turned hard, and he held eye contact to make sure his brother saw how serious he was.

"Well you'd better *pretend* to trust him," Lance said in a tone that came a little too close to sounding like an order. "We don't have a choice. He knows too much, so we're all in this together now."

Yeah, all in this together, Lucas thought. He had never liked having so many people involved in their plans—that was a big part of why things felt so out of control. This, more than anything else, frustrated him. But then again, it would be unwise to let his brother know he was beginning to lose faith in what they were about to do.

Marcus Graham followed Don Seaton down the marble staircase toward the grand entrance of the New York Stock Exchange building. He watched as his employer caught the attention of the old suits of Wall Street, whose careworn faces, engraved by a lifetime of maneuvering amid the battle dust of high finance, showed their jealousy of the spry old billionaire with the shiny blue eyes and skier's athleticism.

Marcus couldn't help admiring his employer's stature in the business world. He wondered, what was it that made the man so intriguing to the media? Was it his billions of dollars in net worth, his groundbreaking software company that had outlived so many competitors, or his legendary heli-skiing and mountain climbing adventures? In the business community, Seaton seemed to have acquired the stature of a retired general, a man who had found inner peace at the end of a lifetime of war.

Cameras flashed as they moved down the stairs. Reporters threw a barrage of questions.

Don Seaton turned to Marcus and said, "Last time I enjoyed talking to the press was in the eighties, back when they were interested because I was building a new type of corporation. But that was a long time ago. These days it feels like they're just out for blood . . . or dirt."

Marcus smiled at the remark, though never taking his alert eyes from the crowd as he scanned each face for signs of tension. "Mr. Seaton, what did the commission discuss during your meeting?" one journalist asked. "Has Cygnus changed its offer?" another queried. "Why were you the only representative from X-Tronic at the meeting?" "Mr. Seaton, what sort of transformation do you anticipate if the merger goes through?" "Mr. Seaton . . ." "Mr. Seaton . . ." "Mr. Seaton . . ." A symphony of camera flashes threw strobelike shadows on the wall behind them.

"Everyone, please!" Seaton said at last. "You need to slow down. I'm an old man, so I'm afraid I can handle only three or four questions at a time." The press corps laughed. Don took a step forward, and with a smile that charmed even the hardboiled veterans, he pointed to the first journalist he made eye contact with. "Go ahead, please."

"Mr. Seaton," the man said formally, as if he were an attorney cross-examining a witness, "Some say you are less concerned about your company's shareholders than about the welfare of your customers and employees. Are you ignoring your responsibilities to the X-Tronic shareholders? If the merger goes through, who do you think will be the victims?"

Seaton nodded as if he had thought long and hard on the question. "As we all know," he said, "a business can be broken down into terms like 'profitability' and 'operational efficiencies.' But the responsibilities of corporations are changing. There is also a new school of business that emphasizes the relationships a business has with *all* its stakeholders: customers, employees, citizens in the surrounding community . . ."

Marcus's thoughts drifted away from his boss's words as he found what his eyes had never stopped looking for: something suspicious in the crowd. Among the dense throng of journalists and onlookers, he found a face that was not dazzled or intrigued. Instead, it was a face like his own: so serious and focused, it was oblivious to the outside world. Focused like the face of a predator about to spring.

Just as Marcus had singled him out in the crowd, the heavyset man began to move, pushing his way through the crowd, getting closer to the steps. Marcus stood loosely on the balls of his feet, watching, waiting, playing a dozen scenarios in his mind. He even glanced around the crowd for a half second in case this was a decoy, making sure that this one man was the only immediate threat and not part of a team. *Nothing.* His eyes shot back toward the man. He was alone. Then Marcus saw the final warning as the man's right hand lowered to his side, resting, fumbling with something out of sight.

"Get down!" Marcus shouted as he moved forward, drawing his gun.

Heeding his bodyguard's command, the older man dropped to the ground. As the crowd stood baffled and stunned, Marcus leaped in front of Seaton and squatted in a low triangle position, partly to shield the billionaire and partly to steady his firing stance amid the crowd. A woman screamed, and journalists milled and collided in panic as the assailant came barreling through the crowd, yelling, his gun half raised. He looked like an amateur, unsure of his aim. The gun waved about as it fired two shots. The first ricocheted with a whine off the thick marble of the stairs; the second grazed Marcus's shoulder. Without flinching from the pain, the bodyguard returned three steady shots to the man's chest. The assailant fell like a poleaxed bull at the base of the stairs. The journalists, shaken but recognizing the opportunity, rushed back to snap their cameras at the unknown corpse. Marcus maintained a strong hold, keeping Seaton flat on the staircase, and yelled at the crowd to stand back from the body. Eyes watering from the pain in his shoulder, he kept his gun trained on the prostrate, unmoving form in its growing pool of blood.

20

———— ·❊· ————

MARCUS SAT IN the back of an ambulance in front of the New York Stock Exchange building. The street was obstructed by three police cruisers and another ambulance. The entryway was blocked off with yellow police tape that brightened with each flash from the police photographer's camera. And as if the earlier horde of journalists hadn't been enough, all the news networks had now sent reinforcements for their coverage of what the media had dubbed "the Wall Street shooting."

Don Seaton sat in a daze among the bustling investigators outside the trading floor. As he watched the NYPD officers moving throughout the corridor, he reminisced on the life he had enjoyed when starting X-Tronic. The addicting passion of being a new entrepreneur, putting his all into an idea—not just a company, but the possibility of developing a product that would change the marketplace forever. It had never been about the money—the money was only a way of keeping score. He would never admit it, but at first he had been terrified by the rapid growth of the company that would eventually make him billions.

He was nostalgic for the excitement he had experienced with his original business partners when they were starting X-Tronic thirty years ago. But life had taken some tragic turns since those days. Even Seaton's legendary life was turning toward disaster. He had just survived an assassination attempt; his own bodyguard had been wounded in the attack. But the most horrifying thing for him to accept was that he had known the man who tried to kill him. Once, long ago, they had been good friends.

Thirty years ago, Seaton was beginning to build X-Tronic and had recruited two childhood friends: Nick Kemper and Jack Ross. All three men were bursting with ideas and the energy to pursue them. But as they developed X-Tronic in San Francisco, in the wake of the software boom of the early 1980s, the company had produced only flat earnings.

Nick, fearing that the company wouldn't succeed, had exercised his stock options and left for another promising start-up in Silicon Valley. But Don and Jack had planned to stay at X-Tronic for the long haul. He remembered working eighteen-hour days for two years with his friend as they prepared for the company to go public. Eventually, they had developed an array of business software applications that dazzled corporations across the globe.

Seaton could still remember the night he and Jack rented a yacht for the company party after the initial stock offering. Drifting under the Golden Gate Bridge at sunset, they had led the toast to all the employees, for everyone's hard work and for the future. It was the pinnacle of their friendship.

Returning to the present, Seaton turned away from the trading door as more investigators pushed into the side room. Looking at them was too painful. He was lost in his memories. The terrible things that happened between Jack and him after X-Tronic went public were too painful to think about. His chest hurt. He needed fresh air.

Seaton took a last swig from his bottled water and looked briefly around the room. The meeting with the committee had gone exactly as he expected, but the assassination attempt had changed everything. He had planned to travel to Denver this afternoon; now it wasn't possible. There was a new agenda. New York had been a childhood playground in his youth, and a place of learning during college. Now he knew that the city still had one final lesson to teach him: betrayal. He pushed open the door to the outside and walked out under the line of American flags hanging low on the six Corinthian columns of the building's facade.

This time Seaton managed to avoid the journalists. He moved through the crowd until he found Marcus sitting in the back of an ambulance. A heavyset young paramedic was washing the flesh wound with saline solution.

"How is it?" Seaton asked his bodyguard.

"Oh, just a little scrape," Marcus replied, wincing as the paramedic wrapped a bandage around his shoulder. "But they still need to take me to the hospital to get it disinfected. It won't take long; we'll still be able to fly out in a couple hours as planned."

Seaton's eyes followed the paramedic as he rose from the padded bench inside the ambulance and, hunched under the low ceiling, lumbered his way forward to the radio by the driver's seat. In a quiet voice, Seaton leaned in and said, "We can't leave the city yet—there are some things I need to clear up first. I've told the pilot we're not planning to leave until Sunday."

"Have the police any leads on the man?" Marcus asked, studying his employer carefully.

Seaton shook his head. "No, they don't know anything. But his name was Jack Ross."

"You *knew* him?"

"He was a business partner of mine more than twenty-five years ago."

Marcus gave his employer a piercing look. "Why would he want to kill you?" he asked.

Seaton looked back at the columns that, in that moment anyway, made the Stock Exchange building look like an ancient Greek tomb. "That's what we're going to find out."

21

———————‹‹✳››———————

T HE DRIVER PULLED up next to a red brick apartment building in the East Village. Seaton and Marcus emerged from the limousine and walked along the cold sidewalk. Bare trees in protective iron grates lined the neighborhood street. Aspiring artists and students relaxed in corner cafés, rotating their lattes and brochettes as they discussed their passions. It was a time in their young lives, Seaton realized, when they had the luxury of leisure time and abundant hope for the future. While they were busy thinking of their futures, he had returned to the neighborhood in search of his past.

"Who's this friend we're meeting?" Marcus asked. On high alert after the shooting, he was making it a point to walk between Seaton and the street. His eyes roved constantly: scanning around every corner, between parked cars, his imagination continuously rehearsing every potential threat.

"An old business partner," Seaton replied.

"You seem to have a lot of those. Is he connected to the shooter, this Jack Ross?"

"He used to be. We all used to be connected before we split over twenty-five years ago. His name's Nicholas Kemper. While Jack went into other software businesses, Nick took his wealth into the music industry after the first big tech upsurge in Silicon Valley. In the early eighties I bought Nick's shares in X-Tronic so that Jack and I could take it public on our own terms. Afterwards, I squeezed Jack out and took over the CEO position that we had previously shared. After I pushed him out of the executive group, Jack sold his shares to me and left the company. All three of us were worth twenty to thirty million each when I took control of the company. But while Jack started a new venture, Nick experimented with some other tech companies in San Francisco before eventually leaving the industry for good, where he finally ended up using his money to pursue an old passion."

"And his passion was music?"

"Punk rock," Seaton said with a hint of amusement. "Nick was quite a wild one during the seventies. He was always one of those guys that were unsettled with the relaxation of the sixties— was never interested in disco, of course. But he took to punk right away, even before anyone really knew about it, when it was still confined to this neighborhood."

"I thought that stuff all started in England."

Seaton shook his head. "Nah. It went mainstream in England, but its true birth was in New York. Some would argue Detroit, but if you ever argue history with Nick, he'll claim with his dying breath that the movement developed here."

"And he'll know something about Ross?"

"I don't know. They don't exactly travel in the same circles anymore. None of us do. Nick's an odd one, that's for sure. He started an independent record company here in New York after the three of us split. Been losing money ever since, but he doesn't care. He can afford it. Apparently, he's always signing no-name bands that remind him of the glory days of punk. Then he spends a lot of money trying to promote them, but none have ever broken through. Like I said, though, he doesn't care. It's more like a *cause* for him. He despises mainstream media. One of those 'independent music for independent minds' kind of guys. He likes to refer to himself as 'the punk missionary,' like he's trying to spread the word—that sort of thing."

"And at one point this guy was a founder of a software company with you?"

"The tech industry attracts all types," Seaton said with a wry smile. "Ah, here we are. Christ, I haven't been to this place in a long time. I told him we needed to meet someplace private, and this is what he suggested. That's Nick for you."

Marcus looked up at the white turnip that stuck out from the wooden door. Giant red letters stood out on the turnip, announcing "CBGB's" and "OMFUG" with an unmistakable we-don't-give-a-shit attitude. It was as if the bar itself were a cocky, disgruntled youth leaning against a brick wall of a bleak city backstreet.

As they entered the bar, the sunlight vanished, and they could hear the strident, raunching tones of a band rehearsing covers from the Ramones. "Beat on the brat with a baseball bat," were the first words Marcus heard from a screaming kid almost as skinny as the microphone stand he held as he gyrated around onstage. A scratched wooden bar top stretched along the right side of the room, while the left side was crowded with empty tables. The bartender, a big man in his forties with leather straps around both wrists, stared intensely out from behind his draft handles. The walls were covered with so many flyers and advertisements, it was impossible to determine their color.

The two newcomers moved to the back of the bar, where a dozen people in front of the stage shook chaotically to the offbeat vibrations. An older man sat at a table in the far corner, alone and away from the crowd. It was the darkest spot in the room, practically hidden from the entrance. The man's age made him seem out of place, though he didn't seem the least bit concerned as he lit a cigarette, illuminating a pale, rough face.

"Hello, Nick," Seaton said as they reached the table. "Thanks for meeting me."

"It's been a long time, Donald," Nick Kemper said, extending a long arm toward the empty chairs at the table. "How's business?"

"It's a handful."

"Dangerous, too, from what I hear." Nick nodded toward Marcus. "This the bastard that killed Jack?"

Nick's hair was cut short, further emphasizing his long face and large, owllike eyes. He wore a drab brown T-shirt underneath a sports jacket. His cigarette dangled loosely between the long fingers of his left hand, and a tumbler of whiskey sat in front of him on the table. His right hand always kept hold of it, even when he was not drinking, as though someone might try to filch it from him at any moment.

His body shook sporadically to the merciless beat of the music. Suddenly he sparkled. "Let's say you and I get a drink, Donnie! For old times!"

"Nick, I'm not here for a drink. I'm here about Jack. For God's sake, he tried to *kill* me this afternoon, and now he's dead."

"All the more reason to drink!" Nick said, glaring at Marcus with moist, shining eyes.

"Why did he try to kill me, Nick?"

"Well, let's see, a few reasons come to mind."

"Damn it, Nick! That was more than twenty years ago! This is something else. I think it has to do with the merger talks with Cygnus. The timing's too critical on this one. He didn't do this on his own . . . Someone got to him."

"And you think someone might have gotten to me, too? You think I'm gonna try to kill you, too? Is that why you brought your goon? Can I expect a complimentary bullet from him as well?"

Seeing the tension build in Nick's face, Seaton could see that his old friend was telling the truth. It was as if he had been allowed a glimpse, behind the ravages of age and a dissipated life, of a time when they were both young men, when telegrams were sent instead of e-mails, when the nightly news was seen on a black-and-white television, when the world still dreamed of colonies on the moon. Don, Nick, and Jack had all grown up in Brooklyn during the fifties. They had played stickball in the streets together and tried to best each other in every pursuit from athletics to girls. Later, with scholarships to New York University in 1958, Jack had studied management, then got his MBA, while Nick took PhDs in history and philosophy. And Seaton, fascinated by the space race and the dawn of the computer age, had studied astronomy before becoming one of the first in his generation to complete a PhD in an entirely new branch of academics: computer science. And after fifteen years of teaching programming at MIT, he would eventually bring Nick and Jack in to help him pursue his vision.

A particularly loud and discordant guitar riff from the stage brought Seaton out of his reverie, and again he asked his old friend, "Nick, why would Jack want to kill me? I need to know if it had anything to do with the merger."

"The merger? Why would Jack care about that? Maybe you've kind of forgotten what you did to him."

"We all had to go our own ways, Nick. And anyway, that was a long time ago."

"Not to Jack, it wasn't."

"I can't believe that!" Seaton shouted, slamming his fist down on the table. But the band was quite a bit louder than one upset billionaire, and no one else in the bar noticed.

Nick shook his head sadly and, releasing his death grip on the glass of Scotch, motioned Seaton closer. "You don't know, do you?" he croaked in a gravelly voice. "Jack was practically living on the streets."

Seaton's eyes narrowed. "What are you talking about? He was running his own software company!"

"It went bankrupt a year ago. He had problems with his product line—some sort of unexplainable glitch in the design. Lost all his customers within three months. The company was overextended for a massive product expansion, so his overhead was through the roof. He had already maxed out his line of credit with the bank. His only hope was to issue another series of preferred stock, but all the investors got cold feet and backed out at the last moment. He even asked *me* to help him out, but I told him I had my hands full with the record label and couldn't afford to invest even a fraction of what he needed."

"Why didn't he come to me?" Seaton demanded. "I would have helped him."

"After what you did to push him out of X-Tronic, do you really think he was gonna come to you for help? He would have killed himself before coming to you. You know that."

Seaton's fierce gaze lowered as he recalled the first time he had betrayed loyalty for money. "I'm not like that anymore."

"You're not the only one who's changed since those days. I told him he should still go to you, but he wouldn't hear it." Nick took a drag from his nonfilter cigarette and chased it with Scotch. An explosive coughing fit overtook him, causing the tumbler to slam back onto the table and sending an ice cube spinning into the ashtray. When the paroxysm finally subsided, he wheezed, "I only saw Jack once after that. It was after he lost his business. He had filed for personal bankruptcy protection, but the court's auditors found that he had tried to inflate the value of certain company assets before the bankruptcy proceeding, hoping to scare up some additional capital from investors. After that, it was open season. Jack avoided a jail sentence by agreeing to give back most of his personal net worth to his company's capital pool, to be distributed according to the bankruptcy. His wife divorced him and took his kids. By the time I saw him, he was broken, unrecognizable—just another casualty in the big city. People don't hire tired old executives with a history of corruption. I gave him some money, but he didn't want anything else. He had become a drifter . . . a lost soul. He was beyond anyone's help at that point. When he left, I had the feeling it was the last time I would ever see him. You don't realize how much he changed after the X-Tronic days . . . Just wasn't as tough as he used to be."

"He should have come to me!" Seaton yelled, smashing both fists down on the table, shattering the glass tumbler on the floor. "He should have come to me! I have money—I would have helped!"

This time, his outburst came during a lull in the music, and people in the bar turned to look at them. "Hey!" the burly bartender yelled, coming around the bar. He got within six feet of Seaton before Marcus had him against the wall with a forearm across his throat.

"Hey, look . . . I don't want no trouble," the bartender said meekly.

"We were just leaving," Marcus replied as he stuffed a fifty in the man's fleshy hand and relaxed his grip. He turned to Seaton. "Do we have everything we came for, sir?"

Seaton stared at Nick with an anguished despair that he had held inside for twenty-five years. He opened his mouth to speak, but no sound came out. "We were like brothers," he finally said. "All of us. Weren't we brothers?"

Nick nodded. "I think that's why he wanted to kill you himself."

Seaton shook his head before turning to walk away. After a few steps, he turned back toward Nick. "If you ever fall, if anything ever happens that you need help with, please . . . ask me. I want you to know, you can always ask me for help."

"Same goes for you, Donnie boy," Nick said through a rising curl of smoke. "Some of the biggest tragedies in history began with just a couple of gunshots, with just one or two deaths. If this is as big as you think, if this is the last act of some operatic tragedy in your life, I want you to know that you can always consider me your brother . . . even in death. Just like poor Jack."

22

---◄※►---

SEATON AND MARCUS left CBGB's and returned to the fading sunlight of the street. Not wanting to attract any more attention than necessary, Marcus had instructed the company driver to park the hired limousine out of sight in a side alley. Now, seeing no suspicious activity, he phoned the driver to pick them up.

"What's the best investigation agency you know in New York?" Seaton asked.

"You mean a private investigator?"

"No, no—a high-end agency. The kind you use to run background research on political opponents or to uncover business deals between executives."

"Kostroma International. They're a Russian-based firm that was founded after the fall of the Soviet Union to help Western executives and investment bankers investigate potential corruption within Russian enterprises before investing in them. Their specialty is corporate espionage. They claim to have a number of ex-KGB agents in their ranks, and they recruit most of their new hires out of various intelligence agencies from around the world. They've grown substantially since they were founded in the early nineties. Besides Russia, they do a lot of work in China and Brazil. They don't have much business in the United States, but they have an office here in New York."

A gray Lincoln Town Car pulled up in front of them, and Marcus stepped forward and opened the door for Seaton while continuously observing the surrounding streets. Even though the vehicle was bulletproof and as well protected as any commercial vehicle could be, he was still apprehensive of the attention that it drew.

"Let's go there now," Seaton said.

"Ralph," Marcus called to the driver, "take us to the corner of Eighteenth and Broadway."

"You know exactly where they're located?" Seaton asked. "How do you know so much about these guys?"

"They tried to recruit me nine months ago."

Seaton bellowed out an uncharacteristic laugh. "And why didn't you join them?"

"And miss out on this kind of luxury?" Marcus replied with a wry grin, his eyes roving the plush interior of the limousine. "Seriously, though, what do you want from Kostroma?"

Seaton looked out the window at the familiar New York streets of his youth. At the mouth of a small side street, a group of boys stopped their game of stickball to admire the flashy Town Car as it rolled past.

"I want to find out exactly what happened to Jack's business," he finally answered. "I need to understand every detail to figure out why he tried to kill me. I owe him that much."

*   *   *

Seaton and his bodyguard stepped off the elevator on the twenty-fifth floor and walked into the gray reception area of Kostroma International. The black marble floor reflected a dim glow from the studio lights spaced along the high ceiling. A thin woman greeted them with an Eastern European accent as they approached the counter that arced around her in a semicircle of flat-screen monitors and information networks. Loud blue eye shadow and blood-red lipstick stood out against her fair skin and blond hair.

"We'd like to see Darryl Mitchell," Marcus said.

"Do you have an appointment?"

"No."

"I'm sorry, but Mr. Mitchell's schedule is full this evening. We're not regularly open on Saturday evenings, but at the moment we're working on a special project. Perhaps I could direct you to one of our risk assessment managers by making an appointment for Monday?"

"My name's Marcus Graham. I phoned thirty minutes ago. I'm an old friend of his; I'm sure he will want to see me if you tell him I'm here."

The receptionist nodded and dialed an extension. After speaking into her headset, she looked up at them and said, "Please take a seat. Mr. Mitchell will be out in a few minutes."

Within a few minutes, a stocky black man with a shaved head walked into the corridor. He wore a Natazzi three-button suit.

Darryl Mitchell reached out a giant pink palm to shake Marcus's hand.

"Marcus, you're back!" he said, flashing an expensive smile. "What's it been—nine months? If you've come to reconsider my offer, you can forget it—you had your chance to join us."

"Darryl, stop begging. It's embarrassing," Marcus bantered back.

"This is my client, Don Seaton. He could use your agency's help with something. Mr. Seaton, this is Darryl Mitchell. We were in military intelligence together."

"A pleasure," Seaton said, shaking his hand.

As the three walked to Mitchell's office, Seaton related the shooting incident on Wall Street and his discussion with Nick about Jack's failed business, failed marriage, and failed life. Seaton asked him to gather as much detail as possible, public and private, about the bankruptcy of Jack's business.

"What kind of specific information are you looking for?" Mitchell probed.

"Anything that can link me to the past two years of his life. I can't believe he would try to kill me over something that happened twenty-five years ago. There must be something that's happened since . . . something that I'm not being told. Your job is to find it. Can you do that?"

"It'll take time."

"I must know within forty-eight hours."

"I'm afraid that's impossible. We can't take on an investigation with such short notice. We have limited resources here in New York and may not get to this till the end of next week."

"I'll pay ten times your going rate if you can get started in the next five minutes," Seaton said.

This brought a chuckle from Mitchell, who shook his head in disbelief. "I can see why I was unable to lure Marcus away from your employ. Okay, Mr. Seaton, but I have to warn you, we're not cheap."

"I'm not poor."

Rolling his chair over to the corner of his desk, Mitchell pressed a button on his phone. "Natalya, please clear my schedule for the remainder of the evening. Reschedule calls, both domestic and international—I don't care if it's World War Three. And have Adam Hawley in my office in three minutes."

He turned back to Seaton. "We'll get right on it."

Seaton nodded. "Marcus will give you our contact numbers. We'll be at the Windsor Hotel this evening, flying back to Aspen tomorrow afternoon. I'll have someone contact you with the satellite phone number on the jet so you can reach us in flight." He stood up and shook Mitchell's hand. "I appreciate your thoroughness and confidentiality in this matter."

"Always."

"I'll wait for you outside," Seaton said to his bodyguard before leaving the office.

"What's really going on here, Marcus?" Mitchell asked the moment they were alone in the office.

"That's what we need you to find out. I've known Mr. Seaton for more than five years now. He's probably the smartest man I've ever met. If this is something he's concerned about, it's serious."

23

⸻•◦✳◦•⸻

OVER A HUNDRED guests had been drinking and reveling at the Seaton estate since midafternoon. They were thickest on the patio that stretched along the back of the mansion. Outdoor heater lamps were connected by lines of Christmas lights, and dangling Chinese lanterns were strung through the woods surrounding the house, giving the party the look of a Chinese New Year's celebration. On a stage at one end of the patio, a rock band was blasting away. Two hot tubs were overflowing with ski bums and flirtatious college girls, all on unexplained sabbaticals from the real world. At the moment, they sat lined up in the bubbling water, holding a long ski with five shot glasses glued to it at equal intervals; tipping the ski, they drank the shots in unison.

Michael ordered two vodka tonics from the outdoor bar. "*Nazdrovya!*" he said, obliging Sarah to look into his eyes as their glasses touched. A trick he had learned in Germany long ago. He was a little nervous that he had convinced Sarah to come to the party with him without telling her about its connection to X-Tronic. He wanted to see the twins' reaction when he introduced her to them, and he needed her to be surprised as well.

"So," he said, "Kurt once told me you're going to be our generation's Bob Woodward."

Sarah smiled. "My brother always had a problem with exaggerating."

"He said you exposed a fraud scheme in the city government."

"That part is true."

"What happened?"

"A project manager in the Public Works Department for Denver had been misallocating funds that were appropriated for two new homeless shelters. He had awarded the contracts to a guy he went to college with. I knew some people in the department, who informed me there could be a conflict of interest in the bidding process. As I dug into the investigation, I realized that the bid was overstated and the contractor managed to obtain additional funds from the city without meeting even half the required milestones in the contract. The manager in Public Works concealed the shortcomings of the contractor, and the two of them pocketed the additional billings."

Michael shook his head. He had seen too many stories of corruption to be shocked, but it was sad to think that someone could be greedy enough to steal from those who had nothing. "Well, the exposure ruined the manager's life," he said. "He obviously got fired, and he'll never get a decent job again—that is, after he gets done serving his time."

"And he would have served it, too, if he hadn't killed himself first."

Michael looked over at her. "He *killed himself* because of your story."

"No," she said, looking dead ahead at the roaring party around them. "He killed himself because he was a coward."

"How'd it feel, breaking such a big story only a few months out of college?"

She laughed. "It made me realize how many stories there must be out there that need to be told. I mean, if I could stumble on that so quickly, just imagine how many other things are happening right now, even as we speak, that need to be uncovered. That story really helped me build momentum for the kind of career I want to have. My editor also gives me a lot of freedom to explore things now."

As he lowered the tumbler from his lips, he glanced above its rim and saw Lucas at the far end of the patio, standing in the center of a small group. "Sarah, there's someone I'd like you to meet."

He took her hand and led her through the crowd, never taking his eyes off his host. Approaching from behind, Michael was careful to block Lucas's view of her. He tapped Lucas on the shoulder.

Turning, Lucas smiled and said, "Michael!" He was wearing a yellow ski coat and drinking a longneck. "I was wondering when you'd show up!"

"I didn't realize the party was starting so early. Thought I might be the first one here."

"No, no. Most came straight from the slopes. Some drove in from Denver, but this place has been slammed for a while now. Don't worry, though—plenty of time left, and we've got some good bands coming on later."

"I'd like you to meet my friend," Michael said, stepping to the side. "Lucas, this is Sarah Matthews. Sarah, this is Lucas Seaton; it's his party."

Michael watched Lucas's face as he pronounced her name. Just as he had been trained, he watched for the deepening of breath, the slight tensing of the jaw, the subtle dilation in the pupils. And he saw all three in the split second before Lucas could regain his composure.

"Sarah—yes, I remember you from your brother's funeral. I'm so sorry for your family's loss. I always liked Kurt."

"You were at his funeral?" she asked in surprise. "How did you know my brother?"

"I'm one of the chief operating officers at X-Tronic. Your brother had been leading our annual financial audit."

Sarah tensed immediately. "Really," she said. "You're from X-Tronic?"

"That's right," Lucas said.

"X-Tronic," she said slowly. "I've heard a lot of interesting things about your company."

"That a fact?" Lucas asked, grinning as if eager to face a possible challenge. He gave her an appraising look.

She nodded. "My brother told me a lot about it once."

"*Did* he, now?" He had turned away from Michael to face her, making it obvious that she had his full attention. He waited, as if daring her to continue.

"Mm-hm," she mumbled, raising the tumbler to cover her trembling lips.

"Hey, this is one impressive place!" Michael said, trying to ease the tension. He had already seen what he was looking for in Lucas's initial reaction. Now he knew he had to get Sarah away from him lest she reveal too much of their suspicions.

"The estate?" Lucas asked, looking around nonchalantly. "Yes, well, it belongs to my father—most things in our family do. But someday my brother and I will have plenty to show for ourselves."

"I bet you will," he replied.

Sarah had stopped talking. She hid behind her glass and eyed the two men with what Michael realized was growing anger.

The wail of an electric guitar erupted behind them, and Lucas turned. "Oh, this is a terrific band. You won't want to miss this."

"We'll be there in a minute," Michael replied.

Their host gave Michael a quick nod and Sarah a stiff smile and was off through the crowd.

Sarah turned and walked in the other direction.

"Hey!" Michael yelled, pursuing her. "Sarah, wait."

She started walking faster. When she heard Michael racing to catch up, she threw down her drink and burst into a sprint. Running past the thinning edge of the crowd, she left the patio and entered the dark trees behind the mansion.

Michael cut between the trees, easily closing the gap between them. She got fifty yards into the woods before falling to her knees. She was panting, head down, her dark red hair covering her face like a long veil. He stopped a few steps behind her.

"Why didn't you tell me this party was related to X-Tronic?" she asked. Her right hand grasped a piece of crusty snow, clenching until it broke apart in her fingers.

"It had to be a surprise when you met him. He would have known if your meeting wasn't a surprise. You had to appear naive."

"Are you trying to torture me?" she asked, still looking down.

"I'm trying to *help* you. Did you see his face when I said your name?"

She looked up. "All I could see was my brother's face."

Michael leaned against an aspen trunk, resting his forehead against the smooth, cold bark. "He was startled, almost terrified." He paused. "It was exactly the kind of reaction I needed to see to believe he was involved in Kurt's death. I believe you now. I believe that your brother was murdered by someone from X-Tronic. And I think Lucas knows who."

"I want to kill him," she said. "I don't want to write a story anymore—I just want to kill him."

"So you *are* working on a story about X-Tronic . . . about your brother. You're not just trying to get a murder case opened. You want to expose anything illegal yourself."

"If he's responsible for my brother's death, I swear to God I'll kill him. I'll fucking stop his heart." Cold air stung her face, making her eyes tear, but she stared on into the darkness—a woman scarred and alone, with a building rage that wanted only to fight anyone foolhardy enough to get in her way.

Michael sensed in her the same inner rage that he himself had felt, on the ice with Dr. Speer a few days ago. She was losing herself to the anger, the same anger that had consumed the doctor after his wife's death. It was all happening again, and in that moment, Michael vowed to do everything he could to help her.

"You don't mean that," he said.

"No?" she said evenly. "Stick around."

Michael's eyes lowered to the corn snow blanketing the pale wilderness around them. Years ago he had learned how to keep his cool under explosive passions of anger. "Do not be overcome by evil, but overcome evil with good," he said, quoting the apostle Paul.

She glared at him. "What are you, some kind of a saint?"

He knelt down beside her. "No, not a saint," he said. "More like the sheep that got lost."

"Aren't we all," she replied. "Promise me one thing, Michael. Promise me you won't abandon Kurt. No matter what happens, promise me you'll help me follow this to the end."

He raised his head and looked out into the dark woods. "You don't know me, Sarah. You don't know some of the things I've done. I don't have the right to promise anyone anything anymore. But if it helps any, I already made that pledge to Kurt—the day of his funeral, when everyone drove away from his casket in the cemetery."

"You're not telling me everything," she said.

"No, I'm not," he replied, still gazing out into the dark. "I'll tell you everything I learn about Kurt and everything I learn about X-Tronic, but there are just some things I can't tell you about myself. I'm sorry, but I don't have a choice in that."

She nodded while pursing her lips and blinking the tears out of her eyes. "You're just like my brother was. He said there were things he couldn't tell me, either. Just don't ever lie to me about my brother. If you promise to tell me everything you learn about his death and X-Tronic, I'll promise to tell you everything I learn. We can find out the truth together. If you really were Kurt's friend, then you owe it to him to work with me."

Michael felt suddenly glad she was beside him. After all his years of working alone, he would welcome her help. He just hoped that in the end, she would prove to be someone he could trust.

Together they emerged from the trees and rejoined the party. The few people who saw them coming in with snow-stained pants gave them knowing smiles, assuming that it was nothing more than a tryst. Holding her hand for appearances, he led her through the growing crowd toward the stage, where the band was finishing a song.

"There must be over three hundred people out here!" he yelled back at her. Even though the music had come to a stop, the yells and whistles from the crowd were all but demanding an encore from the departed band.

A hand grasped his shoulder. "Michael, you sneaky bastard! I've been looking for you all night. And only now, at the end of the show, do I find you."

He turned to find Lance, grinning, in a black wool cap and a ski coat.

"Lance! I just saw your brother a half hour ago."

"Well, you're doing better than me. I haven't seen him half the night." Lance peered at Sarah. "And who's this?" he asked.

"My friend Sarah," Michael replied. After the way she had challenged Lucas, he didn't want to tempt her to take another shot, and he suspected that she wasn't up for it, either.

"Have we met before?" Lance asked her. "You look familiar—I'm sure I've seen you before."

Sarah forced a grin and latched on to Michael's arm. "See honey, I told you all the boys use that line."

Lance chuckled uncomfortably. "Funny girl," he said to Michael.

Michael grinned. "I didn't think they had night skiing at Aspen," he said. "Looks like you're getting ready to hit the slopes."

Lance smiled. "Actually, I was skiing with some people all day on the mountain. We drank so much at the lodge afterwards, we thought it would be fun just to tough it out all night in our ski clothes. Tell you the truth, I don't think I'm gonna last."

"I'm sure of that," Sarah muttered under her breath.

"You're gonna have trouble getting back into the house through this crowd," Michael joked, hoping Lance had missed her words.

"Actually, I'll probably use the servants' entrance. I can get into it from the kitchen," Lance said, pointing to the back corner of the patio. "There are hidden staircases and hallways for the servants to move around the place without being seen. Designed so that my father's well-to-do guests wouldn't have to notice the staff, but it ended up being a great playground for Lucas and me when we were kids."

As Lance talked of hide-and-seek in hidden passageways, Michael noticed two large tags sticking out from the front of his coat. "You've got a couple ski passes there?"

"Yeah," Lance said, looking down; his fingers plucked absently at the tags. "This one's the season pass for Aspen, and this is the Colorado pass. You ski? We'll have to go sometime if you do!" he said, slurring his words.

"Oh, yeah, definitely, I'd love to ski, *anytime,*" Michael replied, bending over to take a closer look at the tags. "I see they changed the design on the Colorado pass this year," he concluded after looking at it for a few seconds. "I actually didn't buy one myself, not this year anyway—busy season and all. But

I have to go up at least a half-dozen times this season so I can still feel like I'm living in Colorado."

"Sure, absolutely! We'll go sometime, I promise," Lance said. "Even if we have to drag you away from work. You can tell your boss you're 'meeting with a client.'" He laughed loudly.

Just then the floodlights from the mansion cast a long shadow across the crowd as the band returned to the stage. Lance slapped him on the back and smiled wryly. And Michael, watching the band take the stage again, also wore a smile, because he had just memorized the fifteen-digit bar code on Lance's ski pass.

As the band started up, Michael turned to say something to Sarah, when his eyes settled on a familiar image amid the throng. His heart skipped as he caught a profile view of what looked like Alaska's face. But before he could move forward to catch a better look, the lights from the mansion dimmed, and he lost her.

24

———·⊪✳⊪·———

JERRY DIAMOND LEANED his considerable bulk back in his chair, sipping his bourbon and gazing out at the Portland skyline. Setting his drink down on the table, he turned back to look at the man sitting across from him in the top-floor bar of the luxurious Continental Hotel. An aging lounge singer in a purple dress stood next to the baby grand piano, singing a slow jazz number.

"So everything's finished," Diamond said to the man.

"No, it's far from finished," the man said in the tone of a professor lecturing a student. "We still have a lot of work to do—you saw so yourself."

"But it works, Winston," the X-Tronic CFO said. "It works, damn it. That's the important thing. If it works, then everything else is just a matter of implementation."

"Yeah, you're right," the man replied, smiling. "The prototype works. That's really what matters. The hardest part is finished...but that brings me to my latest concern."

"What's that?" Diamond said, looking back down at his drink. He had long ago developed the skill of looking casually away from a person just as they were about to ask the impossible of him.

"The financing. It's time to start running the production facilities. When does my team get final funding?"

Diamond grimaced. He knew that his associate would not like the answer. "We can't give it to you just yet. It might take another month or two."

Winston choked on his whiskey and started coughing. He looked back at Diamond with watering eyes. "You're kidding, right? A month or two?"

"Maybe longer," Diamond said with a deadpan face, then took a drink of bourbon.

"Why?" the man asked, leaning forward with both arms on the white tablecloth, palms up. "That could be too long. It's hard to keep things like this a secret, you know. The longer we sit on it, the more likely something will leak."

"That's a risk we'll just have to take. The funding can't be completed until after the merger."

The man's face sank. In a mournful voice, he said, "That's corporate politics—it has nothing to do with me or my work."

Though Diamond was not generally a sympathetic man when it came to funding allocations of X-Tronic's annual budget, he could understand the man's disappointment. They both wanted this project to be finished without any unpleasant surprises.

Reminding himself that the man in front of him was about to make him one of the most powerful and respected CFOs in America, Diamond leaned forward. Now he was the lecturer. He spoke in a calm, reassuring voice. "Look, we can't spend or announce anything until after X-Tronic resolves this situation with the Cygnus bid. A merger would essentially reset all our accounting records with new valuations. The timing's critical; we have to be very careful about how we do this. And we've done everything possible to safeguard access to the project. Only a handful of people outside your team even know it exists.

Nothing will leak."

"Seems like an unnecessary risk to me. I hope you guys in Denver know what you're doing."

"We do," Diamond said, grinning. "Besides, I know your team still has a few small glitches to work out in the software. I could see that much during my tour of the facilities today. This'll give you enough time to make sure the final design is flawless long before we get into mass distribution."

The piano player struck the last chords of the song, and the singer gave a quick bow to light applause. Winston took the final sip from his whiskey and stood up from the table. "I've waited five years for this moment," he said. "I guess I can wait a little longer before it's announced. Just don't let Denver get distracted from what we're trying to do. Merger or not, we're about to change the software industry forever."

"Good night, Winston," he said as his guest walked away from the table. Despite their strained conversation, he had been very excited by what he saw at the Portland facility today. He couldn't wait to return to Denver and let everyone know that their plans were right on schedule. Now it was up to the twins to see that the merger went through without any problems.

25

————✳————

MICHAEL FINISHED DRESSING in the darkened room in the east wing of the Seaton estate. Flipping his nylon travel bag over on the empty bed, he pulled a green fleece from the side pocket. Dawn was breaking over eastern Kansas and wouldn't gray the skies over Aspen for another hour, though songbirds already were stirring in the trees lining the back of the estate.

Keeping the lights off in his room so that no one would see him stirring at this early hour, he zipped up the collar on his fleece and moved toward the door.

The hallway outside his room was quiet, and the room next to his showed no light under the door—Sarah was still asleep. He moved quietly through the gray shadows to the softly glimmering banister that curved down the grand staircase to the front corridor on the ground floor. At the bottom he tiptoed past the display cases of costly artifacts that Don Seaton had collected during a lifetime of travels. He felt like a cat burglar skulking about such unguarded wealth in someone else's home.

Moving to the kitchen, at the opposite side of the mansion, he stopped at a back door to the outside. Pushing it open as slowly as possible, he peeked out into the cold air. Fifty yards across a field of snow stood a stone building. Lance had told him it was originally a horse stable before his father converted it into a garage big enough to house forty cars.

Ten minutes ago, Michael had heard the soft purr of a car engine arriving at the estate. Unable to see any activity from his window's limited view, he had thrown on enough clothes to sneak outside. Seeing the dim lights in the frosted windows of the old stables, he moved across the snowy field in slow, cautious steps. The snow was overrun with footprints from the party, so there was little chance of leaving a trail. Reaching the limestone wall of the stables, he moved along in the building's shadow.

Without warning, a beam of light shot out from the darkness, just missing him standing flat against the wall. He dropped to his knees and hugged the shadow of the building as another car pulled into the front drive of the stables. He heard a car door open and close, then footsteps crunching in snow before disappearing into the building.

Inching his way toward the front of the building, Michael saw a black Mercedes parked with its front bumper pressed against a high snowbank. Tracks led from the car to a small side door, still ajar, next to the main doors, which were closed. Following the footprints, he peeked into the doorway just in time to see a tall shadow shrink and disappear up a ramp to an unseen room.

As he stepped into the old stables, his feet crunched softly on the gravel floor. He crept along, feeling his way, until he came to a makeshift board ladder that led up to a square hole in the ceiling. Realizing this was the best way to move closer to the light without the risk of being seen, he climbed hand over hand up the rungs until he found himself in a huge attic with rafters angling in sharp upside-down V's. The attic's board floor stretched the length of a basketball court.

Looking for joists through the slim gaps between the boards, he crawled along the planks at a snail's pace, gently redistributing his weight with each movement to minimize the chance of creaking boards. After what felt like an eternity in the darkness, with slivers of light shooting through the spaces between the boards and striping the roof above, he had advanced far enough from the square hatch that he could now see down into the main room. A half-dozen men stood in the center of a peculiar cluster of fine automobiles, as if they were a gang of thieves admiring a heist they had just made. In the center stood Lance and Lucas Seaton, speaking in low tones. Michael could not catch a word they said.

Though he did not recognize the other men, he memorized every detail he could. Their suits, too formal and luxurious for a dawn meeting in an old stable, suggested something shady. They appeared stiff and obedient in the presence of the twins, yet their confidence was apparent in their nods of agreement with whatever the twins were discussing. Michael guessed them to be lawyers or bankers perhaps. But whoever they were, they seemed to be working *for* the twins, and clearly they were working in secret.

Realizing that he had learned all he could from his hidden lookout, Michael became acutely aware of his exposed position. Sooner or later the meeting would conclude, and if he didn't make it back into the mansion before then, he could easily be caught out. He turned and crawled back toward the square hatch that led down from the attic. Knowing he would be blind while climbing back down the ladder feetfirst, he peeked through the hole, searching for any sign of life below—he had been forced to crawl so slowly across the attic floor that he could not be certain the meeting was still going on. Somewhere outside in the distance, a dog started barking. He feared that the other overnight guests from the party were beginning to wake. He didn't have much time to get back.

Sensing no movement below him, he started down the ladder. He expected at any moment to hear a voice yell out at him. But no sound came, and soon enough, his feet were back on the ground. He moved to the door and left the stables. The car sat undisturbed out front, and a dim blue glow over the eastern peaks announced the approaching day.

A smile broke over his face as he felt the exhilaration of having escaped undetected, but it was wiped away as he rounded the corner of the building and found himself face-to-face with a short, stocky man standing shin-deep in the snow. He wore a thick cashmere coat so long it dragged the surface. The man's rosy cheeks revealed that he had been in the cold air for some time, but his shiny brown eyes seemed quite focused, as though he could tolerate a great deal more discomfort without being distracted.

"Are we lost, Mr. Chapman?"

But before he could answer, he heard noises behind him. Jerking his head to look back at the stable's side door, he could now see a glimmer of light where he had left it cracked open. The men must be walking down the ramp from the main room and would soon be outside the stables. He had to move fast. "Just stretching my legs," Michael said to the man. "Couldn't sleep . . . feeling better now, though." He walked quickly, trying to move past the man and make it back to the mansion before the men inside the stable came out. But a strong hand grabbed his arm.

"You'll never make it in time. Come this way." And without another word, the man pulled him to the side of the building. They stood in the shadows as the other men exited from the building and exchanged a few final words. Then the Mercedes pulled away as the twins and the other men hiked through the snowy field back toward the mansion.

"Who are you?" Michael whispered.

"Name's Hopkins. I work for Mr. Seaton."

"Don Seaton? What kind of work?"

"I'm the butler. What happens on the property is my responsibility."

"How did you find me?"

"Who said I was looking for you?"

"Who *were* you looking for?"

Hopkins didn't answer. He watched the dark silhouettes moving across the field to the mansion.

"You knew my name," Michael continued.

"Mr. Chapman, I'm required to be familiar with all overnight guests at the estate."

"What were you doing out here?" Michael persisted.

Hopkins turned away from the field after everyone had disappeared back into the house. His shiny brown eyes gleamed at Michael from the shadows, with an intensity that commanded attention. "Mr. Chapman, this never happened. We never met. Neither of us was ever here."

Hopkins paused to make sure there was no misunderstanding. There was none. "Now it should be fine for you to return to the main house," he went on. "The twins never linger on the main floor. But watch the windows. Don't let anyone see you."

Michael moved past Hopkins to look around the corner. "Why are you helping me?" he asked, but when he turned around, the man was already out of sight, around the corner of the building.

26

———————=:(▪※▪):=———————

THE BLACK LINCOLN Town Car turned off the FDR Highway and into the parking area of the Downtown Manhattan Heliport. The DMH, the premier heliport in New York City, catering mostly to top business executives, was only a few miles south of Wall Street, on the L-shaped Pier 6, which stuck out into the East River just north of the Staten Island Ferry.

Don Seaton stepped out of the limousine and walked with Marcus toward the terminal. Even on a Sunday afternoon, the Port Authority of New York and New Jersey was busy coordinating ship activity along the East River. Moving through the small security station, the two men were soon walking with a pilot down the wide concrete pier, to a blue Dauphin AS-365 helicopter. Stepping into the spacious aircraft, Seaton stretched his legs and started reading one of the files in his lap.

The bird lifted off, stirring a wide circle of white ripples that trembled in the river below. Rising into the air, they banked over the Brooklyn Bridge and followed the river as the field of gray buildings faded away behind them. Seaton looked out at the Empire State Building, still an imposing, beautiful feature of the skyline after all these many decades. Sunlight glinted off the countless glass-skinned buildings, making New York look, from the air, like the cleanest city in the world. Out the opposite window, he could see in the distance the Statue of Liberty, standing alone above the cold gray water. Flying over the city, Seaton could not help feeling a sad hollowness. He reflected briefly on the vigorous young man he had once been, and compared him to the sagging face now reflected in the window. And reflecting on the long and eventful life he had lived, he could not but wonder how much further he would be able to go before the end found him. Perhaps, he thought with an uncharacteristic sense of gloom, this would be his last time ever to see New York City.

Within minutes they landed at one of the Teterboro Airports, where they again made their way through security before being escorted to the private Learjet, where Captain Steiner was waiting to take off.

Once they were in the air, Seaton scanned through some additional investigative documentation relating to Lance and Lucas during their university days. "What does all this prove?" he asked Marcus after closing the file.

Marcus was sitting across from him, at one of the small tables near the back of the fuselage.

"It proves they are capable of a lot more harm than we originally thought."

"You can't really conclude that based on just this."

"Sir, I had one of my contacts at the Bureau take a look at this information. She's a profiler, and I figured her opinion wouldn't hurt."

"That's taking things a little far, isn't it, Marcus? An FBI shrink? We don't even know for sure if the boys have been up to anything. So they've taken a different stance than I on the Cygnus merger talks. So they're distancing themselves from my ideas and have been trying to persuade the board to change strategies. I can handle the board, and I can sure as hell handle my own sons."

Marcus said nothing as his boss turned to look out the window.

"Okay," Seaton conceded after his brief objection. "So what did your friend say?"

"She said the thing that most interested her, the one thing that we need to be most cautious of, is that the twins have always been together. She didn't see any evidence of competition between them, no evidence of disagreements or disloyalty. Everything they have been through, they have been through together. They feed off each other's strengths, and they give each other confidence to pursue things that neither would attempt on his own. That was the main warning she gave. She said that as long as they're together, they will continue to be fearless before others. But she also warned that they have become so dependent on each other that if they are ever separated, there's no telling just how unbalanced or destructive they may become."

Seaton felt the jet being gently pushed around by soft turbulence. He closed his eyes. The conversation with Marcus had fired him up at first, but now he felt weak. As a businessman, he found the background history and analysis about his sons very concerning. As a father, he found it terrifying. He was seventy years old, but instead of having a strong understanding of the circles he lived in, he had suddenly found himself blindly feeling his way in life. Everything he had thought true, all the assumptions he had believed and lived by, had melted away. And he feared more than ever that something horrible was taking place in his own kingdom. With his eyes still closed, he could almost feel the speed at which the jet was burning across the skies, taking him toward his distant home in Aspen, where he would prepare for the coming board meeting in Denver. Things were moving too fast, and he feared that everything would soon spin out of control.

* * *

The Learjet 60 XR descended over the Sawatch Range of the Rocky Mountains. It was a little after six on Sunday evening, four hours after Seaton and Marcus had left New York City. The sun had set almost an hour ago. The jet shook as it hit some sudden turbulence: they were passing between Elbert and Harvard, two fourteeners not far outside Aspen, which many pilots called "the Goalposts."

"Mr. Seaton?" a woman's voice called out.

Seaton turned his head away from the black window to find the flight attendant waving at him from the front of the fuselage. She was holding the satellite phone next to a leather ottoman.

"You have a phone call, sir. A Mr. Darryl Mitchell from New York."

He looked at his watch. He would be impressed if Mitchell had already gotten him some information.

"Seaton here. What do you have for me, Darryl? Answers?"

There was a hesitation on the other end, as if Mitchell was choosing his words with care. "With all due respect, Mr. Seaton, I would expect *you* to be the one with the answers. Why did you hire me to find out the cause of the bankruptcy when you knew it was because of X-Tronic?"

Seaton felt as if he had been slapped. "*X-Tronic?* What are you *talking* about?"

"Mr. Seaton, do you recognize the name Chartz Networks? It was Jack Ross's company."

"I've never heard of it."

"I see. Well, it was X-Tronic that single-handedly put Chartz Networks out of business. Your name is involved. I have a copy of an executive memo from you regarding the transaction."

"What the hell are you talking about?" He couldn't believe what he was hearing. None of this made a damned bit of sense.

"Mr. Seaton, from the best I can tell, Jack tried to kill you because you were involved in the legal party that ruined his life."

"What are you talking about! Before this weekend, I hadn't even *seen* Jack for twenty-five years!"

"Then you're going to find this rather interesting. I've obtained copies of court records documenting the bankruptcy proceeding. Do you know why his business went belly-up?"

"Nick said something about Jack's company not being able to get a key product out of the development stage." As Seaton spoke into the phone, he saw Marcus eyeing him from the back of the main cabin.

"The product was a new software application," Mitchell said. "It was designed to help transfer information from scanned documents into actual accounting data that could be uploaded to a company's operating system. Apparently, things were going well on the development side. To raise more capital, the company was planning to issue another round of stock to investors, and their software was scheduled to be completed in less than two years—that is, until a company named RSA Systems brought a lawsuit against Chartz Networks for patent infringement."

"RSA?" Seaton said quietly as the concept settled into his mind. "Oh, my God! How is that *possible*?"

Mitchell continued without acknowledging Seaton's question. "RSA's legal motion forced Chartz Networks to stop all R and D until the suit was settled. RSA brought in a team of expert witnesses that pulverized Chartz. They even got Ross's head software programmer to testify against the company. After six months, the courts found the company in breach of patent laws and ordered it to cease all operations of that specific product line. The problem was, Ross had been gambling everything on that one product. He had no backup plan for something like this. The lawsuit was a fatal blow. Besides owing damages to RSA, he now had no product, no prospects for issuing new stock, and no bank that would extend him capital. He was finished. The board of directors voted to file for bankruptcy and liquidate the company."

Seaton cupped a hand to his forehead, as if to ward off a sudden headache. He could feel everything closing in around him. First Marcus's concerns about his sons, then the takeover threat from Kavanaugh, and then the news from Nick that Jack had suffered a failed life long before his violent death. And now it appeared that all these things might somehow be connected. The only time in his life that could trump his current despair was after his wife's sudden death.

Mitchell paused for a moment to make sure all this was registering with Seaton before he continued. "And Mr. Ross lost everything. In the blink of an eye, all his stock options were worthless. In a desperate attempt to entice investors, he made some inflated reporting of the market value of the company's investment holdings. The courts found this during the proceedings and hit him hard. He filed for personal bankruptcy. Afterwards, he couldn't get another job to save his life. No one wants to hire a CEO who lost ninety percent of stockholders' equity and attempted fraud in his last venture. Neighbors say he started drinking, his wife divorced him, and he eventually fell out of society—that is, until he showed up on Wall Street Saturday morning and tried to kill you . . ." Mitchell paused for a moment. "Mr. Seaton? You understand the connection now, don't you?"

"RSA," Seaton said weakly.

"That's right. X-Tronic acquired RSA just one month after the final settlement of the lawsuit. And RSA eventually hired the lead software programmer from Chartz—the same guy who testified against Jack."

Seaton sank back in his seat. His hand grew weak holding the phone, and he stared absently into the cold winter night. Small mountain towns lay scattered below like illuminated spider webs across the black earth.

"You can imagine, Mr. Seaton, what it must have been like for Jack to take such a rude slap in the face. He would have realized that merger talks take longer than a month. And he also would have realized that no company would offer to take over another company without identifying all risks involved— especially pending litigation regarding the validity of its products' patent rights. I believe that once he realized it was you—his old business partner and childhood friend—who was involved in the lawsuit, it was only a matter of time before he looked for an opportunity for revenge."

"I had nothing to do with the RSA deal," Seaton said, knowing that it didn't matter. "I was on a ski holiday in New Zealand for a month during that time. I only received updates from those in my company who were in charge of the merger."

"And they never mentioned anything about the lawsuit? This is important, Mr. Seaton, because there is such an obvious connection between you and what happened to Jack. It's almost as if someone intentionally wanted to make the two of you enemies."

Seaton didn't respond, though his mind swirled with all the different ways things may have played out behind his back. And he felt horrified that Jack had fallen victim to a situation Seaton himself may inadvertently have created within X-Tronic.

"Who was it, Mr. Seaton?" Mitchell asked excitedly. "Who was it that omitted telling you about the RSA lawsuit? Who was in charge of overseeing the merger?"

For the first time since Jack's death, Seaton allowed himself to mourn the loss of his friend. He turned sideways against the window. Resting his head on the cold Plexiglas, he watched the dark sea of mountains drift by outside.

The jet ripped through a cloud, and he heard the whir of the landing gear motors. They would be landing in Aspen in minutes.

"Who was it?" Mitchell repeated. "Who set you up?"

But Seaton never answered the question. He merely hung up the phone without another word. The answer was too difficult to admit, the truth too terrible to reveal.

"My sons," he whispered to his reflection in the window. "My God, what have they done?"

The tires chirped on the cold runway. He was back in Aspen, yet he could take no comfort in being home, for he knew that his life was changed forever. The one thing he had feared for more than a decade was finally happening, and it had taken him too long to realize it. He was devastated by the realization that he had failed to protect the only thing that really mattered.

Closing his sad eyes, he felt the jet roll to a stop in the dark winter paradise.

27

————◦◦※◦◦————

MICHAEL'S FATHER SOUNDED eager for news. "So busy season is in full swing?" It was Sunday evening when the call came, and Michael was just back from being in Aspen with Sarah.

"Oh, yeah," he replied. "'Busy' doesn't begin to describe it."

"And your mother says you've been put on the X-Tronic engagement. That's exciting stuff, son. One of the best companies in the country. Nice job."

"Thanks, Dad," Michael said into the phone, feeling a sudden pang of guilt. He hated not being able to tell his father the whole truth: about the peril his job was facing at the firm, his growing suspicions of fraud at X-Tronic, and his hidden agenda for Glazier.

"How are your classes?" Michael asked, hoping to steer the conversation to more comfortable ground. "Find your next protégé yet?"

Ernest Chapman laughed. "There are one or two possibilities, I think. But none even half as good as you were." He paused. "Your mother and I went to visit your grandfather's grave up in

Haddem. It was his birthday, so we took a nice wreath for his tombstone."

"I wish I could have gone," Michael said as images of his grandfather flitted through his mind. The clearest, most potent memory was of himself, age seven, sitting on his grandpa's right leg and steering the old brown Ford pickup. His grandpa was the only one who would let him "drive" at such a young age. Those were innocent times for Michael, still years before he was old enough to hear the story of his family's history in Elk County, Pennsylvania in the 1950s, before they had to move away to Kansas. It was his first real lesson about both the good and bad sides of business. And although his father hadn't said so, Michael suspected that his grandfather's shame had much to do with his father's becoming a professor of accounting and finance. It was as if, when his father stood before a classroom to teach business ethics, corporate responsibility, and proper accounting practices, he was making amends for what his own father had done many decades earlier.

They chatted another ten minutes about weather, fishing, and hometown politics. After hanging up, the stories about his family's history in Bethel, Pennsylvania newly stirred up within him, Michael found himself more driven than ever to keep investigating the mysteries he had uncovered at X-Tronic.

*   *   *

Alaska's heart sank when she walked into the Funky Buddha and saw her three paintings still hanging on the wall. Even after lowering the price on each, she still hadn't gotten a nibble. It seemed, no matter what she did, she just couldn't sell her work. Moments like this made her really question her dreams of being a professional artist.

Spotting the owner's gangly frame behind the bar, she forced a smile. "Still no buyers, huh?" she said.

"Sorry," he said in a tone of genuine sympathy. "We haven't really been selling anybody's work this month," he said, cocking his head to the paintings over the other booths along the wall.

"At least tell me people noticed them," she said.

"Oh, sure. They love your stuff—your booths are the most popular ones in the whole place. They just aren't buying anybody's, that's all."

For so many years now she had tried to keep optimistic about painting, but lately it was getting harder. All her life she had felt a little different from others, a little strange, almost like an outsider. She had loved painting for as long as she could remember. As she grew up and had to deal with her mother's leaving and her father's accident that left him blind, there had been times when the only moments in her life when she felt balance and control were while painting. It had become her personal escape from the world. Later, near the end of high school, with the building pressure to choose a career to study, she had feared she could never fit into the kinds of careers that even her closest friends were thinking about. There had just been something different about her, and for a long time she had worried she would never find a path of her own.

Finally she had decided to pursue the uncertain career of her passion. Studying art history and painting at the university had felt like living a dream, but it hadn't prepared her for the difficulty of continuing that dream after she finished college. Now she had been following this path unsuccessfully for years, and she was beginning to feel stuck. She could no longer envision where her life was taking her, and that scared her. And as much as she loved painting, she worried that pursuing it might be ruining her life.

"You don't mind if I leave them up, do you?" she said quietly. "I know you usually have a three-week limit."

"We'll keep 'em up as long as you like," he said. "I kind of like them anyway—be sorry to see 'em go."

"Thanks, Rory," she said. "You're a pal." She felt that she should say something else, but the melodic ring tone of her cell phone broke into her thoughts. "Is the upstairs open?" she asked the owner.

"Sure," he said, "but no one's up there. Go right ahead."

She answered the phone as she moved toward the stairs. "Hey, Dad," she said, trying not to sound as off balance as she felt.

"Hey, angel," the raspy voice said. "Save any souls lately?"

"No time," she replied with a wry chuckle. "Still too busy trying to salvage yours." She was feeling a little better. She loved talking to her dad, loved hearing that gruff laugh.

"I'm a lost cause, kiddo. You'd be wise to cut me loose."

"Oh, shut up, Dad. What kind of way is that to talk to your daughter?"

"The bank called again."

Alaska grimaced. Now she knew why he had called. It was never just to talk. It was always to tell her either good news or bad news. For the past six months, there seemed to be only the latter.

"What did they say? Can they give you another extension?"

"I talked them into it," he said. "I think they feel bad 'cause I'm blind and live alone. Maybe it would be bad publicity to foreclose on someone like me. Still, I don't think their charity will go much further. And I'm not even sure what good the extension will do—I've gotten next to nothing from record royalties in the last five years. I think *that* golden goose is finally cooked and eaten. I need to talk to someone about foreclosure and bankruptcy. I've never understood how those things work, but I'd better start learning fast. Maybe there's some protection."

"Damn it, Dad, why'd you send me to Berkeley to study art if we were starting to have money problems? Do you know how much that *cost*? And do you know how hard it is to make money painting? I would have made different decisions if I'd known back then how much trouble we were in. I could have done something to help us."

"Aw, angel, you've always wanted to be a painter, ever since you were a little girl. I wasn't gonna rob you of that."

Her eyes were tearing up now as she looked down from the empty rooftop bar onto the cold, gray city street below. She felt so powerless to control events in their lives.

"Well, at least I've known about this for a little while, Dad. I'm going to help us through this. I've got a job waiting tables at a nice restaurant downtown. And I've got other things going that could make a lot of money. I'm painting some of the best work I've ever done. Just hang on a little longer, okay? Things are going to get a lot better for us again, I promise."

"I'm so sorry you have to worry about this, angel. It's not fair you should have to carry this burden. I'm not the greatest father."

"No? Well, you happen to be the greatest dad *I've* ever had, so there. I love you, and I've loved the life you gave me. It's time I gave a little something back. I have to go now, Dad, but I want to talk more later on. Can I call you this evening?"

"Anytime, angel."

When the call ended, she was in one of the main outdoor booths on the vacant balcony. Her father's voice had kept her strong and motivated, but the moment his voice was gone, she felt overwhelmed by sadness. It wasn't fair. Things weren't supposed to be this tough. She wasn't supposed to have to make the decisions she had made during the past month. She felt hollow inside, and sick that she could do nothing to protect her father.

It was the two of them against the world, as it had always been: her mother leaving them, the accident that left him blind, and now the money problems. Just one bad thing building on top of another over the years. But she wasn't going to let the world beat them. Not anymore. If it meant protecting her daddy, she would do a deal with the devil himself.

28

A T SEVEN O'CLOCK Monday morning, Michael sent an e-
mail to the Cooley and White audit team at X-Tronic,
saying he wouldn't arrive until midmorning. Then, grabbing one
of the two briefcases of the contract copies, he drove downtown
to the corner of Stout and Seventeenth. The towering gray
buildings shaded the crowded streets and alleys in an urban
setting that now seemed foreign after so many weeks working in
the sunny suburban Tech Center. Navigating his way through the
pedestrian throng on the final leg of its morning commute, he
arrived at the elegant brass doors of the United First Bank. The
oldest financial institution in the Rocky Mountain region, it had
remained an archaic, stand-alone bank, keeping its long tradition
of conservatism and discretion—the very qualities that made it
most attractive to Michael in this moment.

He went to the front counter and asked to speak with an
account representative. Within moments, a slender woman in a
dark business suit crossed the marble floor to meet him. She led
him to her office, where he selected a medium-size safety-
deposit box. He then gave the woman his instructions: he was to

call the bank and verify a rotating password on a weekly basis to confirm the continued storage of his briefcase. "I will call every Monday before noon," he said. "If I should ever fail to make the call, please contact this person and give them this message, along with full access to my deposit box." He slid a sealed manila envelope across the desk. Looking down at it, she was visibly startled to see the name of the addressee.

*   *   *

Sarah left the *Denver Post* building Monday night and crossed Colfax into Civic Center Park. During the day, the small park sat as a peaceful, open medium between the State Capitol building and City Hall, nearly two hundred yards of lovely stone pathways stretching between the two seats of government, wandering past fountains, sculptures, flowerbeds, and benches. But by night, most pedestrians had vanished, and the trees lining the lawns made it a dark and shadowy place. Traffic circled endlessly around the area on the edge of downtown, and police cruisers were often seen in the vicinity, which kept the area fairly safe, but the roaming homeless, hustlers, and other street people gave some visitors a heightened sense of danger. But not Sarah. Denver was her town, and nothing could harm her as she moved through its shadows.

Walking across the dark hollow of the small Greek amphitheater where Hamlet had died on a dozen summer evenings, she paused to look at the lingering Christmas lights of City Hall. She hesitated before walking up the steps where she and Kurt had sat with friends watching *King Lear*'s tragic end. They had planned to catch *A Midsummer Night's Dream* this June—something that would bring her to tears when the ads started popping up around the city in May.

Choking back the tears, she headed toward the lights of the Central Library, winking through the park's dark trees, and followed this beacon as homeless people shifted like zombies in the darkness around her.

Reaching the other side of the park, she crossed the street and walked a half block along the five-story castlelike structure before reaching the library's main entrance. She took the escalators up three floors and walked over a bridge to the entrance of the Western History section. Moving through the small security station, she realized how clever Michael had been to arrange the meeting here. For this was where many of the archived historical documents of the Old West were stored, and that meant added security measures. Everyone who entered this part of the library walked through metal detectors and had to check in all possessions: cell phones, backpacks, computers, and even notepads and pens. Librarians gave out wooden pencils and small squares of white paper so that people could hand copy things from the various historic documents, journals, and manuscripts, but nothing could be photocopied and absolutely nothing could be checked out. She realized Michael had picked this place because they could arrive alone without drawing notice but also have security and privacy. It would be tough for anyone to smuggle a surveillance device past the security station to record their conversation.

She walked into an elliptical-shaped reading room with a large wooden structure in the center that looked like the base of an antique oil rig rising up through the wood and glass ceiling. Moving past the dozen or so people in the large room, she crossed to the edge, on the other side of some tall bookshelves, and passed three private meeting rooms until she found Michael waiting inside the fourth.

"Thanks for coming," Michael said when she came in. He sidestepped her to close the door, then adjusted the blinds over the windows before going back to the table. "These are good rooms." When he sat, he looked at her as if trying to discern something from her expression. "Are you ready for this?"

"Yeah, I'm ready," she said. "Now, tell me what the hell's going on inside X-Tronic."

"All right. Well, I finished looking through the revenue contracts, and they didn't support the revenue the company was recording. I recalculated everything for the past year and concluded X-Tronic was overstating revenue by three times what they should have reported. Profits were overstated by much more."

Sarah was digesting this news. She needed to focus on the facts and understand the mechanics of what Michael had found—only then could she piece everything together to discover what had happened to Kurt.

"So how does this work?" she finally asked. "I'm no accountant. Break it down for me."

"Okay," Michael said, arranging some of the scraps of notepaper the librarian had given him on the tabletop. It seemed he had written things on each piece before she arrived. "X-Tronic's a software company, right?"

"Right."

"So what do they sell?"

"Software."

"They sell software *licenses*: the right to use their software for a period of time—often three years, but the terms can vary."

"Okay."

"But they only develop software for businesses, mostly large corporations. So they also sell different types of software products attached to their main operating system software. They have inventory applications for manufacturers, payroll applications for companies that don't outsource payroll services, purchasing applications, accounts payable, revenue and accounts receivable, and corporate accounting and financial reporting applications."

Pausing a moment, he appeared to refocus his explanation, as if he was worried he might fail to communicate the significance of what he had discovered. "The business software helps a corporate client with their accounting. Everything a company needs for its employees to record all the accounting activity, keep track of all the money coming in and going out, all the business transactions and journal entries, all that. Everything needed to create management reports so that the big suits can make the right decisions about whether to open a plant, lower prices, purchase a competitor, fire a manager, kill a product, or get a new loan from a bank so they don't run out of money at the end of the month. Everything, right?"

"Yeah, I get it." She had been watching him point to the variously labeled bits of paper on the table, depending on what he was trying to describe. She had not seen this side of him before: he spoke fast and jumped around the different business issues faster even than her brother had the few times he had described his job to her. Seeing this behavior gave her confidence—even if she couldn't grasp everything he was saying, he wouldn't lead her astray in his analysis of what he had seen in the company. In short, he knew what he was talking about.

"So," Michael continued, "a sales rep at X-Tronic sells a mixed bag of products in one large contract to a big corporation. Everything is broken down by license and product. The contract says a company will pay so much for twenty users for the payroll license for three years, thirty users for accounts payable licenses for three years, twenty users for revenue licenses for three years, and so on. They usually bundle the products and license levels to give corporate clients a good deal, et cetera. Okay?"

"Sounds like a mess to me, but yeah, I've got the gist of it." Sarah felt suddenly exhausted. Her mind was working fast, and so far she was keeping up with his explanations, she had to stay on her toes. Part of her wanted to take a moment to digest what he was saying, but she didn't want to break his momentum. She sensed he was about to get to the most important part.

"Well, here's the thing with the accounting rules," he said. "If a company pays X-Tronic three million dollars for the license rights to use a bunch of different software products for three years, X-Tronic can't record that as three million dollars in revenue."

This confused her. "Why not? They made the sale, right? They have a signed contract? They got the money, right?"

"Oh, yeah, they get the money right away. The problem is, technically they haven't *earned* the money yet."

"What do you mean they haven't earned it? They must have spent a fortune developing their software products. They sold the software to a company to use. They get the three million. You don't call that revenue?"

Michael shook his head. "Like I said, they didn't *sell* the software. What they sold were license agreements so that the company could *use* the software over a three-year period. The three million they get is a *prepayment* for those three years. Just like if a person had to pay their rent for three years in advance— the place they rent from would have to break those prepayments into thirty-six even amounts and recognize the revenue as each of those months occurs."

"Why the hell would a company pay that much in advance?"

"That's just the way this kind of contract works. I'm sure they could be modified if the company wanted to. The point is, from an accounting point of view, the three million is supposed to be booked to an account called 'unearned revenue.' In other words, X-Tronic can't consider the money actual revenue until time passes during the term of the contract: the three years."

Sarah felt a little overwhelmed, but despite the complexities of what Michael was describing to her, she felt as if she understood. The company had collected money in advance for services it would perform over the next three years, but it was reporting in the accounting statements that it had already performed the services, thus fraudulently declaring the money *earned* revenue instead of *unearned* revenue. She still didn't have all the ins and outs, but she got the thrust of it: X-Tronic was using bad documentation and false calculations to pretend it had made more revenue and profits during the year than it actually had.

"In any accounting fraud," Michael continued, "it's really hard for just one person to cook the books. Companies generally have a lot of checks and reviews in place, so you typically need at least two people: one to lie about the numbers, and the other, the reviewer or supervisor, to cover up the lie. If you have more than two people, it's even easier to cover things up. Now, everyone in accounting has different responsibilities, so of course the fraudsters can't be just anybody—they have to be the right people."

"And X-Tronic has the right people doing this?"

"Oh, I think so," Michael said. "I think they have the CFO, the two COOs, and the CEO, as well as some others. That's everyone important for the revenue contracts. With a team like that, they could make up almost any number they wanted for revenue as long as it wasn't so inflated it might raise a red flag for a stock trader or a security analyst."

Sarah considered this. The implications of a fraud this big by the top executives at one of the largest software companies in the country was enough to make even the most veteran investigative journalist salivate.

But suddenly her emotions took over, and despite all the financial crimes Michael was trying to explain to her, Sarah came back to the only reason why any of this mattered to her. Somehow, her brother had fallen into this nest of vipers at X-Tronic. Between the shock she felt and the grave concern she saw on Michael's face, she could only imagine what must have been going through Kurt's mind since he discovered the same crimes and tried to sleuth out their sources. She wanted to hurt everyone who had robbed her of her brother, but she forced herself to maintain control. She was out of her element and knew she must rely on Michael, not only as a journalist's source but also as an expert analyst on financial crimes.

"So you think I should write about it," she said. "You want me to expose them."

"Yes—but not yet. I still haven't gotten all the information about what's happening."

She knitted her brows. "How much more do you need?"

Michael shrugged. "I'm working with someone to determine all the potential criminal aspects of what we've seen. He's really smart, and I trust him. He's helped me out before, and I think he can help me now. He'll understand this stuff better than anyone, so I want to check with him in case I'm missing some angle on what's happen or why."

"And you can't tell me who they are, I suppose?"

"Sorry, I wish I could," Michael said honestly.

Sarah hated not having answers, but she liked Michael and trusted his judgment. "You think there's something more going on besides the inflated revenue, don't you?"

Michael shifted around some more scrap paper, looking up at her just long enough to make sure she was watching as he pointed to the different pieces of paper. "From what I can tell, X-Tronic is creating a huge one-year spike in revenue this year," he said, stabbing a piece of paper in the center of the new pattern he had created. "It looks like they've been doing it the past few years, too, but by not as much. This year they're doing it to almost every contract. It's not sustainable."

"What do you mean, 'not sustainable'?"

"Well, say they entered into new contracts this year for three hundred million. Normally they would report revenue of a hundred million this year, a hundred million next year, and a hundred million the year after. But since they're reporting everything up front, they're really digging themselves into a hole in future years. In future years a stock analyst would definitely see a drop in revenue, which is a huge red flag that something's wrong with the company's numbers."

"X-Tronic could just do it again next year?" she offered.

"They could try, but they'd start out in the hole because of the two hundred million they can never record as revenue in future years—even though they have to keep servicing those contracts."

"So they're eventually going to get caught!"

"Normally, yes. These things are short-term lies. They always get caught after a number of years of lying, if not sooner—there is usually no escape in the end. That's what happened to Enron, and it happened to Bernie Madoff. In the end, time almost always catches up to this type of accounting lies. But if the merger with Cygnus goes through, X-Tronic can hide the numbers forever, because all their accounts get revalued. It's called an *open balance sheet* audit. It's something unique— happens only once: when one company gets bought by another. The bought-out company's accounting records get revalued in order to be merged with the other company. And in future years it's too complicated to make accurate comparisons of premerger versus postmerger financial results, because the company's operations are now combined with another company's operations."

Sarah knew he was trying to explain everything to her in the simplest terms he could, but it was still a little confusing to wrap her mind around. To her, the important thing was that X-Tronic would legally be able to reset the accounting records—erasing its fraud and starting the books fresh—if it got taken over by Cygnus. It was as if the accounting lies were the bodies of people the mafia had killed, and Cygnus was a new casino they could build on top of the unmarked graves to make sure the bodies were never found. Cygnus wouldn't even know it had inadvertently helped X-Tronic cover up the crimes.

"And you think most or all of the top executives are involved?" she asked.

"I don't see how they could not be."

"You said the CFO, Jerry Diamond?"

"Almost certainly."

Sarah realized that this was matching closely with some of the documentation Kurt had mentioned in the notes she found. "You need to be careful. You're heading down the same path Kurt must have been on. You may even be farther down it than he got. If they find out what you're doing, they'll kill you, too."

Michael nodded. "I think someone's following me. Not all the time, but sometimes I see a black Mustang with tinted windows, and I'm sure it's the same one every time."

"You should tell someone."

"I'm telling *you*," he said, as if that were enough. "I'm telling you because, if anything happens to me, I don't want you to keep digging around in all this. Print an article about everything you have, but don't wait for more information. Put this out in the open so it'll be harder for someone to come after you. You have to promise me that. I'm the best source you're ever going to get inside X-Tronic. Trust me. If I'm gone, you can't continue. Cut and run and put up a giant red flag for the whole world to see, and wait for the cavalry. They'll come, I guarantee you. You have to promise me you'll stop if something happens to me."

Sarah was a little surprised how calmly Michael spoke of his own potential death, and it was sweet the way he was trying to protect her. But there was no way she would stop investigating the story and print some unfounded article if something happened to him. The more time she spent with Michael, the more she liked him, but as far as she was concerned, X-Tronic was more her investigation than his. And no one could ever ask her to stop digging for the truth.

"Promise me," Michael repeated.

"I promise," she said just to satisfy him. *I promise to do everything I can to hurt those bastards who killed Kurt. I promise to push even harder if something happens to you. And I promise never to give up, no matter how many years I have to search before I find the truth about everything that's going on in that company.*

Michael seemed content with her response. She watched as he slowly picked up the scraps of paper he had used to help explain the fraud. On each piece, he had written the name of a person at X-Tronic, a division of the company, or a department or accounting concept or transaction type. What she couldn't help noticing, though, were all the extra pieces of paper pushed to the side that he hadn't pointed to during his explanation. On one, he had written *Cooley & White*. She realized that Michael must have been making extra notes for himself before she arrived. He was still trying to figure this all out! He had a lot of the pieces, but not all of them. As she watched him pick up the pieces of paper, she had the eerie feeling that they were looking at the barest tip of the rot. They had no idea how deep it went, or what they were really up against.

29

———————✴———————

WEDNESDAY MORNING, DON Seaton got out on the passenger's side of the red Hummer and walked down the snowy sidewalk toward X-Tronic's entrance. Thick snowflakes drifted down, imbuing the corporate campus with a cold solitude that reminded him how utterly alone he was in his quest to save the company. When he first created X-Tronic thirty years ago, he had been surrounded by a group of loyal friends, a faithful few who were young, ambitious, and ready to conquer the world with him. But now all his old friends were gone. Even his wife had been taken from him so many years ago that she seemed part of another life. It had been a fight, building X-Tronic into the multinational giant it was today. Having fought and won so many battles, he had once hoped to retire to a quiet life in the mountains—a man who had seen everything the world could offer and who no longer needed anything from it other then to enjoy a life without conflict. That had been his ultimate dream— that and to see his corporation learn to flourish without him. But now everything was falling down around him.

For the first time in his long life, he shuddered at what the future might bring. Entrusting his sons with the keys to X-Tronic, he had done everything possible to groom them as the future leaders of the empire he had built. But they had abused the power they were given—that much he was sure of. But the question remained: had they abused their power merely to speed their own rise in the corporation, or had they done much worse by conspiring in an out-and-out betrayal of their father? He was not attending this morning's corporate board emergency meeting just to fight the Cygnus takeover bid; he was also hoping to save what little he had left of his family.

He walked across the marble floor of the corporate entrance. The security guard, caught dozing, stiffened in his chair and returned his nod. Feeling tired and alone, he crossed the floor to the elevators and pressed the button, and as he waited, his eyes fell on *The Oath of the Horatii*. He studied the scene in the painting as if he had never seen it before. Though he had bought it to impart a feeling of dominance and courage to his employees, he now suspected that the artist may have had a darker theme in mind. Perhaps he wasn't celebrating the soldiers' courage at all. Even though they were willing to die for Rome, perhaps the focus was really on the weeping women in the background. Perhaps the artist was himself weeping for the fall of the Roman Empire, for the loss of one of history's greatest societies.

"I've always thought this a remarkable painting," said a deep voice beside him.

Startled, he turned his head away from the painting to find Jerry Diamond standing next to him.

"Truly remarkable," Diamond continued. "Have I ever told you that?"

"No," Seaton replied.

"Well, it is. The courage of the soldiers to fight whatever enemy they encounter. And they're so young, too. The courage of youth can be impressive, don't you think?"

"There are many kinds of courage," Seaton replied. "Perhaps it's the father who is the most courageous."

"The father?" The CFO gave him a puzzled look.

"It's the father who is giving the swords to his sons, even when he knows he may be sending them to their death. You see, the soldiers are courageous because of their ignorance—they're too young to really understand how big a sacrifice they may be making. It's the father who can see the big picture, who truly knows how much they are about to lose. But the women are the ones who weep. You see that. The father stands in front of his sons without shedding a tear, even though he's crying on the inside because he knows he is about to lose them. Now, *that's* courage, Jerry: to lose your sons because of their actions and not shed a tear."

The elevator chimed behind them, and Diamond turned and moved toward the opening doors, but Seaton lingered a second, his sad eyes gazing at the Roman scene captured by a long-dead artist. He suddenly regretted buying the painting. It was too beautiful to be imprisoned inside a corporate lobby. Every day it seemed that life was draining from X-Tronic. For too long the grand entry had been a mask for the fading glory of a stronger, more vital past. As the elevator doors closed on the poignant scene, he made a mental note to donate the painting back to the Louvre, where it deserved to be—back out in the world, surrounded by the nobler elements of humankind, far away from the coming events at X-Tronic.

Lance felt more alive now than at any time he could remember. The board of directors meeting was in fifteen minutes. Waiting in his office for Lucas, he thought of how he had rehearsed this meeting in his mind until no possible variation of events or discussion could surprise him—nothing, that is, until he saw the hangdog look on his brother's face as he walked in.

"Well, guess this is the big day, huh?" Lucas said in a less-than-convincing tone.

"Yup," Lance replied, hiding his concern, "this is it . . . Say, you ready for this?"

But Lucas seemed unable to meet his gaze. And for the first time in nearly a year, he realized there was something wrong with Lucas: a disturbance so deep that not even his own twin could see the problem. This sudden, mysterious distance between them was troubling, especially now, only minutes before the showdown that, it seemed, he had been preparing for his whole life long.

"I'm ready for it," Lucas replied.

"You sure? You don't seem all that amped."

"Just a little nervous." Lucas was looking out the far window. "What if things don't go the way we expect?"

"What's wrong, bro?"

Lucas looked at him but said nothing.

"C'mon, what's going on?" Lance insisted. "We're about to walk into the most important meeting of our lives, something we've spent years working for. What are you not telling me?"

Lucas turned from the window and faced him without a word.

Lance stood and, moving around the desk with remarkable speed, grabbed Lucas's shoulders and forced him to look him in the eyes. "Brother," he said, trying to sound calm, "what are you not telling me?"

Lucas looked at him with apologetic eyes. "Nothing," he finally said. "I just wonder if there isn't another way to do this."

"Another way?"

"A way that doesn't hurt Dad."

"What are you talking about!" Lance asked, gaping. "There *is* no other way. Why would you even think this? Don't do this to us. Everything is set up. Don't betray me."

These last words seemed to bring Lucas out of his fugue, for he seemed once again aware of the world around him. Straightening the slumped shoulders and filling his chest, he said, "Sorry. It was just a thought. I don't know why I said that."

Lance stepped back, unable to shake the feeling that his brother just might be a lot less like him than he had always thought. But they were still together on what they were doing. They might have different reasons for the choices they made in life, but in the end, they were still the same choices.

"Jesus, Luke," he said with a disarming grin. "For a moment there I wasn't sure who you were."

"It's still me," Lucas replied. "That was stupid what I said. I'm ready for this."

"Okay, then. No more pussyfooting around. This is where we reveal our intentions. This is where he realizes he's lost his company and that we're every bit as strong as he was when he was young."

"He can't blame us for doing what he once did."

"He won't blame us," Lance said. "That's not his style. He'll blame himself." Then, for Lucas's sake, he added, "After the shock wears off, he'll be impressed that we did this."

Lucas smiled at this, and Lance knew that his drifting brother had found his rudder and was back on course. He looked at his watch, saw it was time to head to the boardroom, and pointed at his office door.

As he and his brother walked down the palatial hallway in their Savile Row bespoke suits, Lance felt himself almost bubbling over with excitement. They were only moments away from beating their father at his own game, taking power away from the man who had made billions taking power from others. It served him right for betraying his business partners, for failing to save their mother in that tragic climbing accident, for abandoning his sons to a childhood of boarding schools and hazing and headmasters so he could continue chasing power and money while his sons grew up as orphans. And now, after all these years of solitary success, dear old absentee, eyes-on-the-prize Dad was finally going to lose the thing he cherished most in all the world: his *real* baby, X-Tronic.

30

—⊶✱⊷—

W ALKING INTO THE dark boardroom, Don Seaton found ten people waiting for him. They all stood up around the massive wood roundtable that he had chosen thirty years ago because it reminded him of his childhood romance with Arthur and his knights. He nodded at the men in waiting and approached his designated chair. Lance and Lucas were seated opposite him. Jerry Diamond sat two places to Seaton's right, his shaved head wearing a diadem of half-reflected small cone lights in the ceiling. The other seven men who sat around the table were X-Tronic's outside directors, who, along with the elder Seaton, made up the board of directors. On the table in front of each place lay a copy of the summary packet for the meeting's agenda.

Seaton wondered whether he might be losing his zeal for leading his company through the brawling, eye-gouging chaos of the corporate world. He thought of how far he and X-Tronic had traveled together across time since he took the helm twenty-five years ago. Looking around the table at the faces of the current board members and select officers, he thought of the vanished faces of those who had sat with him at this very table in the beginning. Nick Kemper, the enfant terrible astounding the early board members with his eccentric brilliance, now sifting through New York's seamier bars looking for young bands he could develop into real talent. And the young and energetic Jack Ross, who had made up for his ignorance of software programming and computer engineering by demonstrating one of the most brilliant business minds Seaton had ever known, now lying in a steel drawer tucked into a wall of the Milton Helpen Institute of Forensic Medicine, under the care of New York's chief medical examiner.

Seaton forced himself to let these thoughts go, for they would only depress him more, weakening the very instincts that had kept him focused and strong as he survived one threat after another over the years. He knew now what his sons must be planning, though he couldn't see how they planned to get away with it. He feared he had been given only the barest glimpse of the depth of their planning and maneuvering over the years. They were threatening him from the darkness of his own past, like demons rising from the graves of all the souls he had let down or betrayed in his life. No, it wasn't so much his sons he must face, as the darkest deeds of his own past.

He looked across the table at Lance, then Lucas, holding the eyes of each for a few seconds before turning his attention to Paul Kirkland, a skinny man who looked more like a farmer than a board-appointed secretary. "Shall we begin," Seaton said. "Paul, is everyone accounted for?"

"Everyone's here," Kirkland replied, nodding around the table. "Everyone's ready."

Seaton closed his eyes and took a second to collect himself. Though he had lost his sons' faith, he still believed he could control the board, believed they would once again choose to follow his vision for the company's future.

Opening his eyes, he took a centering breath and sat up straight. "If history has taught us anything, it's that empires rise and fall." He paused. "As do corporations."

The others in the room remained silent, watching him with a mixture of puzzlement and curiosity, guessing at where he was trying to take the first discussion of the meeting.

Seaton continued. "Rome destroyed itself internally, over a period of years, before it eventually fell to barbarians from outside. The fundamentals on which it had built its society had dissolved under the weight of its success as those with power were corrupted and failed to honor the work and morals of those who had built the society before them. And as with Rome during the start of its decline, I fear that the fundamentals that made X-Tronic great have been disappearing even as our company is growing."

Having said enough to begin his first point, Seaton paused to survey the room for individual reactions. He saw Paul Kirkland look at William Steel, the chairman of the board, whose tan, pockmarked face was frowning. Lucas seemed to shift uncomfortably in his chair before settling into an aggressive breathing rhythm, like an adrenaline-charged fighter before a bout. Lance seemed perfectly relaxed, even grinning when he flashed a glance at Jerry Diamond, who, to Seaton's sudden dismay, was staring at the center of the table with gleaming eyes, one hand over his mouth in an unmistakable attempt to hide a smile. And for the first time, the terrifying idea occurred to Seaton that his CFO could be in league with the twins. But before he could follow the thought to its possible implications, Lance cleared his throat to speak.

"Your concerns are unfounded and misconstrued, Father."

"It's 'Mr. Seaton' in this room." He had snapped the words a little more sharply than intended as his frustrated mind still raced to work through the serious damage the twins may have done if they had Diamond's help.

Lance swallowed. "Mr. Seaton," he said stiffly, "X-Tronic has not fallen, and it never will fall. The stock price is at an all-time high, we're on the verge of reporting record profits that will beat every analyst's estimates, and even one of our top competitors is now groveling at our front steps, begging us to approve an acquisition bid. X-Tronic is as strong as it has ever been."

Seaton interrupted Lance with a quote he had memorized long ago. "'Many shall be restored that now are fallen, and many shall fall that now are in honor.' Horace said that, and Benjamin Graham felt it was so important that he reminded the world of it. Everyone at this table needs to take a careful look at why X-Tronic appears to have been doing so well these past two years. I'll tell you one thing: it hasn't been because of organic growth. We've grown through numerous acquisitions of smaller competitors under the shroud that they served the expansion of X-Tronic. But sometimes acquisitions only mask the lack of growth within the core corporation."

"Mr. Seaton," Jerry Diamond said, "growth through acquisitions is every bit as successful for a corporation as any internal growth could be."

"Tell that to Steve Jobs and Apple," Seaton shot back. "How many years did Microsoft's stock lag after its initial success with Windows and Office Suite? Meanwhile, Apple grew internally, and its success exploded. Gentlemen, this might be coming as a news flash to you, but X-Tronic has suffered from a serious brain drain over the past few years. We need to refocus our efforts on R and D. Not just a minimally acceptable level of research, either—I want the best programmers and software engineers in the world begging for jobs at X-Tronic. And there are two sides to R and D: the research phase, to make the technological advances; and the development phase, where the new technology is further enhanced to make it a marketable product for consumers. Some of the greatest technological advances in history came through pure research, with no end product in mind. I want research laboratories built on our premises, for pure research only—no strict financial oversight or restraints. I don't want anything to impede the innovation of our researchers. As they develop the technology, we'll have a separate team whose primary goal is to further develop that technology into a product we can sell in the marketplace."

"You're talking about an enormous financial investment," Diamond said.

"It will be worth it down the road," Seaton replied.

"You don't know that," Lance said.

"We have to invest in the future or we'll die," Seaton battled back.

This time Lucas jumped in. "We're investing in the future by merging with Cygnus."

"That's not an investment," Seaton said. "That's joining the enemy out of fear of competing with them."

Lucas's eyes widened. Lance shook his head violently.

"Now, hold on, Mr. Seaton," William Steel interrupted from beside him. "I happen to think a merger with Cygnus could be the best way for us to compete in the marketplace."

"I disagree," Seaton said.

"Wall Street would love it," Diamond argued.

"That means it will be good for the shareholders," Lucas added.

"Not necessarily," said Seaton. "There are a dozen reasons why the merger would be a bad idea."

"Really," Lance said, laughing. "Name one."

"The cultures are too different," Seaton said with fire in his voice. "The two companies could never be combined as long as Kavanaugh is Cygnus's CEO. He'll shake up the divisional structures and try to control the creative operations in a way that will stamp out any innovation by our development and design teams."

"We believe we can control those aspects of the merger," Lucas said.

"You can't *possibly* control them!" Seaton said, his voice rising from the frustration of having to battle everyone in the room at once. "You can't control them, because you can't control Kavanaugh. I'm telling you, if you let him get control of X-Tronic, he will destroy everything that has made this a great corporation. He'll combine our software products and client relationships into the assembled behemoth that Cygnus has become over the years."

Lance, who seemed to have had enough, stood up to speak. "Mr. Steel," he said, addressing the chairman of the board, "with all due respect to *Mr. Seaton,* I believe that everyone in this room is well aware of his personal opinion of Mr. Kavanaugh. However, I believe that in the best interest of the shareholders, it is the board's responsibility to review the proposed merger by examining the report in front of us."

"That is enough!" Seaton growled, getting to his feet. "It's not a personal opinion but a *fact:* Kavanaugh destroys companies that merge into his."

"With all due respect, sir," William Steel interjected. "I believe your son has a right to speak here."

"His *son?*" Lance said to Steel. "It's 'Mr. Seaton' in this room." Lance's gaze turned toward Seaton.

Seaton stood, vulnerable and alone, while both his sons looked at him from across the table with the same rebellious strength that he recognized from his own youth. How long had they been positioning themselves in the power struggle for X-Tronic's leadership? How long had they been planning to confront him at this meeting? And how long ago had Jerry Diamond decided to join them? A lot of backroom dealing had been going on—even Steel's last comment hinted that the chairman of the board had already decided to side with the twins on the merger. And the horrible realization hit him that he may have lost control of his company long before ever setting foot in this boardroom.

Slowly Seaton lowered himself back into his seat. The betrayal he felt in this moment squeezed his chest and choked his throat. He closed his dry lips and stared at the table in front of him, willing his right hand to stop shaking. Unable to control the quivering, he pulled his hand back from the tabletop and put it in his lap.

Now Lucas cleared his throat to speak for the first time. "Look," he said, "Mr. Seaton is right: companies rise, and they fall. But while focusing on pure research sounds good in theory, we all know there are serious risks to such a strategy. Hundreds of millions of dollars could easily be wasted on haphazard research goals that never materialize into any salable product. I don't believe that's a risk X-Tronic should be taking right now. In fact, both Lance and I see the offer from Cygnus as X-Tronic's best opportunity for continued future success."

Now Lance put his hand on Lucas's shoulder to signal that he was taking control of the discussion again. "Let's get right to the point, everyone," he said. "We are here today to vote on whether to give the shareholders our endorsement of the Cygnus offer. Goldman Sachs has been retained as our M and A advisor, and their valuation report—which is in the board summary packet you've each received—outlines their evaluation of the offer as 'fairly priced based on current market conditions.' Therefore, the only decision we have to make is whether or not we believe that an allowed takeover of X-Tronic by Cygnus will result in the strengthening of our corporation as the resources of the two companies are combined. As you all know, Mr. Kavanaugh is the CEO and majority shareholder of Cygnus, and he is prepared to offer retention clauses for all top executives at X-Tronic. Many mid- and entry-level employees of X-Tronic will be laid off during the restructuring efforts after the takeover, but all top management will remain in place. This will help ensure that X-Tronic continues to grow through our current strategies."

Lance paused a moment before nodding to Diamond. "Now, I believe Jerry is planning to take us through the numbers in the report, to better explain the details of Cygnus's proposed merger and the potential advantages of the corporate restructuring and combination of market share, and so on."

"Thank you, Lance," Diamond replied in his deep baritone. He lowered his shaved head and picked up the report in front of him. "Everyone please turn to page four," he said, flipping through the glossy soft-bound packet. "I'd like to start with what the improved margins will look like after combining the revenue streams . . ."

Seaton reluctantly picked up the report. As he half-listened to Diamond's presentation, he flipped through page after page of rosy projections and best-case-scenarios presented as if they were near certainties. Nowhere was there proper risk analysis, or contingency plans should the businesses find combining difficult. Nowhere was there discussion of Seaton's worst fear: Kavanaugh's history of betraying a competitor's management and culture *after* the merger was initiated. But despite his growing concerns, there was nothing he could say to persuade the other board members, because when he looked up from the report he saw nothing but gleaming smiles. All the other board members were fast falling in love with the merger proposal. They loved the image of power they thought the company would have after the merger. And they were further comforted knowing that Lance and Lucas and Diamond were all for it. And Seaton, as everyone well knew, saw the merger with a jaundiced eye because of his personal dislike of Kavanaugh.

Turning back to the proposal, he knew he had lost control over everything. He didn't need to wait for Diamond to finish his little dog-and-pony show to know that the board would vote overwhelmingly to recommend the merger to X-Tronic shareholders. He looked at the twins. They were both watching him: Lance's lips were clamped tight, as if to fight off a smile; Lucas's eyes were moist, as if waiting for something he hoped would happen. What were they thinking right now? Seaton had misread what was happening. He had thought it a simple case of the sons attempting to supplant the father because they didn't respect him and had ambitions for his power. Now he understood: there was a much larger conspiracy in his company, trying to oust him from the throne. But why would the twins need to form a conspiracy, and why would Diamond join them? Something else nagged at him, eclipsing even the horrible realizations of what was happening: a bad feeling that beneath it all lurked a deeper, darker secret—one that would explain *why*.

Seaton's hands had stopped shaking. At least *that* small blessing had been granted him. Folding them together on the table, he raised his head and sat upright. Despite the crushing weight of everything he had realized in the past ten minutes, he vowed to show the same strength and courage that a revolutionary martyr might display while facing the firing squad. But he wasn't dead yet, he reminded himself, and as he half-listened to Diamond drone on, his mind searched and circled, looking for a way to survive the conspiracy that he had been blind to for so long. Everyone in the room thought his reign over X-Tronic finished, but he would not go gently into *that* good night.

31

⸺⸱◦✸◦⸱⸺

"**I** SAW YOU last weekend," Alaska said.
       He snugged the cell phone against his ear. "Where?" he
asked, testing her. After the long workweek, he had been too
busy to expect her call.

"The party in Aspen. Who was she—that girl you were
with?"

"Just a friend," he said. "Who were *you* there with?" It
bothered him that she had avoided him at the party. Perhaps he
was making too much of their short time together. Maybe the
connection he was so sure he felt with her had just been a silly
illusion.

Alaska didn't respond for a moment, and he could tell she
was hurt. She had never been this subdued. The gentle side
didn't fit her; it wasn't like her at all. Who *was* this—a different
personality altogether? Things had started so well for them, but
now they seemed to be sliding backward. All these thoughts
flitted through his head as he lay on the couch, speaking on his
cell phone and listening to the light Saturday morning traffic
from the street below.

"Michael?" she asked. Her voice sounded so innocent, so peaceful, and he realized how much he had missed her over the past week.

"Why didn't you talk to me at the party if you saw me?" he asked.

"You seemed happy with your friend."

"I was," he said with a toughness that surprised him.

She was silent again.

"Alaska?" he said, unsure whether she was still there.

"Do you feel like being alone?" she asked.

"Why were you at the party?" he asked.

"Visiting my father for the weekend—I grew up in Aspen, remember?"

"And the Seatons' party?"

"Aspen's not that big, you know. I was having lunch with my dad and saw some old friends who had heard about the party, so I went with them for a bit. I don't know anyone that lives there. I only knew that the old software billionaire owned it. But it doesn't mean anything to own something in Aspen. People are seasonal. Who knows who's actually staying in any of those houses at any given time?"

He had hurt her, and he knew it. "Sorry. I just wasn't expecting to see you there, that's all." He waited for her to respond, but when she didn't, he said, "Alaska, look, I really want to see you again. Let's do something today." He stared up at the bars of morning light angling across his ceiling. "Something outside . . . in the sun. I've been distracted by work this past week. Let me make it up to you."

Even before the call ended, Michael wondered what the hell he thought he was doing. Glazier wouldn't have approved. He should be focusing all his energies on X-Tronic, but something about Alaska made him temporarily lose interest in his work. The fun he had with her, and seeing the no-regrets way she lived her life made him realize more than ever how his own choices were burning him out. Before they had met, it had been so much easier to tackle all the late nights and weekends on the job, but now he could see so much more that he wanted out of life besides his work. Alaska represented a hope he held out for the life he might have when he was finished with X-Tronic and Cooley and White. And even though he knew he should be disciplined and stay focused on his work until he was done with his audit of X-Tronic's books, right now he needed more than ever to be around her, if only to remind himself that things were going to be good again in his life when all this was finished.

After an hour's drive into the mountains, Michael and Alaska tromped through the snowy entrance to the Weather Lake Lodge, where a clerk helped them fill out the proper payment and insurance forms before herding them past vacationing families and college students. The clerk took them out the back door and pointed at a snowmobile. "Stay within bounds," he said, handing them a colored map of the resort, "or you'll risk spending a night in the Loveland jail." He seemed amused at the joke.

"Avalanches?" Michael asked.

"Oh, yes, avoid those, too," the clerk replied, laughing his way back to the lodge.

They could hear the rumble and whine of other snowmobiles in the distance. It reminded Michael of the feeling of being in elementary school and realizing that his class was one of the last ones let out for recess, only to find the other kids halfway through their games. "Come on," he said. "This'll be fun!" He switched on the ignition as Alaska climbed on behind him. "Hold on!" he yelled over the motor. She wrapped her arms around his stomach and leaned into him as if her life depended on it. He squeezed the throttle three-quarters of the way back, and the snowmobile shot out toward the field like a dog unleashed for the hunt.

Swinging dangerously close to the wall of trees, Michael felt her grip tighten around his waist as she screamed in jubilation over the roaring engine. Discovering that she liked it only encouraged him, and he didn't let off the throttle until they had shot out into an open field where a dozen other snowmobiles were zooming about.

He spun it in tight circles before turning toward the nearest stand of trees, then brought the vehicle to a crawl as they entered a white forest.

"Turn the engine off!" she screamed into his left ear after they had gone some distance from the field. His right hand came down to cut the engine. She immediately heaved sideways with surprising strength, pulling them both off the seat into a cushion of snow. He curled into a ball and began laughing as she moved to straddle him. She pulled the edge of his ski cap over his eyes and held it there as she began kissing him.

Releasing him, she flipped onto her back and nestled under his armpit until they were both looking up at the vanishing point beyond the pale black-spotted trees that rose above them.

"Aspens are my favorite trees," she said.

"Why are they your favorite? Tell me." He felt her thigh pushing again his.

"They just are," she answered, giving him a soft elbow in the ribs.

"*Ouf!*" he grunted.

She dug her face deeper into his side. "Let's just lie here for the rest of the day."

"We're paying for the snowmobile by the hour," he replied. "*Ouf!*"—another elbow jab.

"Don't be such an accountant."

"Hey, watch it, missy. I can handle being called a lot of things, but a bean counter has his limits."

She laughed. "Seriously, what made you want to be an accountant, anyway?"

Michael was silent for a moment as he looked into his past. "My father," he said. "Also, my grandfather."

"They were *both* accountants?"

"My father's an accounting professor at Kansas State. He's actually one of the best in the country. My grandfather, on the other hand, understood almost nothing about accounting, but he really encouraged me to be like my father when I was growing up. I got started on that path at an early age, and I was decent at it, too. So here I am."

"Lying in the snow in the mountains with your future ex-wife," she said with a big grin. "Didn't turn out so bad for you, did it?"

"No, I guess I got pretty lucky. What about you? Any luck with your paintings?"

"No luck," she said. "I checked all the places again last week, but still nothing. I graduated with an MFA from Berkeley two years ago and have been painting ever since. But I've only sold a few. It's really hard to sell art these days—not quite as stable a career choice as doing accounting."

"At least you're doing something you enjoy. Accounting's not always that great; trust me. My current job is killing me. I'm locked away in an office building all day long, straining my eyes and constantly stressing over issues with the client, juggling heavy workloads with short deadlines."

"If you hate it so much, why don't you just quit?"

"Can't," he groaned. "I've made commitments I can't break." He watched as a clump of snow fell from a branch high above them and broke into a cloud of powder as it fell through the branches, showering them in a light haze of crystals. "My dream is to someday become a chief financial officer for a company. I want to be the head of the overall financial aspects of a nice small company, so I can help it grow, so I can feel like I've accomplished something worthwhile in the business world. And to get a job like that, I need to get a lot of experience in one of the big international accounting firms. So that's where I'm at now: just doing my time in the trenches so that someday I can be a general."

"So we're both chasing dreams," she said, rolling onto her side and wrapping her arm over his chest.

"The only problem with dreams," he said sullenly, "is that they always feel so far away." He had been referring more to himself than to her and hoped she hadn't been offended. But his concerns vanished as she leaned in and began kissing him again. She always had the ability to make him forget all the problems on his mind, as if taking him into another world where everything was perfect. And at that moment, he realized that he had more in common with Alaska than with anyone else in his life.

32

⸺•◦✳◦•⸺

•

THE LEARJET 60 XR dipped down out of the clouds and glided toward the festive night lights of Austin, Texas. Don Seaton looked out the window at the illuminated State Capitol Building. After circling the city, the jet approached an outer airport from the south and landed on a black runway lined with emerald lights. Seaton and Marcus descended the stairs and slid into a bulletproof limousine waiting for them.

Going through downtown, Seaton noticed that winter was almost nonexistent here. Along Fifth Street, people dined in chic ethnic restaurants surrounded by some of the best live music venues in the country, while, only a block away, college students from the University of Texas seemed to treat every night as if it were spring break.

The limousine turned up a narrow neighborhood road that wound up a small hill covered in stately cottonwoods and live oaks. Pulling in front of a spacious white house, the car stopped next to a stone staircase that rose up a low hill to a wraparound porch.

As they got out, Marcus scanned the area for any movement

among the shadows. They were in one of Austin's most prestigious neighborhoods, with century-old mansions fronted by iron gates. The only movement Marcus could see was a plump silhouette at a second-floor window. Nodding his approval, he followed his employer up the stone steps.

The heavy door opened just as they stepped onto the porch, and out stepped the same plump body that Marcus had seen watching them from the window.

"Mr. Seaton, I still can't believe you insisted on coming all this way," the man said. "Luckily, I could work you into my schedule. As you know, I'm very busy these days."

"Busy trying to take over my company," Seaton said to Fredrick Kavanaugh.

"Among other things," Kavanaugh replied.

"Fred, you need to withdraw your bid from X-Tronic."

A wide grin crossed Kavanaugh's face, turning into hearty laughter. "Don, your tactics are remarkable," he said. "You come to me with a request like that when you know I have no intention of turning away from X-Tronic. This is a desperate ploy, even for a man who has lost the faith of his own board."

"How did you hear about that?" Seaton demanded.

"We all have our sources, Don. You of all people should understand that."

"Fred," he said, stepping closer to his adversary, "I came to you tonight not to ask you for a favor, but to warn you of the consequences if you continue to pursue this folly. I will not let you take control of my company. X-Tronic is in the middle of something right now that I've been planning for years, and I won't let you ruin things. You know my history. You know what I do to companies and people that challenge me. You know what I'm capable of."

"Things aren't what they used to be, Don. Times change. X-Tronic is falling apart from the inside out. Your house is no longer in order. Your precious company isn't as strong as it once was, and neither are you."

Seaton motioned with his eyes for Marcus to return to the car. As his bodyguard retreated down the steps, he turned back to Kavanaugh. "Fred, you don't have any idea what you're getting into on this one. I came here to warn you. What you do with that warning is up to you."

"You didn't come all this way to do me any favors, Don. You took the time to come here because you're searching for a miracle. It just shows me how desperate you really are. Now, I don't know exactly what kind of trouble you guys are having up there in Denver, but whatever it is, I can promise you one thing: once I take over X-Tronic, I'm going to find out everything that's been going on. And here's a little warning for you, Mr. Seaton: you'll be the first piece of business I take care of. You were great in your day, but that day is over. I hope you haven't done anything too desperate to try to hold on to your company. I used to have a lot of respect for you, and I'd hate to have to be the one to make you pay for your mistakes."

Then, without another word, Kavanaugh stepped back inside his palatial house and shut the thick wooden door.

Seaton stood there on the porch for a moment, trying to calculate just how desperate his situation was rapidly turning. It was sobering to think that Kavanaugh's informants gave him such a clear view inside X-Tronic. But Seaton wasn't giving up hope. His investigation into the events surrounding Jack Ross's demise had turned up the name of a man working in Portland who had once worked for Ross—a man who, Seaton hoped, held the secret behind everything that had gone wrong with Ross's business. When he turned around, he heard Marcus starting the car engine on the street below. Moving away from the great, brooding mansion, Seaton hurried down the stairs.

33

———•❋•———

THREE HOURS AFTER leaving Austin, Don Seaton's Learjet rocketed past the snow-covered mass of Mount Hood, descending toward Portland. A steady, chilling winter rain drenched the world outside.

After learning from Darryl Mitchell about Jack Ross's bankrupted company, Seaton had come to follow up personally on the new information. According to Mitchell, Dr. Winston Sharpe, the head researcher for Jack's company, who had later testified against Jack, had taken a job with an X-Tronic subsidiary in Portland. Sharpe must surely hold the missing piece to the puzzle surrounding the fall of Jack's company.

The jet's tires compressed on the wet asphalt, and the engines roared in reverse thrust, shaking the cabin and pulling Seaton forward in his seat. The world passing by outside the window began to slow. After coming to a stop, Captain Steiner opened the cockpit door and entered the cabin.

"Bit of a rough landing, Captain," Seaton said.

"Yes, sir. But I saved you twenty minutes by cutting along the river. The tower recommended circling up around the west end of the city because Mt. Saint Helens had been showing some activity in the past few days, and they're concerned she just may go up again. I told them I could bank the jet above the river gorge and slide in at a safer altitude from the east. The tower was fine with that as long as I was—most pilots wouldn't have tried it."

Seaton smiled. "That's why you're my guy, Captain Steiner—you're a hell of a pilot, and you know what you can and can't get away with in the air."

"Yes, sir," Captain Steiner said with a grin. "Just trying to prepare myself for the day you ask me to do something really crazy."

"I appreciate that," Seaton replied. "Let's just hope I never have to ask. At my age, you start to get concerned about the odds finally catching up," he said with a grin. "Now, Marcus," he said, switching gears and turning to his bodyguard, "let's go see this Dr. Sharpe. It's time for me to find out the truth about Jack's company."

The Range Rover climbed through the hilly streets of Portland. It was late enough on this rainy night that hardly a soul could be seen.

"We're almost there," the driver said, pulling into the underground garage of a massive twenty-story building.

"This is a residential building?" Seaton asked. Something didn't feel right. The absence of other vehicles in the parking tunnel made the place feel more like an abandoned factory than a luxury condominium complex.

"No, sir. This building houses the research labs for Acheron Technology. Acheron is a partially owned subsidiary created by RSA after X-Tronic acquired RSA last year. This place is strictly for R and D activity. The scout team tried to contact Dr. Sharpe at his home, but we were told that he's working at Acheron tonight. Apparently, he's heading a research project that needs to perform some upgrades to the corporate servers overnight. I don't know any of the details about the upgrades."

Seaton thought for a moment. Two weeks ago, he had never heard of Acheron Technology; now he was looking for its head researcher of a software development program that had been kept under wraps for more than a year. The more he learned about the numerous side businesses his sons had started, the more it unsettled him. He could feel his plans for X-Tronic slipping away. And now it may well be too late to undo his mistakes, to fix the instability that had developed in the company over the past few years.

"And you're sure Dr. Sharpe is here?" Seaton asked the driver.

"That's the information I have, sir."

The Range Rover stopped in front of three elevator doors at the far side of the tunnel. As Seaton and Marcus got out, the bell dinged and a big man in a business suit stepped from an open elevator. He waved at Seaton.

"Mr. Seaton," he said, "I'm Hayden Sorenson, head of security. Dr. Sharpe is waiting in the executive conference room on level eighteen. I'll take you to him."

Seaton felt a little alarmed to be inside a $400 million research division of his own company, which he had not even known about.

"This way, sir," Sorenson said as they stopped on the eighteenth floor.

Clearly, they were in no ordinary office. The inside of the building had been gutted to make room for the large research apparatus and equipment sealed inside glass rooms. Seaton was surprised to see that the hallway split into a large circle, which left an open rotunda looking down onto a lower floor. He realized that the space had been designed to operate factory-style research equipment—something he had seen only in some of China's top research institutions when he toured Hong Kong last year with a group of U.S. technology executives. He had no idea that X-Tronic had developed the same advanced system of laboratory work in a downtown corporate setting—indeed, he had thought the technology still two or three years away for his company.

"What is this place?" Marcus asked.

Seaton stopped by the rotunda's opening and leaned on the banister to look down at the research floor. Two young women were hunched over computer terminals, while an older man ran through a data checklist on the inside panel of a giant server sitting in the center of the room. Next to the server was a glass room, where a bundle of network cables snaked into a device that looked like a large copier-printer. Another research programmer fed a bin of paper into the device before returning to the two women to look at the computer monitors.

"What are they doing?" Seaton asked Sorenson.

"I'm afraid that's a question you'd better ask Dr. Sharpe."

Seaton had to bite back the impulse to demand an answer here and now, but he realized it would be best to wait a few more minutes for the complete story. Stepping back from the banister, he shot Marcus a quick glance to communicate his growing concern, then followed Sorenson along the corridor.

They stopped in front of two cherrywood double doors. "He's in here, Mr. Seaton. I'll be outside if you need anything."

Inside, they saw a tall man with close-cropped gray hair standing at the far end of the room, facing away from them with his hands clasped behind his back. A colorful sign on the side wall near the entrance showed the logos of X-Tronic and Cygnus mounted side by side. They were linked, as if already joined in a single company.

"My God," Marcus said, "this place isn't owned by just X-Tronic. Cygnus is a part owner." Turning to his boss, he said, "Mr. Seaton, we're inside the enemy's camp!"

34

———⋅◦✳◦⋅———

"WHAT THE HELL is going on here?" Seaton demanded of Dr. Sharpe, across the conference table. Sharpe stood motionless while Seaton paced back and forth like a caged panther. "I have so many questions, I don't even know where to begin!" he said in a commanding voice.

Sharpe stood with his hands still behind his back, waiting patiently for a chance to respond. "I'll tell you anything I can, Mr. Seaton," he finally said.

"You'll tell me *everything*!" Seaton yelled, slamming his palm on the conference table. "What happened to Jack Ross? What happened to his company in the end? It collapsed because of the failed test results of the software glitches for your star program, right?"

"The Redshift Project—yes, that's correct."

"You testified that it couldn't work, that it couldn't be completed, isn't that right?"

"That's what I testified, Mr. Seaton. You know this already—it's public record."

"Was it true?"

"Of course it was true . . . at the time. I'm a researcher, Mr. Seaton. I'm not going to perjure myself, and I'm not going to lie to you."

"C'mon," Seaton replied. "I have all the pieces to the puzzle: Jack Ross's indictment, his company's bankruptcy, your mysterious Redshift Project and its failure, your testimony at the hearing, and your subsequent acceptance of a position with Acheron Technology. I just don't know how the pieces fit together yet . . . but you do."

"Mr. Seaton, you don't know what you think you know. Things aren't what they seem."

"Then why don't you just tell me how things are? My God, man, you *worked* with Jack. You know he didn't deserve what happened to him."

"It could have been avoided," Sharpe said reasonably. "Jack could have avoided all of it if he had just listened to me."

"What happened, Dr. Sharpe? This is the only time I'm going to ask you nicely. Tell me everything now, or I'll get the authorities involved to the full extent of the law."

Sharpe raised his chin a notch—the proud intellectual who refused to be intimidated by a power establishment of inferior minds. "I did nothing illegal, Mr. Seaton; you can rest assured of that. Jack was pushing for the development of our Redshift Program. We were working on a groundbreaking combination of software codes and linking algorithms that could read a scanned document with a fourth-generation artificial-intelligence demand program. We were trying to upload readable data from documents into a user-friendly analysis and data-processing function." His eyebrows rose, and he half smiled, as if he now expected Seaton to give him an award for his achievement. "The technology had the promise of giving corporations a program whose operating system could process scanned images as regular data, depending on a particular company's industry." He raised his index finger. "For example, the program could be customized for a large heath care provider, in which the scanned patient charts from hospitals could be uploaded automatically into the company's data and billing files. The program would focus on and detect patient information, such as name and address, and also specific billing information for the accounting records. This could eliminate millions of data entry jobs for large corporations across the globe. That was the Redshift Project, Mr. Seaton. It had the potential to be one of the most groundbreaking business software programs introduced in the last five years, and it would have made Jack Ross a billionaire."

"But you had some bugs you couldn't get worked out," Seaton sneered.

"It's more complicated than that. We had some serious problems with the development of the software, it's true. The system worked only eighty percent of the time. The other twenty percent resulted in corrupted data transfers from the scanned documents. We were still developing the AI process of identifying various combinations of handwriting so that the system could learn to distinguish symbols over time, just as a person does, but these were problems that I believed could be solved given the right resources. But Jack didn't want to do what was necessary to allocate those resources. I felt we needed to partner with a larger software corporation to obtain the funds necessary to finish developing Redshift. Jack refused that suggestion and insisted on a ridiculous plan to raise twenty million through a new stock offering. It was a ridiculous idea— twenty million wouldn't have been anywhere near enough funds to resolve the problems."

"But you solved that problem, didn't you, Dr. Sharpe?" Marcus put in. "You found another way to get funding to complete your research."

Seaton understood where Marcus's question was going. "You contacted X-Tronic, didn't you, Dr. Sharpe? You contacted X-Tronic on your own to make a deal."

"He contacted both X-Tronic *and* Cygnus," Marcus said, remembering the dual logo outside the conference room.

"I contacted more than just X-Tronic and Cygnus, but it was those two companies that had the most interest in moving forward with a joint venture project. Oh, yes, at first they individually tried to outbid each other for complete control of Redshift—Mr. Seaton, you should have seen how aggressive your own sons were during the negotiations. But in the end, neither company wanted to take on the entire risk of the project. You see, we could not guarantee success in solving Redshift's problems . . . not until now."

"Not until now?" Seaton asked. "That's what we saw in the rotunda coming in—that was Redshift. You've completed it?"

"Nearly."

"And so you squeezed Jack out of the project by sabotaging the remaining research to ensure that he wouldn't be able to raise additional money. You had already had secret discussions with X-Tronic and Cygnus to make sure they would snap up the remains of Jack's company after the bankruptcy hearing. You arranged to be hired as the head researcher on the project so that you could continue your work with nearly unlimited research funding." Seaton seethed with anger as he worked through everything that had happened to Jack and his business. "I bet you couldn't wait to be backed by two of the biggest software companies in the whole country, as opposed to having to scrape by in a small tech start-up company like Jack's."

Sharpe ran both hands through his hair and looked as if he might explode. He turned away from the other men, toward the wood-paneled wall, and found himself again facing Seaton, this time through the large mirror in front of him.

"You have no idea the constraints that Jack's financial limitations were putting on my research," Sharpe said, no longer able to conceal the frustration still locked in his memory. "Redshift will revolutionize the way corporations capture and process data. The software could potentially replace an estimated ten to fifteen million jobs worldwide within the first year alone. This is the very essence of technological innovation: to replace a human job with a technology that can do it faster, cheaper, and more accurately."

"And so you had no problem whoring yourself out to the highest bidder," Seaton said, "leaving poor Jack betrayed and bankrupt."

"That's quiet an accusation coming from you," Dr. Sharpe replied. "Jack and I spoke often. He told me about the circumstances in which he left X-Tronic. I know all about what you did to him twenty-five years ago. And now you have the gall to say *I* betrayed him? That's rich."

Seaton backed away from the table as if his armor had been stripped away, leaving him defenseless in battle. The man had struck the one spot that could still hurt—the Achilles' heel that still left the billionaire vulnerable.

"Who owns the majority of the Redshift Project?" Seaton asked, blotting out the memories from twenty-five years ago so that he could stay focused on the current problem.

"Acheron Technologies was created by X-Tronic and Cygnus as a separate legal entity after Jack's company filed for bankruptcy. Acheron is a private company with only institutionally owned shares: half by X-Tronic and half by Cygnus. Neither company is a majority shareholder, so neither X-Tronic nor Cygnus has complete control over the project—it is a true joint venture. Redshift is nearly completed, but no one has complete control over it."

"But someone *will* have control," Seaton said, turning to look at Marcus. "After X-Tronic accepts the takeover bid from Cygnus at the shareholders' meeting next month, Cygnus will have complete control of Redshift. That's why Kavanaugh is so desperate to take over X-Tronic. He knows that if he can squeeze me out of the game, combine his company's resources with X-

Tronic's, and gain complete control of Redshift, he'll be in a position to make Cygnus the most powerful software company in the world."

Even as he said this, Seaton was dumbfounded at having been so blind to events at his company. Everything was falling merrily apart. How could he hope to stop something so carefully orchestrated by so many people for what appeared to be years?

He felt a sharp pain in his chest. He must have reacted to the pain, because Marcus suddenly moved toward him.

"Sir, are you all right?"

Seaton nodded as he leaned on the conference table. Sharpe also took a few steps toward him, as if he suddenly wanted to help the man he had been arguing so bitterly with for the past ten minutes.

"Sir," Marcus said stiffly, "I think you need help. We should go to the hospital. Let me call someone."

"Don't you dare!" Seaton said, strength returning to his eyes. "I'm fine," he added in a softer tone. He turned to Sharpe. "I want to see everything: your research data, your accounting records, even your company e-mail account. And don't even think about contacting anyone in Denver about this. Let's get the head system administrator on the phone right now—I want them here in the office within the hour. We're going to lock down your network to prevent outside access." His eyes bored through Sharpe. "You report only to me now. You do exactly what I say, and you may just possibly avoid jail time."

Seaton sat at the table and waited while Marcus led Sharpe out of the room to get things rolling, while the head of security waited just outside the door. Seaton had to think. If there was any hope of saving his company, he had no time to spare. But would he have the strength to see the fight through to the end?

35

THURSDAY EVENING, ALASKA walked into the downtown Hyatt. Cold air brushed behind her as she pushed through the revolving doors into a lobby devoted to luxury. Wearing a long, black leather jacket over her clothes, she kept her head lowered, allowing her black hair to fall over the sides of her face, leaving only a glimpse of her nose below big blue sunglasses. She walked toward the reception counter carrying a large briefcase.

"You should have an envelope for me," Alaska said to the chubby young man working behind the counter.

"Name?" the man asked with a servant's smile.

"My name's Alaska," she answered.

"Last name?"

"Look for Alaska. That's under the 'A's.'"

Stiffening visibly, the man turned and flipped through a shelf under the counter before retrieving a manila envelope with her name printed in large black letters.

Grabbing the envelope, Alaska ripped it opened and found a sheet of paper bearing only the number 2219. She folded the paper and put it in her jacket pocket after sliding the empty envelope back to the man. Then she turned away and walked toward the elevators.

Getting off at the twenty-second floor, she found the room and knocked twice. She saw movement of shadow and light under the door; then a shadow went over the spy hole. The briefcase was heavy, and she tried not to think about its contents. A chain rattled behind the door, followed by the solid thud of the bolt being unlocked. The door opened.

"Here it is," Alaska said. "Everything he had hidden. It's all here."

Lucas Seaton smiled and stepped back for her to enter the room. Walking past him, she saw Lance standing by a large window with a panoramic view of downtown Denver. Setting the heavy briefcase on a center table, she turned and waited for one of the twins to speak.

Lance glanced at the briefcase. "That's it?" he asked.

"That's everything related to your company," she said, stone-faced. "Those are copies of everything he had in his apartment. I also think he has a second copy of everything, which he keeps somewhere else."

"What makes you think that?" Lucas asked.

"You told me your network showed over two thousand photocopies during the late-night hours when only Michael was in your building. The number of pages in the case was closer to a thousand."

"Well, even if he has another copy somewhere, at least we now know exactly what he does have," Lucas said to his brother.

"The problem could be more complicated than that," Lance reminded him. "I think we need to have a little chat with him." He turned from the window and looked at Alaska for the first time since she had entered the room. "You've gotten to know him pretty well over the past three weeks, haven't you?"

She held his stare with gleaming eyes, showing a strength and independence that would not back down.

"Yes," Lance said, seeming to read her expression. "You got to know him well. So tell me, what kind of man is Michael Chapman? What's he really like outside of work? We need to understand how he thinks."

Alaska turned and stared out the window at the bright moon that had climbed over the sea of lights below them. "No one really knows Michael," she said. "Sometimes I don't even think *he* knows who he is. He's very smart, but you already know that. One moment he's laughing and chatting away like he's the life of the party, and then the next moment he'll get quiet, and suddenly you realize that he's studying you. It's when he gets like that you realize he's hiding something—something from his past, maybe, or some plan he has for the future—I don't know. But you know that no matter how much he studies you, he'll never really let you inside his mind." Alaska closed her eyes as she fought off a pang of guilt. "Michael's a good man, but I don't think he trusts anyone. He's alone and sometimes he's lonely, but he still won't let himself trust anyone. I don't know what made him like that."

Lance smiled as if secretly admiring Michael's traits. "Thank you, Alaska. That's what we needed to know. You've done a good job."

"So it's over?" she asked. "I'm finished with the job?"

"Yes," Lance replied. "You're finished. I want you to avoid Michael from now on. Don't ever call him again. If he calls, don't answer. No communication whatsoever. If he should somehow get in touch with you, if for some reason it can't be avoided, call me at this number and let me know." He handed her a piece of paper. "We may need to bring you back into things if our other plans don't work out."

"What 'other plans'?" she asked. "You said you just wanted to know what he was looking at. What are you going to do to him?"

Lance acted surprised at the trace of concern in her voice.
"Do you really care?" he asked. His voice seemed to warn her
against answering incorrectly.

"No," she replied, realizing it was the only response they
would accept. She had to be careful. "It doesn't mean anything to
me. I was just curious."

"Well, don't be. You've done your job; it's better if we just
leave it at that."

"I understand," she said.

Lucas walked toward the door. "The rest of the money will
be wired to your account tomorrow. You may go now."

Alaska told herself not to feel any regrets as she stepped into
the hallway and heard the door close behind her. She had been
forced to make a choice, and she had made it, and now, she told
herself, she could live with it. She had liked Michael a lot, but
that was nothing compared to how much she loved her dad. Her
life had been going nowhere for too long, and her father
desperately needed her help. She couldn't have passed up this
opportunity to try to take control of their lives again. She still felt
like an outsider, and now, perhaps, even a little lost because she
had betrayed Michael, but she had done the thing she needed to
do most: empowered herself to help her father.

Walking down the hallway, then waiting for the elevator, she
let the memories wash over her. She saw Michael, approaching
her in the strobe light of the nightclub basement when they first
met, but she pushed away this image with the memory of her
father, spending hours teaching her to play the electric guitar
when she was thirteen. Then she remembered birds singing in the
trees in the Capitol Hill neighborhood below Michael's
apartment the morning after they first made love, and finding
him waiting for her on his high-rise balcony after she woke in his
bed. Again she abandoned the image for one of her father,
bailing her out of the Aspen County Jail her senior year in high
school after she got arrested with some friends for vandalizing

the principal's station wagon. Then she remembered how close she had felt to Michael as they lay together talking in the snowy woods after snowmobiling, but she replaced the feeling with the memory of her father's proud face the day she graduated with a BA in fine arts.

The elevator doors opened, and the nice-looking older couple inside paused their conversation as she entered the car. She felt out of place in this elegant hotel. The doors closed, and the car began descending, and Alaska swore she would have no regrets. But as the couple behind her resumed their soft conversation, she thought about Michael again and wondered if there might have been another way to handle things.

After Alaska left, Lucas came over to the table. Lance had already opened the briefcase and was flipping through the documentation.

"That son of a bitch," Lucas said as Lance turned over page after page documenting the fraudulently reported software revenue contracts. "How much does he have?"

"A lot more than we thought," Lance replied.

For a moment, neither brother said another word. They both understood the situation. They had been here before, and they knew what they needed to do if they wanted to survive.

"We need to tell *everyone* about this," Lance said, as if the shock of what he was seeing had finally receded enough that he could collect his thoughts. He cut a glance at the briefcase. "This is a hell of a lot worse than Falcon thought. As if we didn't already have enough to do in the next few weeks . . ."

Lucas slapped both hands against his head and made an animal growl. "That *motherfucker*! What the fuck is he doing? Who the *fuck* does he think he is, getting involved in our affairs? Does he think he's some kind of hero? Are you *kidding* me? What is it with this guy!"

"We can control this," Lance said as calmly as he could manage. "We've known he was a potential problem for a while now. We've been prepared for this. We can handle it. This just means we're going to have to do some things we didn't want to do, that's all. But we can handle this. We *will* handle this."

"I'll handle it right fucking now!" Lucas said, almost shouting.

Lance had seen this rage too often in his brother lately. "No," he said, putting his hand out. "Not like that. Don't be stupid. Right now we still have options."

"Yeah? What options are those?"

Lance pulled his cell phone out of his pocket and slid it across the table. "Call Falcon," he said.

Lucas picked up the phone. "And tell him what?"

"Tell him we need to meet."

"That's it?"

Lance nodded. "Tell him it's about Michael."

"He'll want to know more," Lucas said as he began scrolling down for Falcon's number.

Lance walked toward the television and grabbed the bottle of Grey Goose vodka standing next to the ice bucket. "Tell him to come here," he said. "Give him the room number and everything. And tell him to bring his laptop so we can access Cooley and White's network." He pointed with his chin at the briefcase full of documents. "We're going to be here a while."

As his brother selected the number and waited for an answer, Lance poured vodka into the two tumblers he had filled with ice, making sure to give his brother less vodka and more ice than he gave himself. Then he set Lucas's glass on the table, near where he stood talking to Falcon on the phone. Ignoring the city lights that stretched out below him, he watched his brother pacing behind him in the window's reflection. Michael Chapman had now become more dangerous to them than they ever could have imagined, and for that, Lance would never forgive Falcon. But there was good news in all this, for now the bond he had felt with his brother through all the strenuous, scary events of their life—a bond that he had begun to question recently because of his brother's compassionate weakness toward their father—had been fully renewed and rejuvenated by the threat Michael now posed to them both. For everything that had gone wrong with the plans during the past two months, for all the obstacles and perils that had come their way, he had never felt more powerfully connected with his brother than at this moment. Their motivations and intent were once again united. And together they were unstoppable by anyone who got in their way.

*   *   *

When Falcon phoned Thursday night to say the twins needed to change the Friday meeting, Michael knew something had happened.

"It looks like they have another appointment, so we'll meet at the Adolphus downtown Saturday," Falcon said.

"Anything specific we need to discuss?" Michael asked, hanging on to every minute sound. Had they finally figured out that he was up to something? The black Mustang that kept showing up—someone was watching him. He had been careful, but maybe they saw something. If they had, they would have scrambled immediately, evaluating their exposure and deciding just how much of a threat he was. But what would be their next move? *Stay calm,* he said to himself. *You still have one advantage: they have no idea who you really are. They don't know your past or what you're capable of.*

"There's nothing specific they want from the meeting," Falcon said. "Just an overall update on everything we still need to wrap up before concluding the audit in the next two weeks. Oh, also . . ." He hesitated a moment, as if distracted by something on his end of the line. "Also, we should probably go over our discussion related to the Cygnus acquisition bid."

As Michael flipped his cell phone shut, he turned to look out the dark window of the café, watching the slivers of light from auto headlights shooting by.

"Would you like another latte?" a voice asked.

In the window, he saw the reflection of the server standing behind him. Without looking, he nodded. Then he watched as the reflection pulled farther back into the kitchen, and the server's image appeared to be standing in the middle of the street, where a car ran over it.

He turned back to the spy novel he was reading. Desperate to take his mind off his problems for a few hours, he had taken the paperback to a hideaway café to escape his grim reality. But now his own life was beginning to adopt the same characteristics of the solitary hero of the story. The hero in the novel had swum halfway from a boat to shore, but now he was exhausted, and the idea of drowning was beginning to seem like a reasonable solution to his woes. Michael understood the character's feelings only too well.

The server set the latte on the corner of his table, slid the ticket next to it, and left without a word. Michael picked up the novel, put money on the table, and left the drink untouched. He walked out to his car and started the engine. Then, without putting it in gear or releasing the hand brake, he sat and listened to the soothing purr of the motor while looking up through the moonroof at the few stars that had broken through the city's shield. He sat unmoving in the car for nearly ten minutes, gathering the strength to continue his swim to shore.

36

———⚹———

MICHAEL WALKED INTO the Adolphus Hotel and across the immaculate white tiles that stretched the length of the lobby. To satisfy the dress code of the private lounge room, he wore a charcoal suit over a smoke-gray shirt. The escalator carried him to a gathering room with Flemish tapestries, furniture reminiscent of the Gilded Age, and a Victorian Steinway piano.

Falcon and the twins were already there, and Falcon began the meeting the moment Michael joined them. "I was just discussing the progress of the audit," he said. "As I was saying, we obviously hit a few snags this year due to staffing, but Michael's done a great job getting everything up to speed since he came on." The twins nodded, and Michael gave an appropriate smile of acknowledgment. "There were some areas where we needed some reclassifications. Nothing new—nothing in the past week, anyway—so you should be up to date on those issues."

"What about software revenue contracts?" Lucas asked. "How did they look?"

"Well," Michael began carefully, "we looked at those. I believe there were a few carve-out adjustments, naturally. There always are during audits—nothing we haven't expected." Michael was doing his best to dodge their probing. The unusual meeting probably meant that all three knew he had uncovered the fraud. His only advantage was that they didn't know *how much* he understood. They still thought they had surprise on their side.

"How will that affect revenue?" Lance asked with a doggedness that made him nervous. Lucas was watching him, while Falcon seemed distracted by a spot on the carpet.

"It won't affect it much. About seven million was reclassed—not much for a company this size. I don't think investors will see the company under a bad light as a result of that," he said with a note of finality, as if daring them to dig deeper.

"And there's nothing else you've found? No other concerns that we should know about?" The three seemed to be looking through him, and for a moment it was obvious that the unspoken fraud was the very issue that all four were now thinking of.

Realizing that he was on the ropes, Michael knew that if he answered too quickly, he would appear scared. Then he had an idea. He realized that they had not called this meeting to bully him. Scaring him into silence was just not their way. He could almost see it in their eyes: they would not trust loyalty through intimidation. They would trust the only thing they understood, which was *greed.*

Time to gamble. Michael had to make them believe he was not intimidated. He had to make them believe he was like them.

"No," he finally said, displaying a confident smile. "We have conducted a very thorough audit of the financial statements. If there were any issues or concerns relating to revenue recognition, stock options, *fraud,* or any other disclosure items, we would have brought them to your attention by now. But I'm happy to say—for *all* our interests—that there have been no other findings of any kind. Over the next two weeks, our plan is merely to wrap up our final testing, finish any adjustments to the numbers, and get the financial statements issued as they are."

He watched closely as all three reacted differently. Lance smiled, nodding his head in a springlike motion that slowly wobbled to a halt. Lucas eyed him more carefully, as if waiting for him to add to his statement. And Falcon, lacking any visible reaction, merely looked at the ground in meditation, waiting for someone else to respond.

"Well," Lance said, "that's what we were hoping to hear. Yes, that's very good. Nobody wants any surprises this time of the year."

Over the next twenty minutes, the tension slid away. Falcon rejoined the conversation as they began discussing the disclosure of necessary items in the financial statements. It all became very routine, as if they all had forgotten their unspoken fraud. And Michael, having a difficult time playing through the haphazard disclosure issues relating to the financials, might have forgotten altogether his implied agreement to remain silent with the conspirators, but for the occasional glares from Lucas in his peripheral vision.

37

———— ·ː❉ː· ————

MICHAEL WOKE AT ten thirty Sunday morning to the
soft sound of snow falling against the window. Last night,
he had turned off his cell phone, cut himself off from the world,
and gone to the Church alone. A few drinks had helped him
escape the dilemmas at X-Tronic for a while. Staring up at the
ceiling, he could not recall how much he had drunk or what time
he had finally come home. He sat up in bed and looked at his
clothes, strewn in a line from his apartment front door to his bed.
He got up and took a warm shower. Continuing his Sunday
morning routine, he stuck a frozen ham-and-egg muffin in the
microwave, turned on his sleeping cell phone, and waited for his
breakfast. But a surge of vibration from the cell phone made him
forget his boredom. He dialed his voice mail, eager to see who
had tried to reach him during his twelve-hour sabbatical from the
world.

Five new messages. The world must have spun off its axis
during the night. The first was his mother, begging him to call
home immediately. Her voice shook. The second call was his
mother again: ". . . *very important, Michael, please call home.*

The third: "*Michael, where are you? Please, please call.*" The fourth: his brother: "*Michael, where the hell are you? Don't call Mom anymore; she's not up to talking. Call me.*" The fifth: his brother again.

All five messages were from this morning: the first at 7:30, the last just twenty minutes ago. With a feeling of dread, he dialed his brother.

"Michael, Jesus! Where've you *been*?" Cody answered.

"I just woke up."

"You talk to Mom yet?"

"No, your message said to call you first."

There was silence on the other end. His brother's voice cracked. "Michael, it's Dad. He had a heart attack this morning. We've been trying to reach you for hours."

"Oh, my God. Is he . . . ?" His words sounded as if someone else had spoken them. His father, invincible, immortal, had never shown a sign of weakness for as long as Michael could remember. Michael's grandfather had had two heart attacks before the third one killed him, but Michael had thought his father at least ten years away from being at any real risk.

"How's he doing?" he asked, focusing his thoughts. "They take him to St. Mary's?"

"Oh, no, Michael," his brother said in a half-muffled voice, as if his mouth was pressed against the phone. "Dad didn't make it." His voice cracked. "He's *gone,* Michael."

"Wha . . . ?" The word fell apart before Michael could finish forming it.

"Mom found him on the floor in the den downstairs. He was already dead. He'd been working on something early this morning."

"Oh, God . . . ," Michael whispered as the impossible reality hit him like a sledgehammer. Lowering himself to the carpet, he leaned against the wall and looked out at the city skyline. It had stopped snowing.

"Michael, we need you here," Cody said.

"Yeah," he replied, not bothering to wipe away the tears that now blurred his vision. "I do, too."

"You okay to drive? It's a long ways across Kansas."

"I don't know," Michael said, still trying to process the reality that their father was gone.

"Be careful. Call if you need to talk while you're on the road."

When the call ended, Michael sat motionless on the floor of his apartment, looking out at the snow-covered neighborhood below. He felt as if he had done nothing, become nothing, during his father's entire lifetime. It just wasn't time yet to lose him. Leaning against the wall, he curled up and wept, pressing his head to the cold window and listening to the whisper of traffic rushing by on the street below. Then, after several minutes of trying to find the willpower to stand up, he got to his feet and slowly packed what he needed to go and see his father buried.

Five minutes later he was in the car, heading for Kansas, with the Rockies gleaming white in his rearview mirror.

38

---※---

A WEEK AFTER his father's funeral, Michael found himself alone in an elevator riding up toward X-Tronic's twentieth floor. The past week's events felt like a blur in his memory. It was beginning to soak in that his father was really gone and that his world had changed. The funeral had been difficult for him. It was the memories of his father's strong, happy life that had most torn at him as the minister spoke the final words at graveside. Michael felt ashamed that after all the sacrifices his parents had made for him, he wasn't living a happier life in Denver. All he had been able to do was hold his weeping mother while his eyes looked blankly at the casket. If only he had known how little time his father had, he could have made another trip back home, or even just one more phone call. But there was no warning, just *bam!*—gone. And now came the lifetime of regret.

He had planned to pick up the pieces of his life after he finished at Cooley and White. He had often imagined what it would be like, once he was finished, to tell his father about everything he had been doing these past few years. But now he would never have that chance. He had waited too long. He had lost more than he could bear, and now he was angrier than ever at the people who had poisoned X-Tronic and killed Kurt in the process. His father's death had quickened him with a sense of strength and urgency that he had never felt before. It was clear now: he had to stop the crimes before things went any further. And that meant stopping the conspirators before they could publish their bogus accounting results to the financial world. At this moment, he knew that he would do whatever it took to expose the rot he had discovered at X-Tronic.

The moment Michael returned to the audit room at X-Tronic, he knew that something was wrong. Only half the document files remained along the wall of the room, and the conference table was bare. The room looked abandoned.

He unpacked his laptop, booted it up, and logged on to Cooley and White's remote network. Opening his e-mail account for the first time in eight days, he scanned down the list of two hundred unread messages. Half were for basic administrative announcements from either the firm's Denver office or the national headquarters in New York. The remaining messages related to X-Tronic. He scanned through them. Things had moved fast, starting the Monday after he left for Kansas. Jerry Diamond had e-mailed Falcon to discuss moving up the issuance date for the financials. Apparently, Diamond had wanted to release the annual financial disclosures to the SEC two weeks ahead of schedule, and Falcon had agreed. A number of correspondences had gone between the CFO and the audit committee.

With a sinking feeling in the pit of his stomach, he realized they had done something horrible while he was gone. His dismay grew with each e-mail chain between the conspirators that he saw. The nightmare scenario he had so feared was now unfolding before his eyes.

He read through more e-mails, his concerns growing. Both Diamond and Falcon had taken advantage of his absence by going forward on issuing the 10-K annual report. And the Seaton twins had been included on all the final e-mails. According to the e-mails, X-Tronic should already have issued the financial statements to the public. He couldn't believe what he was reading. If Cooley and White had issued its audit opinion and allowed X-Tronic to issue its fraudulent financial statements last Friday, then the market would already be responding to the falsified reports. Tens of thousands of investors would already be pouring their money into the software company's stock, whose financial position was grossly exaggerated.

Michael opened his Internet browser and typed in the Web address for the Securities and Exchange Commission. On the SEC's Web site, he navigated through the hyperlinks until he found the listing of all filings for X-Tronic within the past two years. Looking at the top of the list, he saw that the company had filed its 10-K last Friday. The financial floodgates had been opened to the public. He took a long, deep breath as he stared at the SEC's Web site. It was all over. He had done everything possible to prevent this, and it hadn't been enough. To confirm his fears, he went to the *Wall Street Journal*'s Web site, entered X-Tronic's ticker symbol, and discovered that the stock price had increased by fifteen percent since the opening bell two hours ago.

Just as he got off the Web site, Falcon walked into the audit room. "Morning," he said cheerfully, dropping a computer bag onto one of the leather chairs.

Michael was startled by the sudden intrusion. He hadn't expected to see Falcon here at X-Tronic, but then again, all bets were off on just what *to* expect.

"Hi, John," he said. "I didn't realize you were coming out this morning. I'm not sure where Andrea and Dustin are, but they should be here soon."

"No, neither of them's coming back out," Falcon said, fishing his laptop out of the computer bag. "They've both rolled off this engagement."

"I don't understand," Michael replied, sitting bolt upright. "How much work did you guys get through last week? Are we still hoping to get the financials issued by the deadline?"

"Actually, a lot's changed," Falcon said breezily, suddenly intent on properly connecting the cords to his laptop. "Haven't you checked your e-mails?"

"No," Michael lied. "Just getting to it. With the funeral and everything, I didn't have a chance to check any messages until now."

"Mm-m," Falcon mumbled. "I'm sorry about your father."

"Did something change when I was gone?" The concern in Michael's voice was clear, but at this point he didn't care how much of his fears he revealed.

"Yes," Falcon said, threading the network cord through the access hole in the table. "X-Tronic was able to get us a draft of their financials a lot quicker than we expected. And the audit committee wanted to speed up the process of issuing the report so that the report could provide information valuable for the merger talks." He paused to look around the room, as if trying to remember where he had left something, then seemed to give up the idea. "Anyway, I was comfortable with all the test work that had been done, so I just spent the week out here with Andrea and Dustin to finish up all the critical test work. Everything went well, and X-Tronic filed its ten-K Friday afternoon."

"They've already *filed*?" he asked, feigning surprise.

"Yes," Falcon said with glowing eyes, playing the part of the supervisor relaying good news to a subordinate. "That's why Andrea and Dustin have rolled off onto other engagements. I still wanted you to be out here for the next two weeks to clear all remaining documentation and review my points. It probably won't even take that long," he said, double-clicking something on his computer. "Once you're done, you can head back to the office. You're on an interoffice engagement in New Delhi for about six months. Exciting, no? You leave in a couple of weeks."

"*What!* The firm's sending me to *India?*"

Falcon gave him a surprised look. "It's a good opportunity. The engagement is very important to the firm."

"John, that's insane! I can't leave the country for that long. My father just died—I need to stay close to my family." Michael couldn't believe what he was hearing. He felt as if he were stuck in a whirlpool, spinning around and around, getting pulled ever closer toward the center, from which there would be no return.

"This is something that the firm has scheduled you on. I'm sorry, but you'll have to talk to the scheduling committee about it. But before you do, think about what a great opportunity an international rotation would be to advance your career at the firm."

Michael knew that Falcon had influence with the firm's scheduling committee, which must be how he had suddenly been shunted off to a project that would take him far from the Denver office and the X-Tronic engagement.

Michael nodded to acknowledge both that he understood and that he had no more reservations. Six months in the middle of India . . . dropped from X-Tronic . . . kept in the dark about the push-up in the SEC filing—how could this be happening! He pulled a workpaper binder from the center of the table and opened it to a seven-page document created by Falcon. It listed small, trivial questions—nothing of any real importance, but they would still take time to answer. He flipped the page to see if any of the numbers in the trial balance had been adjusted to the correct amounts. They hadn't been changed. Each false number, each financial lie, was signed off and approved by Falcon and the concurring partner. He drew his gaze down the laundry list of numbers marked with blue and black letters, and knew that he was deep in the lion's den, surrounded by enemies.

39

———— ·❈· ————

TROY GLAZIER SAT hunched over a thin file on his desk, flipping through the pages with meticulous concentration. His dark suit only made the graying of his hair more apparent. At six three and two hundred twenty pounds, he was a big man even when sitting down. His large nostrils flared as he read the stressful pages, giving his face a dangerous appearance. Suddenly his phone rang. His dark eyebrows knitted as he snapped up the receiver.

"This is Troy," he said in his perpetually annoyed voice.

"Glazier, it's Chapman. I hope you can talk."

"Go ahead," he replied.

"Have you seen this morning's *Wall Street Journal?*" Michael asked.

"Not yet," he answered, as if that were on his agenda.

"You need to. There's a nice article about X-Tronic's record earnings reported on the filing of their ten-K."

"What the fuck are you talking about?"

"X-Tronic filed its financial statements with the SEC last Friday. I was out of town. They jumped at the opportunity to issue the statements while I was gone."

"All right. Just settle down. Even if you had been around, you wouldn't have been able to do much to stop them."

"Glazier, I'm still on the engagement for another two weeks. I'm doing trivial bullshit wrap-up documentation, but it gives me access to X-Tronic's facilities. I think we still have a chance to expose this, but I'm going to need your help for it to work. Whatever you have on your plate right now, drop it—this is too important."

"I'll be there tonight. Someone will call you back with my flight details," he said before a brief pause. "What do you want me to bring from the kit?"

"From the kit? Everything!" Michael paused. "I have to get back to the audit room before Falcon gets suspicious."

"See you tonight," Glazier said, hanging up. Afterward, his brown eyes stared at the dead receiver. He ran his thick fingers through his short-cropped hair. He couldn't believe Chapman had made it so far. None of the others had even come close. Moving around the desk, he opened the door to a loud bull pen and waved at his administrative assistant.

"I need you to get me an afternoon flight to Denver," he yelled at her.

"When do you want to come back?" she asked, picking up the phone.

"I have no idea," he replied as he walked down the hallway. "Better make it one-way." He got to the elevator, looked at his watch, and yelled back over the row of cubicles to his assistant, "I'm going to the range for twenty minutes. Pull the files on Michael Chapman, X-Tronic, and Cooley and White's Denver office. Transfer all information to the encrypted hard drive on my laptop. And include a copy of X-Tronic's ten-K that was filed last Friday, along with any press releases by the company, or articles in the *Journal*." The elevator door opened slowly, revealing his stocky reflection in the mirror. "Oh," he yelled back one last command, "have a full surveillance kit sent up from IT!"

Glazier rode the elevator down to the basement floor and went through a security checkpoint before entering the underground firing range of the U.S. Treasury Department's headquarters in Washington, D.C. He nodded at the range master, put on the muffled ear protectors, and proceeded to an open booth. Snapping a full magazine into his third-generation Glock 22, he raised his arms, steadied the gun, and fired ten quick rounds into the distant paper target's chest.

40

MICHAEL STOOD AT the back of the crowd, leaning against the blue-carpeted wall of the concourse as an airline agent opened the arrival gate. The first passengers emerged from the Jetway. Soon people flocked out the door. A well-tanned couple with clothes too bright for Denver—visiting from Florida, he assumed. An older woman with legs as thick as Michael's waist, laboring up the slight incline. A group of kids, excited as he had once been, jumping and laughing. Then a seven-foot giant, ducking through the tunnel in his travel warm-ups, listening to his headphones—a basketball player obviously, but whether college or professional, these days it was hard to say.

Then Michael saw *him,* walking through the gate in a cool gray suit, like a wolf reserving its energy for the kill. It had been a year and a half since he last saw Glazier in person, but the man hadn't aged a day.

Michael held back, dipping his eyes below the rim of his baseball cap, waiting until the tide of reuniting families, friends, and lovers passed. As people moved away, the lone man in the gray suit looked about for someone to greet him, but no one did. Then his eyes lit on Michael.

"It's been a long time," Glazier said, walking toward him and extending a hand.

"Too long," he replied.

They moved through the airport, grabbed two heavy cases from the overcrowded baggage claim, and made it to Michael's car in record time. After throwing the bags in the Audi's trunk, he paid the parking attendant and headed for town.

"Tell me everything," Glazier said. "What exactly do you have on X-Tronic?"

"I only have evidence that exposes the fraud. They covered their tracks well, so I don't have anything that implicates the specific people involved—that part will be difficult."

"But you know who they are?"

"Yeah, I know."

This seemed to satisfy Glazier. Michael had known the man for years, and for all the bold, decisive posturing, he would often fall back on the suggestions of a trusted subordinate.

"So I'll take a look at the documents you have," Glazier said. "I'll show them to the director. If she's convinced we have a case, we'll file charges against X-Tronic and Cooley and White. We'll get indictments, start pulling people in for questioning, put on the pressure, and watch the conspiracy unravel."

"And destroy the company in the process, like Enron or WorldCom?"

"If that's what it takes."

"Yeah, why not?" Michael snapped, tensing his grip on the wheel. "Look how great that turned out before. How many innocent victims were there from the Enron fallout? Twenty thousand? More? Investors, businesses, employees who were ready to retire. How many people lost their life savings?"

Glazier's chest rose as he took a deep breath. He seemed to be preparing to face a long-anticipated challenge. Unreeling his seatbelt, he twisted in the passenger's seat to face Michael. "Those companies imploded because their executives had created an illusion of strength on their books—a financial mirage to entice investors. And if a formal investigation against X-Tronic reveals similar findings, then they'll implode, too, just like the others. That's financial markets theory one-o-one. We can't delay legal action against them just because you think you can distance the company from the conspirators."

Glazier turned back around to stare out the windshield. Sunlight reflected off the wet road from melted snow, creating what looked for a moment like a dazzling river of light.

Michael wondered if his grandfather had been forced to endure a similar conversation in Bethel, Pennsylvania many decades earlier. But where his grandfather had failed, Michael was better prepared. He also knew that both his grandfather and his father would have wanted him to try.

"We have options here, Troy. We need to try to limit the damage to victims."

"In the end, your efforts probably wouldn't even matter. The only way to do this is by the book."

"Come on, Troy. Who are you trying to kid? You *know* what I want to do. You brought the kit, didn't you? I'm only proposing we rewrite the book a bit. Look, you already have me as an inside person. We could keep this quiet and still bring down those responsible for the fraud without destroying the company."

"What are you trying to do?" Glazier asked. "You know, you're starting to scare me."

Michael grinned. "If you think you're scared now, just wait till you hear my idea."

Downshifting from fifth gear to third, he punched it, rocketing the Audi forward from sixty to ninety miles an hour in under five seconds. He had felt an aggressive impulse to let Glazier know that—at this moment, anyway—Michael was in control. It was Alpha driving 101. But what he could not communicate to his case officer was his struggle with the way everything was unraveling at X-Tronic. He was struggling to hold on to the idealistic beliefs that had first lured him into becoming a Treasury agent. The things he had seen at X-Tronic and Cooley and White were the dark parts of a world that clashed with everything his father had taught him growing up in Kansas. Despite all that had happened, Michael was grasping at the hope that he might still find something good amid all the evil that had occurred—and all the new evil that he feared was still to come. His father had taught him that businesses could be good for society, as long as their leaders were not corrupted by wealth or power, and Michael wanted desperately to believe that what his father had taught him could still be possible in the world he was now immersed in.

41

——◦※◦——

"WHAT IS THIS place?" Glazier asked, glancing around the giant barroom.

Michael didn't answer right away, because he was distracted by the pulsing energy of the cavernous two-story club. They had found refuge at a horseshoe-shaped bar that opened to a room crowded with tables and booths of noisy, mingling happy-hour patrons.

"It's a club called B-Fifty-two's. Used to be the loft for *The Real World* when it was in Denver years ago."

"The real what?"

"*World*—it's a reality show on MTV where a bunch of college-age kids live in a city loft together and do stuff."

"What stuff?"

"I don't know, just stuff."

"I'll never understand your generation," Glazier said.

"MTV's not my generation anymore; it's frozen in youth. Besides, I think I'm under surveillance, so it looks better if we go out for a few drinks."

Cocking one eyebrow, Glazier put his beer back on the red-stenciled bar top. "You're in pretty deep, aren't you? We fully appreciate your situation and will do anything to make your transition out easier. You know you've become a legend in our little circle. The director personally asked me to let you know that. No other agent has gotten as far as you have."

"Then I envy them."

"Oh? You regret your decision? Look, I know it hasn't been easy, but it's all for the greater good, so don't be too hard on yourself. Hell, if you want to blame someone, blame me."

"Oh, I do."

"Attaboy," Glazier said, picking up his beer. "You always were a quick learner."

Michael brushed off Glazier's comments and turned to watch the attractive bartender, laughing at something a customer had said. Her long, jet black hair reminded him of Alaska. "I gave you the number for Lance's ski pass. Did it get you anything?"

"Yeah," Glazier answered. "The Colorado Pass database system showed that his pass was used at Vail the day Kurt was killed. But it's only circumstantial evidence. Vail's a big mountain; this doesn't prove he was ever at the exact scene of the crime."

Michael shook his head in frustration. He knew that Glazier was right—a good defense attorney could dismiss the evidence as inconclusive.

Glazier leaned toward him. "Now, tell me why you won't let me indict the whole bunch of them and plaster headlines of fraud allegations across the Dow Jones Newswire."

Michael set his glass down. He understood why Glazier was so quick to turn X-Tronic into a public circus: it would speed the investigation, help justify Treasury's covert project, and prevent the company from doing any more harm to investors. But he couldn't shake the feeling that they were still missing something. He turned his gaze away from the striking bartender.

"I know both John Falcon and Don Seaton will find a way to distance themselves from the conspiracy," Michael said. "They're too smart to risk exposing themselves. I'm sure they have a dozen contingency plans. You've worked in fraud investigation for almost ten years. You know that people who commit fraud spend more time working on the fraud than doing their regular jobs. And these guys are the best you'll ever see— trust me; I've seen what they can do." He watched for a reaction, but Glazier stared back at him with only stern concentration. "And I swear, if you try to go after them with only a few dozen boxes of documents, you'll find they've spent the last four years picking up every stitch to cover themselves. We need confessions on tape. That's our best chance."

"And you think they were willing to commit *murder* to keep this a secret?" So Glazier still had doubts about Kurt's death being linked to X-Tronic.

"Governments kill thousands in wars over political conflicts. Lovers kill out of jealousy. Street criminals kill for petty cash. Kids shoot their classmates because their peers have made them outcasts. You look at all the things that have happened in history, and do you really think, even for a second, that plenty of the world's millionaires and billionaires wouldn't commit murder to make sure they keep their fortunes and their freedom? Do you know what prison is like for someone with their background? White-collar criminals, by definition, have psychologically distanced themselves from the victims of their crimes to the point that they have almost convinced themselves that there *are* no victims. They lose touch with reality; they justify whatever it takes to survive. They have no conscience and are some of the most selfish criminal minds of all."

"And what if this doesn't work?" Glazier said, ready to consider Michael's plan at least hypothetically. "What if they never make any phone calls to discuss the fraud after we set them up?"

"The most important thing is bringing down Don Seaton and John Falcon. If we can isolate the rumors of the corporate fraud to the key individuals responsible for it, we may be able to limit the damage this does to X-Tronic without destroying the lives of the fifty thousand people who work there and hurting the millions of people who are invested in it."

Annoyed by Michael's resistance to pressing charges immediately, Glazier snapped, "Look, you can't save the company. X-Tronic will be destroyed."

Michael flinched at the last word. "I can't believe that. I refuse to believe there isn't a way to take down the conspirators without punishing innocent people."

"This is going to be tricky, and it's not going to be black and white—it'll be a thousand shades of gray. And it will be impossible to bring these guys down without killing X-Tronic. I'm sorry, but there's just no other way."

"There *has* to be a way." Michael leaned back, not breaking eye contact. So what if Glazier had more experience in these matters—he wasn't going to give in.

"You need to listen to me on this: you *can't* save this company. Sometimes you just have to do some wrong things in order to serve the greater good. That's just the way the world works."

Michael glared at Glazier, studying the man's qualities as much as his words. "But what about values?"

But those were just words, Michael realized. He knew the real reason he had to pull X-Tronic from the flames. But he couldn't tell Glazier. He couldn't let his case officer discover just how emotionally invested he had become. The unfolding events were following in such close parallel with his own family's tragic history—with things that, though they occurred long before Michael's birth, had somehow cursed him all the same.

"*Values?*" Glazier said. "This isn't Sunday school. You need the values to make the tough choices in life, the choices where you have to break eggs. Some good people will suffer in the short term, and that will be the hard part of finding the courage to make this decision. But in the long run, you will have made the best decision for the most people."

Glazier paused and looked around. A crowd of young professionals was laughing and chattering and flirting at the bar. Michael wondered if the man was remembering younger days, when he might have made the same idealistic argument to save X-Tronic that Michael was now making.

Glazier turned back around and ran a pawlike hand through his hair. "It's only rational to doubt what you're doing," he continued. "But that rationality makes you realize that the only responsible thing is to bankrupt a company that employs fifty thousand people, if it helps preserve an entire nation's economic structure and strengthen the financial institutions that support it."

Michael looked down at the bubbles rising in his beer. In a tired voice, he said, "Who are we to make God's decisions?"

"We're the United States government, that's who."

"And I suppose the government's going to be God enough to absolve me of the guilt I'll be carrying to the grave, too?" He downed the rest of his beer.

"I guess we'll both find out."

And there they sat, in somber contemplation of the events they were about to set in motion. Michael wouldn't admit it, but he was glad to have Glazier in Denver.

A dance room upstairs pulsed with loud electronic music. After talking over it for a few moments, Michael suggested, half in jest, that they go and "check it out," and to his amused surprise, Glazier agreed. As Michael walked through an ornate archway at the top of the stairs, red lights lit up the rising "smoke" on the dance floor, and silhouetted dancers raised their clawing fingers through the cloud, like zombies emerging from some hell world of his own design.

42

————— ꞏ⠶✳⠶ꞏ —————

M ICHAEL GOT TO X-Tronic at seven thirty on the
designated morning. He had developed the bait yesterday.
Glazier had obtained the federal warrants to tap the phone in
Diamond's office at X-Tronic and Falcon's offices at Cooley and
White, as well as to set up receptor codes on nearby cell towers
to intercept their cell phone conversations.

Falcon was going to be with other clients for the rest of the
week, so Michael was alone in the audit room. He logged on to
his e-mail account and pulled up the draft message in his unsent
folder in Outlook.

He reread the unsent e-mail one last time. His final draft
spelled out to Diamond and Falcon that he had found some
issues with the financial statements, which he thought should be
communicated to the SEC and the NYSE. After rereading the e-
mail, he hit *Send* and watched the electronic hourglass process
slowly, giving him too much time to reflect on what he had just
put in motion.

He flipped open his cell phone and speed-dialed the number.

"This is Glazier."

"I just sent the e-mail."

"Okay. My team will be listening for anything. Be sure to let me know when they open the message."

Michael heard a knock on the door. "I have to go," he said, and flipped his cell phone closed and snapped it back onto his belt clip.

Lance Seaton walked into the room. "Good morning," he said. "Looks like everyone's abandoned you." He looked around the room. "Do anything fun this week, or have you been working too much?"

Michael read something in the twin's voice . . . a warning, perhaps?

"A little of both. I have an old friend from out of town who's working in Denver this week."

"Did you show them the mountains?" Lance said, moving to the table and resting his hands on the back of a tall leather chair. The white sleeves inched out from his suit jacket, revealing turquoise cufflinks.

He shook his head. "No time. Just staying in the city."

"And they're still here?"

Michael hesitated for a moment that was almost too long. He had just seen a message pop up on his computer. It was an automatic return receipt message. He had set up his options so that whenever someone first opened an e-mail from him, he would get a reply notifying him. He read the subject name on the message: *Return Receipt—Jerry L. Diamond.* His heart quickened; it had begun.

"Michael?"

"Oh, sorry. Yeah, he's still in town, but he's flying back Thursday night."

"Mmm, that's too bad you won't get a chance to go to the mountains."

"Yeah. I'm sure we'll do it next time. He's even considering a move here in a year or so."

"Hey, that's great," Lance said with a grin. "Listen, Michael, I know you've had a very hard few weeks, with your father's death and all. Well, Lucas and I are taking off work this Friday to go skiing at Vail before the weekend crowds rush in, and we wanted to see if you'd like to join us."

Another message popped onto his screen: *Return Receipt— John S. Falcon.*

He had to concentrate to hide the building tension, relieved at least that Lance couldn't see the laptop's screen from where he stood. "I haven't been skiing in a month," Michael replied in what he hoped was a wistful tone.

"Then it's settled," Lance said, stepping back toward the door. "Besides, we're the client, and you have to make us happy. Just e-mail me your address. Lucas and I'll pick you up around eight. Traffic to the mountains shouldn't be bad on a Friday morning. We'll talk again Thursday."

The moment the door closed behind Lance, Michael redialed Glazier on his cell.

"Yeah?"

"They've both opened their e-mails—Diamond four minutes ago, Falcon two."

"I know. Diamond called Falcon, but they didn't say anything we can use. He only told him they need to grab a coffee. They're meeting at a place called Sancho's Café in fifteen minutes."

"Glazier, you've gotta be there—it's on the corner of Fifteenth and California."

"I'm already heading there with a small team."

"Listen, I know these guys. They'll pay attention to anyone that looks like they're worth money, so you can slob it down— jeans and tennies—and they won't give a damn about you."

"It's already covered," Glazier said. "You just let me know if *you* hear anything on your end." And he hung up.

Michael stared at the e-mail screen on his computer. There was no going back now.

Michael worked the rest of the day on minor aspects of the audit, leaving only long enough to grab a sandwich from the cafeteria and bring it back to the conference room. By throwing himself into resolving the review points from Falcon, he managed to occupy himself enough to escape the remaining puzzles surrounding the X-Tronic scandal. He was almost certain he had put together all the pieces to the conspiracy, but his mind still wavered on the final resolution, as if there was still some remaining question he couldn't quite pinpoint.

At four thirty that afternoon, as if it were not important enough to bother sending earlier, he got an e-mail from Falcon: *Please meet me in my office at 8:00 tomorrow morning.*

43

------*------

WHEN MICHAEL KNOCKED on the open door, Falcon waved him in and motioned for him to sit in the black netted chair on the opposite side of the broad maple desk, where he waited for Falcon to end his phone call.

"That was quite an e-mail you sent yesterday," Falcon said, hanging up the phone.

"Yes," he replied. His mouth felt dry. He was too nervous to risk babbling. Glazier had told him to keep his answers short at first, to give Falcon the chance to set the tone of the meeting. Even though they were alone in the room, the recording device Michael wore under his clothes made him feel as if an audience of thousands were listening.

"And you really have concerns that you think should be communicated to the SEC?"

"I do," Michael replied, trying to steady his breathing.

"Then I think it best that we work everything out this morning." He paused to open a desk drawer, and to Michael's surprise, he pulled out a palm-size microcassette recorder and set it on the desk. "I hope you don't mind my recording this conversation. I feel that conversations of this importance should be thoroughly documented in case there are any questions later on."

What was Falcon *doing*? The entire reason he had sent the e-mail was to get the man to reveal something incriminating—obviously, he had completely underestimated him. Falcon wasn't going to reveal anything. In fact, he was going to use their conversation as insurance if he should face federal prosecution. The partner would try to distance himself from X-Tronic, and Michael had walked right into the trap.

Falcon pressed the Record button. "Now, Michael Chapman, please continue. Tell me exactly what concerns you have regarding your audit test work of X-Tronic Corporation relating to its year-end financial statements."

Michael was silent for a moment. Falcon had been playing him since he put Michael on the Performance Improvement Plan five weeks ago. He wished he could just get up and leave without saying another word, but that would give Falcon a perfect excuse to yank him off the job.

"Well," he finally said, "I think X-Tronic is incorrectly recognizing its revenue and isn't nearly as conservative as it should be."

"You're concerned about insufficient *conservatism*?" Falcon asked, as he raised an eyebrow.

Michael knew he needed to be careful with his wording. It would be possible to defuse the situation if the partner could make it look as if Michael were merely being too cautious with his concerns for X-Tronic. But if he mentioned the fraud, Falcon might insist on a full investigation for the record—an investigation that Michael would no longer control.

"Yes," Michael said. "I was looking over some of the revenue contracts we tested, and I came across situations where X-Tronic incorrectly recorded too much revenue."

Now Falcon was silent for a moment. "What's the dollar amount you think they overstated?"

"Two hundred forty thousand dollars."

The number was merely something he had pulled out of the air. The import thing was to make sure the amount seemed too small to warrant correction of the financial statements. He was peeling his lie back from the truth, trying to reveal just enough of a false concern that Falcon might dismiss the warning without taking any action against him—just as when a hustler barely "misses" a billiards shot, leaving his opponent none the wiser.

"And did you extrapolate that sample to the entire company?" Falcon asked.

"Yes. The estimated misstatement for the entire company is two point one million," he lied, knowing that the real number was closer to four hundred million. He couldn't give Falcon the chance to act surprised and have the statements reexamined. Then the crafty partner could reopen the audit, announce a restatement effort, send out another team, burn X-Tronic's reputation on Wall Street, and conclude that Michael had been completely incompetent on the engagement, thus destroying any chance of connecting Cooley and White to X-Tronic's fraud. Michael had to lie.

"As I recall, listing scope for X-Tronic is two million, correct?" Falcon asked.

"That's right," Michael answered. He knew what Falcon was getting at. Every audit engagement had a materiality listing scope—a threshold amount, calculated based on a percentage of the company's assets or revenues, above which known mistakes on the financial statements must be corrected. Any accounting error less than the listing scope need not be corrected, because it was deemed too small for any investor to be concerned about.

"Mmm," Falcon mumbled. "Is it possible that our materiality is a little too low? I recall that we were conservative when we first calculated it."

"Are you suggesting we change materiality after the fact?" This time it was Michael's turn to say something for the record, and he fought hard not to grin.

"Of course not," Falcon said peevishly. "Materiality can't be changed after so much work has been done. But since it is the partner's ultimate responsibility to feel comfortable with the audit test work and financial statements before signing off, I would like you to document what you found with this revenue testing and what you think the changes should have been: the two point one million. I'm comfortable signing off on not making those changes, because of the relatively low dollar amount. Now, was that your only concern?"

"Yes."

"Then I'll consider the matter closed."

"I'll document our discussion in the workpapers," Michael replied.

"And, Michael," Falcon began, as if there was still an important matter that they had not yet discussed, "regarding your e-mail, I appreciate your concern, but I think you may have overreacted when you suggested we contact the SEC about this issue. In the future, if I were you, I would be cautious of blowing things out of proportion before I had a chance to discuss things with the appropriate people."

"I understand."

The last thing Michael remembered hearing as he walked out of Falcon's office was the loud click of the tape recorder being turned off. Furious, he realized that Falcon had evaded his perfect trap without even a scratch.

Michael left downtown and drove south toward the Denver Tech Center. Sunlight glistened off the light-rail track and the corporate buildings in the distance. He speed-dialed Glazier.

"What the hell happened in there?" Glazier asked.

"I don't know," Michael replied.

"He knew you were recording the conversation?"

"No, I don't think so. But he's now been able to protect himself with his own recording, so it'll be even harder to make a case against him."

"That's unfortunate. However, I do have some good news," Glazier announced. "Diamond wasn't as cautious. He called one of the revenue managers at X-Tronic this morning. They had a short conversation about your e-mail. I believe I got enough to show that Diamond was involved in devising the illegal reporting of the contracts. I'm taking the original tape with me to Washington to meet with the director and the secretary, but I'll leave a copy in your apartment. It's good, Michael—really good. We've got Diamond!"

Michael felt something relax in his chest, and even though no one could see him, he tightened his lips to conceal a smile. He knew better than to get too excited, but he couldn't deny how great this news was. Conspiracies of this size never stayed together very long after one or two members were cornered by authorities. He shifted gears and zigzagged through a knot of slow-moving cars on the freeway.

"Diamond—one out of five," he said. "That still leaves Don Seaton, the twins, and Falcon. We have to get 'em all, Glazier. Your flight leaves in three hours?"

"Yeah. I'll be back next week after meeting with the director. We'll decide which indictments to start with. By then a judge will let us know if we have enough evidence to seize records at both X-Tronic and Cooley and White. Within a week, I'm hoping to organize a federal task force and have our agents raid X-Tronic to lock down their financial records. I'll need your help to do the same to Cooley and White. It's going to be big, Michael. The U.S. government is about to declare war on X-Tronic."

"I wish there was another way," Michael said, imagining the broadcast coverage on network news as a hundred federal agents ran into X-Tronic and Cooley and White to box up financial records and lock down the IT systems.

"Trust me, Michael, this is the best thing that can happen."

"What about Kurt's death?"

"Something'll turn up as we unravel the fraud. You just focus on the twins—they seem to be the key that links everything together."

Ending the call, Michael realized that he still had the recording device Glazier had given him from the surveillance kit. Falcon hadn't given him anything incriminating on the recording, but there might yet be a use for the device. Michael would be skiing with the twins tomorrow, and one of them just might say something to hang them.

BRYAN DEVORE

44

---◦◦❋◦◦---

W ITH A FRESH layer of powder and an eighty-inch base, the ski conditions were sublime. Michael sat between the twins on the Vista Bahn express lift, which took them halfway up Vail Mountain. From there they caught a second lift to Patrol Headquarters—the resort's highest point—where they would ski toward the backside of the mountain. Vail's world-famous back bowls offered acres of wide-open, natural terrain that fell hundreds of feet down steep surfaces like the inside of a giant bowl. Such difficult and committing terrain meant that only the most advanced skiers and boarders dare enter.

Dangling from a steel cable fifty feet above the ground, they glided up the mountain, only a few feet above treetops festooned with beads and bras—reminders of wild times in Vail Village.

After reaching the top peak, they skied away from the lift as the chair whipped back around to head down the mountain. Lance took the lead, cutting along the trail toward the back bowls. Lucas was right on his brother's heels, just as he had been since birth.

The trail, well above tree line, edged along the rim of China Bowl, which dropped like a steep staircase for over a thousand feet before leveling off near the trees far below. The entire world opened in front of Michael as he looked out at the tiered mountaintops. He paused, gathering his nerve before launching out over the lip, when suddenly, Lance turned right on his edges, shot from the edge of the rim trail, and jumped off the ledge into China Bowl. Legs pumping like pistons, he attacked the moguls. Lucas leaped off after his brother. And with little option for retreat, Michael exhaled his fears and plunged over the drop-off.

He soon found himself falling behind the aggressive skiing of the twins. Not wanting to be left behind, he tucked into a low ball and pointed his skis straight down the mountain, quickly accelerating to a speed far beyond his comfort level. But he had to keep up with the twins or risk losing them for the day.

Going as fast as he dared, he barely managed to keep up with them as they moved closer to the trees on the far left side of the bowl. His thighs were burning from the violent pounding across the moguls that stood like frozen waves along the steep slope. Focusing desperately through the tinted plastic of his goggles, he fought to keep in control on the challenging terrain. And for the first time that morning, he knew he was in real trouble—the twins were just too good to keep up with.

Jarred and shaken, he tried to go faster yet. But he caught too much of a mogul with his left, and his tips crossed. At that speed, he had no time to react, and his legs were yanked out from under him, sending him sprawling face-first onto the unforgiving terrain. His skis snapped off, fluttering upward as he bounced across the rough moguls, coming to a halt fifty feet downslope.

Stunned from the battering impact of his crash, he gradually rose to his feet. The twins where yelling enthusiastically from below—apparently, his misfortune had been cause for much amusement. Michael gathered himself and trudged up the slope to collect his scattered gear. Before snapping on his skis, he took off a glove and reached inside his jacket to rub the upper left side of his chest. He hadn't registered the pain until now. And as he felt the bruise, a sudden panic rose within him. He turned his back to the twins far below, unzipped his inside coat pocket, and pulled out the recording device. Its case was smashed, the battery panel ripped away. It was destroyed.

"Fuck!" he growled to the snow, realizing that he now had no way to record a conversation with the twins. He looked over his shoulder and saw them waving their poles at him. Mouthing another curse, he skied down the side of the bowl toward them. He slid to an abrupt stop next to the twins, spraying snow onto their legs.

"That looked painful," Lance said.

"More than you know."

"Let's cut through the trees for a while," said Lucas.

"Yeah," Lance agreed.

Michael paused. Was this how it had happened—how they lured Kurt into the trees? An instinctive fear settled in the pit of his stomach as the twins continued to coax and wheedle him into the thick woods, away from the relative safety of the open slopes.

"I'm not much for skiing in the trees," Michael said. "I'll just head on down the trail and meet up with you guys at the Orient Express," referring to one of the lifts near the base of the bowls.

"Well, we're not really sure where we might go," Lucas said. "Every time my brother and I go into the trees, well, you wouldn't believe some of the places we end up."

"Yeah, better follow us so we don't get separated," Lance added. "Come on. We'll go slow, if that's what you're worried about."

"I really don't think I ought to," Michael said, hoping yet to convince them to stay in the open.

"How disappointing," Lucas said as he turned and skied into the trees. In seconds he was out of sight.

"Don't worry about him," Lance said. "He's all talk. The thing is, we were going to stop and smoke some bud, so we need to get away from the trail. Come on. We won't be long." And Lance pointed his skis into the trees and followed his brother's trail until he, too, had vanished.

"Fuck," Michael muttered. Then, almost instinctively, he looked back for a last glimpse of the open slopes before following the faint trail into the shadows, leaving the bright, sunlit world behind.

45

—————————◦❖◦—————————

HEARING VOICES IN front of him, Michael turned to cut farther down the mountain, brushing his shoulder against a snow-laden spruce bough along the path. Then he saw the twins, who had stopped on a wide ledge overlooking a drop-off. They had thrown off their gear and were sitting around one of their ski packs. He slid to a stop beside them.

"Hey! You made it!" Lucas said with a salesman's smile.

"I figured it was better to face my fears," Michael replied. He sidestepped in his skis to get closer to the drop-off.

"And why would you be afraid of us?" Lucas asked.

"No, silly, he means he doesn't like skiing in the trees," Lance laughed.

"Jesus!" Michael said, as he looked out over the drop-off. His eyes followed the small cliff that angled down the side of the mountain. "That's a long ways down!"

"Oh, yeah, you should be careful," Lucas said casually.

Lance pulled out a small nylon case from his inside coat pocket and opened it to reveal a thin metal pipe and a small bag of pot.

"Boys, I don't know about you, but I'm ready for a smoke," he said with a wry grin.

Leaving his skis attached to his boots, Michael sat with his uphill side on the snow. He removed his helmet and gave it to Lucas, who wanted to compare the pattern of vent holes with that of his own helmet. Meanwhile, Lance carefully laid a pinch of marijuana in the pipe bowl, packed it gently with a fingertip, and brushed a flame from his lighter along the rim. Holding the smoke in for a few seconds, he exhaled with a sheepish grin.

Then Lucas took a hit and passed the pipe to Michael.

Michael looked blankly at the pipe for a moment, wishing for a healthy shot of Polish vodka instead. But eventually he put it to his lips and took a puff, held it, and began coughing uncontrollably. The twins laughed like a pair of hyenas.

"Not much of a smoker?" Lance asked.

"It's been a while," he replied.

"So," Lucas said as he took the pipe back and had another puff, "how's the audit going? Since we've already filed, I can't imagine you'll be around much longer." He passed the pipe back to Lance.

"Oh, yeah. Absolutely. I should be wrapped up any day now," Michael said sarcastically.

Lance passed Michael the pipe again and motioned for him to take another hit. He did, this time managing to keep the smoke down for a few seconds.

Lucas said, "The merger talks are something that we're watching very closely, just to make sure no issues come up. Now that the financials have been issued, we should be getting close to a decision. The board of directors has already met to discuss the new offer from Cygnus. They were forced to up the ante once Wall Street became aware of our record growth this last quarter. It's going to be very difficult for any other parties to get involved in a bidding war now that the stock is more expensive. Cygnus is determined to acquire the company, and because of certain assurances we've received, we want to make sure the two companies don't face any opposition."

"Sounds perfect," Michael replied.

"There's only one problem," Lucas added. "If any negative publicity surfaces during the next week, well, it could change minds very quickly. Investors may become wary of any new risks. The stock price could drop, which would start to make it look very attractive to large competitors or even some venture capitalists who might want to purchase the company and cut it up into pieces for a profit. We also want to avoid hitches in the SEC approving antitrust wavers for the merger. It's imperative for X-Tronic's future that we not have any problems during this critical time."

"Can't imagine there would be any problems," Michael said. "You guys seem to have everything pretty well covered."

Lucas stared intently at him, watching closely for any reaction. "I'll just say this straight out," he said. "We know you've uncovered some information about the company that could be very damaging if it became public."

Michael was silent.

"Well," Lucas continued, "it's in our interest that this information remain out of the public eye. You understand, it could hurt a lot of powerful people. In fact, I can assure you that there are very powerful men who will make sure that this information does not become public."

Michael looked back at Lucas but said nothing—the powerful marijuana was affecting him, making it hard to concentrate.

Lance watched him carefully while Lucas continued to talk. "Now, just so we understand each other, I want to make sure you know exactly what information we're talking about."

Now it was Michael's turn to speak. He blinked a few times, and slowly he managed, despite the drug's effects, to bring his immediate surroundings into focus.

"Yes," he said. "I understand *completely* what you're talking about. I have no desire to do anything that would jeopardize anyone's financial position in the company. In fact, I would very much like to become someone of financial position *myself*." Michael spoke the words slowly. He just wanted out. Away from the isolation, from the trees, and from these two people who may well have been involved in taking Kurt's life. Right now he would say *anything* to escape.

Lucas's expression revealed nothing. But out of the corner of Michael's eye, he saw a smile spreading across Lance's face.

"And what do you think it would take to become someone 'of financial position'?" he asked with raised eyebrows.

"Two hundred thousand dollars in stock options. Judging from the options I've examined so far, I'm sure the two of you could make that happen. Nothing that would take away from the piece of the pie—in fact, I'm merely proposing that we make the pie a little bigger. I also want an annual salary of a hundred and fifty thousand and a position on any strategic subcommittees involved in the company's expansion into Asia. I know X-Tronic's growth strategies, and I want to be a part of the company."

"Doesn't that breach your independence?" Lucas asked.

"You let me worry about my professional obligations," Michael said coldly. "Besides, I'm tired of working for Cooley and White. A new job with X-Tronic would be very attractive to me."

Lance smiled. "You want us to make you rich while also grooming you for an executive position. Perhaps I've underestimated your ambitions, Michael. When I first met you, I thought you were just another accountant."

"And I thought you were just another rich kid that had gone to Harvard to learn how to count all his money," Michael replied. "Now, do we have a deal?"

Lance took another puff from the pipe. "Yeah," he said, looking out at the clearing. "We can reach an agreement like that."

"Don't you have to discuss it with your father?" Michael asked, disbelieving the twins' initial response.

"My God!" Lucas remarked. "You really don't know what you've discovered, do you?"

"What do you mean?"

"Our father's not part of this," Lance answered. "He's an old man and knows nothing about X-Tronic these days. The poor fool still thinks he's leading a healthy corporation. If it wasn't for the work Lucas and I have done these past few years, the whole world would know how much trouble X-Tronic is in."

The revelation hit Michael like a concrete truck. "What! I thought your father was overseeing all of X-Tronic's dealings. Who the hell's in charge of all this?"

Lance laughed. "Someone you haven't met. Have another toke and think about it for a second. See if you can guess."

Michael took the pipe, put it to his lips with a shaking hand, and pretended to inhale. He turned away from the brothers, looking down the mountain, hoping they would trust him.

His mind raced as he began assembling all the pieces. Everything that Glazier and he had concluded about the conspiracy relied on the premise that Don Seaton, with Falcon's help, was the mastermind behind the fraud. But now, as he concentrated on the motivation to inflate X-Tronic's financial numbers, the desires of the twins to gain complete control of their father's company, and the ramifications should the fraud be revealed to the public, he realized—for the first time—that there was another possibility. A sudden fear struck him as he realized how big the conspiracy really was.

Suddenly, his eyes caught a quick movement in the reflection of the silver pipe. He spun around as his left hand pulled up one of his ski poles. The pole rose just enough to block the metal baton that Lucas swung at his head. Michael's movements were limited because of his attached skis, but he managed to reach upward with his free hand and grab the front of Lucas's neck with his gloved hand. Screeching, Lucas lunged into him. Michael's body inched toward the edge until he could feel himself beginning to fall. As he slipped over the edge, he kept a strong grip on Lucas's neck, and they both toppled over the edge.

46

---◦◦✳◦◦---

MICHAEL'S FACE WAS pressed into the snow, and he could feel a surge of pain somewhere in his upper back. Gradually his body began to work, his arms pushing him up onto his knees. A swooshing sound came from the trees somewhere above him. It took him a few seconds to register where he was, that Lucas had tried to kill him, that he had fallen over the cliff. Looking up, he studied the rock face from which he and Lucas had fallen. Then he noticed the swooshing sound again, coming and going as if trying to torment him. Invisible swooshing, pounding inside his head while the rest of the world was silent. Only this one sound existed. Then he remembered that Lance had not fallen over the side with Lucas and him. The swooshing, closer now, was Lance, skiing around the drop-off to aid his brother.

His brother! Michael looked around frantically before spying him, lying some forty feet away. Lucas! How had he managed to land so far away when they both had fallen from the same place? Staggering to his feet, he fought the stabbing pain in his back as he slogged through the deep snow. Reaching Lucas's inert form, he grabbed a shoulder and turned him so that he was no longer facedown in the snow. But turning him over, he felt the unnatural limpness and strange angle of the neck.

Feeling suddenly sick, Michael backed away from the body. He looked around the area and spotted the scattered skis and poles. The swooshing sound coming through the trees above him grew steadily louder; he didn't have much time. Hurriedly he gathered his gear and struggled frantically to reattach his skis. The deep snow fought him, keeping him from clipping his boots into the bindings. The swoosh magnified into a roaring in his ear as he panicked, cursing the uncooperative bindings. He prayed they hadn't been damaged in the fall. He could see color in the trees, moving like a phantom, gliding through the snow, growing closer. Finally he heard and felt his first binding engage. Standing on one ski, he could now get some leverage, and he shoved downward—and was in. Lowering his head and taking a deep breath, he stabbed his poles into the snow and lunged forward with all his strength. Moving fast along the snow, away from the base of the cliff, he disappeared into the thick trees down the mountain just as he saw Lance jump a small ledge and blaze toward the cliff base.

Michael skied as fast as he could, desperate to get through the trees and off Vail Mountain. He had been moving for perhaps ten seconds when a scream floated down from the trees behind him. Lance had just found his brother's body.

Picking up speed, Michael darted toward a sliver of sunlight that showed the open trail beyond the trees. He ducked a mat of low-hanging branches and shot down into a small ravine before rising toward a mound at the edge of the trees. As he came to the jump, he exploded from the trees into an open trail thronged with dozens of skiers. Waving his arms frantically for balance as he flew through the air, he hit the ground hard and immediately began stabbing his poles into the snow like an Olympic skier racing for the finish line. He was afraid Lance might come after him. The twin was the better skier, and it would have been easy to follow his tracks through the woods.

He had to catch two lifts before making it back to the front of the mountain. Eventually he made it to the final run approaching Vail Village. He rushed down with a wave of skiers, hoping to lose himself in the crowd. As he left the slopes, he skied past the standing ski racks, almost to the sidewalk, and there unclipped his skis, tossed his poles next to them, and shucked off his red coat. He didn't know what Lance was capable of, but he wasn't taking any chances in case his description made its way to an emergency dispatcher. For all Michael knew, he was now a hunted man—wanted for killing the son of one of the most influential people in Colorado.

Moving through Vail Village, he entered a sporting shop, took off his ski boots, and bought hiking boots, a blue Denver Broncos jacket, and a gray ski cap he could pull down low over his head. He struck up a conversation with some college girls walking toward the east parking garage and ended up getting them to drop him in Breckenridge on their way back to Boulder. In Breckenridge he sent an e-mail to Glazier from a cyber café and then used his Department of the Treasury credit card to rent a Volvo S60. Leaving town, he turned west on Interstate 70 and headed deeper into the Rocky Mountains. He needed to make it to Aspen as soon as possible.

47

MICHAEL EXITED FROM I-70 at Glenwood Springs. The interstate had taken him halfway to Aspen; the rest of the journey would be through mountain back highways. The sun had set, and a giant moon slowly rose over the peaks rimming the steep canyon he had just passed through. Isolated lights of scattered houses dotted the hillsides above the mountain town.

He pulled into a BP gas station nestled close to the highway. As he filled up, he leaned against the Volvo's trunk and looked along the quiet Main Street, lined with a small grocery store, a fly-fishing shop, and a one-name law office. But an unnerving feeling overcame him when he saw a police cruiser creep by the gas station. Its tires crunched the snow as it turned in and stopped at the pump opposite Michael's. The engine idled powerfully, then went dead. As the officer got out, Michael turned his face away, feigning a sudden interest in the gas pump handle. He didn't know if Lance had reported him to the authorities, but his instincts told him to avoid any attention. He watched in the reflection of his car window as the officer worked the gas pump.

The radio at his shoulder spat out occasional chatter: somewhere a patrol car was setting up a DUI checkpoint targeting spring breakers in the area. Michael recalled that Colorado had three times as many DUI arrests in March as in any other month, because of college students flooding the ski resorts during semester recess.

"Hear about that storm coming in?"

Michael cringed when he heard the officer address him. He forced a smile and turned toward the man, a broad-shouldered veteran with a square jaw and eyes that seemed to miss little.

"Storm?" Michael replied, shaking his head. "Nah, haven't heard."

"Yep, big 'un, crossing over the mountains from the east— and it's moving fast. Should be here in a couple hours. Denver got hit hard. Beating the hell out of the Front Range right now. I-Seventy's closed east of the Eisenhower Tunnel. Sixty inches in some places—hope you're not going east!"

"Nope. Heading west to Grand Junction," he lied.

"Should be okay, then," the officer smiled, as if pleased to have helped him avoid a serious mistake.

The gas hose clicked as it stopped fueling the Volvo, and Michael replaced the nozzle on the pump. Even though a cold burst of wind had just brushed his face, he could feel a layer of sweat forming on his back. He walked past the police cruiser and headed inside. He wanted to leave as soon as possible. The policeman's presence was nerve-racking, but he couldn't risk paying at the pump with plastic in case people were looking for him.

He entered the store and proceeded to the checkout. An old woman in an orange sweatshirt sat behind the counter reading a Hollywood gossip magazine. She looked up at him with tired eyes.

"I'm sorry, honey—didn't realize you were there," she said. "Old age is blurring my eyes, I'm afraid."

He smiled as he waited for her to ring him up. She moved slowly, taking an eternity to press the keys. She paused midway to ask him a question that he didn't register, and he mumbled a forgettable reply. *Hurry the hell up!* he thought, smiling at her. *You're killing me.*

When she had finally finished, he turned to leave. Outside, he noticed that the police officer had disappeared, though the cruiser was still waiting next to his rental. The restroom, he remembered, was around back. He walked across the lot, praying that his paranoia was unfounded, that his instincts were wrong. Snow flurries spun and wafted lightly in the air, not really falling so much as circling his face, a teasing prelude to the approaching storm. He was just ten feet from his car. A few more seconds, and he would be gone.

"STOP RIGHT THERE! PUT YOUR HANDS IN THE AIR AND SLOWLY TURN AROUND! SLOWLY!"

Michael's heart raced. He turned slowly around to see the officer hiding in the shadows at the side of the gas station, his gun drawn and pointed at Michael's chest.

"Easy, now," Michael said calmly.

"MICHAEL CHAPMAN! YOU'RE WANTED FOR THE MURDER OF LUCAS SEATON. SLOWLY KNEEL ON THE GROUND AND GET DOWN ON YOUR STOMACH!"

"Easy, now," Michael repeated.

"NOW!"

Michael could see the shocked face of the clerk staring out through the window, her magazine forgotten. He sank to his knees in the snow and lay on his stomach against the cold, grease-stained concrete. He turned his head sideways to speak to the officer.

"I'm a federal agent," he said. "Radio your captain and have him contact the deputy secretary's office at the Treasury Department in Washington. They will confirm my status."

"You have the right to remain silent," the officer began, moving cautiously toward him.

"God damn it, are you listening to me? I'm a federal agent, and I—"

"I don't care if you're the president of the United States— there's a warrant for your arrest in connection to the murder of a Lucas Seaton. Boy, do you even realize you have been the target of a statewide manhunt for the past two hours?"

"Just be careful with that sidearm, Officer. *'Always remember your surroundings when securing a suspect with a fire-strike weapon'*—isn't that what they taught us? I'm not sure your range instructor from the academy would approve if you discharged your weapon over several thousand gallons of gasoline."

The officer seemed a little taken aback by Michael's rote recitation of the firing safety language from cadet school. "If you really are a federal agent, you'll have no trouble clearing this up at the station."

"I'm undercover. I have powerful enemies and can't risk resurfacing."

"Son, I'm taking you in whether you like it or not."

Michael turned his face back down to the concrete. He closed his eyes and listened intently, focusing on the distance and direction of every sound, imagining the world beyond his sight. He knew the procedures the officer would follow in securing a suspect: kneeling on his back while temporarily holstering the firearm to get out the handcuffs. He knew the timing of the procedures. In Alabama he had learned them by heart.

The officer bent down and put one knee in his back. Michael would have a one-second window, maybe two, to make his move. He heard the rattle of the handcuffs coming off the officer's belt . . . the soft slide of gunmetal against leather as he holstered his weapon. Michael levered himself sideways with his legs, which moved his body just enough to throw the man off balance. The officer punched him on the head, but the blow was ineffectual, scraping along his right temple. Michael spun on the ground and flipped the cop to his side. Frantic, the man made a clumsy effort to get his pistol out, but as he got his hands on the gun, Michael threw a hard back elbow into his groin, causing him to curl into a fetal position with a whimper. Cradling the man's neck between forearm and biceps, he squeezed, and within three seconds the officer was unconscious.

As Michael removed the radio and gun from the police belt, he turned back toward the shop to see the old woman speaking frantically into the phone. She was squinting in a vain effort to see the details of his car.

He ran to the Volvo, and within seconds he was on the street and picking up speed. As he left Glenwood Springs, he heard the police radio crackle beside him on the passenger seat. "Officer down! I repeat, we have an officer down at the corner of Sixth and Laurel! White male suspect on the loose. Consider armed and dangerous. I repeat, an officer is down!"

*   *   *

As Michael drove past the town of Basalt, snow fluttered in the Volvo's headlight beams like a swarm of luminescent white moths. Aspen was only a half hour away. He spotted a fast-approaching vehicle in his rearview mirror. The headlights disappeared as he rounded a bend; then they reappeared before vanishing again. Eventually they appeared again and remained in his mirror, gaining on him fast.

He glanced at the gun lying on the passenger seat and wondered just how far he would go to avoid being captured. The silent police radio was beside the gun. The last communication he had heard was that of the on-site officer informing the dispatcher that they were going to examine the store's surveillance cameras to identify the vehicle type. Then the officer had informed all units that the suspect was in possession of a stolen police radio and that all further communication would be coordinated through cell phones. That was the last word from the radio. Michael was a little surprised that the police hadn't used that knowledge to feed him misinformation to help catch him. At least, that was the sort of tactic he had learned at the academy in Alabama. By now they would have contacted the U.S. Marshal's Office in Denver. He could only hope that the storm currently hammering Denver would delay the marshals' response.

His attention turned back to the headlights that were now right behind him. He waited for sirens and flashing lights. Twenty minutes had passed since he left Glenwood Springs, and he was certain the police would have identified his vehicle by now.

Suddenly, the car veered to the left and shot past him—a red Ford Blazer full of college students, with snowboards clamped to the roof. Just as he rounded the next bend, he saw the Blazer's brake lights redden the snow kicked up behind it. Then he saw the reason it was slowing: a hundred yards beyond, a Highway Patrol cruiser was parked on the highway with lights flashing. Flares glowed along the snowbanks. He was trapped. Already too close to the roadblock to turn around without attracting suspicion, he could only proceed toward the police car. All his efforts had been futile. He would never reach Aspen now.

The Blazer stopped fifty yards from the roadblock. Michael was slowing the Volvo when the Blazer suddenly sprang to life, spinning around, accelerating, whipping past him. Immediately the officer rushed to his car and speeded after the Blazer. Michael watched the flashing lights fly past him in pursuit. The cop must not have noticed that he was driving a Volvo. He thanked the drunken college students for foolishly trying to avoid a DUI and, in the process, pulling the officer away from the checkpoint. He crawled the Volvo past the now unmanned flares.

He should be in Aspen in ten minutes.

48

"HOW THE HELL did this happen!" Glazier's voice rang through the corridors of the U.S. Treasury Department headquarters in Washington, D.C. "I was just with him in Denver yesterday!"

"Get me someone from State and someone from Justice," he snapped at Shannon, his assistant. "I want to talk to the ground man, the U.S. marshal they dispatched. They're not declaring open season on one of my agents. I want the governor of Colorado on the phone in the next two minutes—make it happen!"

Deputy Secretary of the Treasury Jack Willis hurried down the hallway toward the Financial Forensics and Fraud Investigative Division. His round spectacles and thick, curly hair were a messy counterpoint to the dark three-piece suit. Arriving just in time to hear the end of Glazier's rant, he put a pudgy hand on the big man's shoulder.

The irate Treasury agent whirled around. "Jack!" he said. "Aspen's gone off the reservation. He's on the run, and everyone in Colorado with a badge is looking for him."

"Aspen?" Willis said, already considering the implications. Like Glazier, he knew the code name for each of the twelve undercover Treasury agents placed inside various accounting firms across the country.

"Yeah. He's gone off the grid. No one on my team's heard from him in almost a day, and now we're getting reports there's a warrant out for his arrest."

"An *arrest warrant?*" the deputy secretary repeated, trying to digest this new and worrisome development.

"For murder!" Glazier emphasized. "They're saying he killed Lucas Seaton! They're also saying he tried to kill a cop in Glenwood Springs."

"Jesus Christ, Troy!" Willis breathed. "Where do we think he is now?"

"We don't know, sir. His last known location was in Glenwood Springs. God knows what's happened to him in the past twenty-four hours. The authorities are saying he killed Lucas on the ski slopes in Vail."

"Just like—"

"Right. It doesn't make any sense."

"Revenge?"

Glazier shook his head. "He'd been working this case for months. It's taken him over two years to get deep enough into the firm to get this assignment—he sure as shit wouldn't jeopardize the investigation now."

"Well, I would say it's jeopardized now."

"I never should have left Denver," Glazier muttered. "I'm going back to Colorado tonight." He turned to Shannon. "Have a chopper meet me on the roof, and have a jet waiting when I get to Andrews."

"I'll do what I can from here," said Willis.

Glazier leaned back into the conference room to grab his case, then bolted for the elevators.

"Troy!" Shannon yelled at him, holding her cell phone to her ear. "All runways are currently closed in Denver. The entire mountain region is under a massive winter storm. They're not letting any air traffic in. All flights have been grounded, and most of the highways are closed. No one's getting in or out of the state."

"Just have that jet ready. And tell the pilot he's going to have to find a way to set us down in Denver—I don't care if it's on the damned interstate."

"Troy!" the deputy secretary yelled after him.

Glazier turned to look at his boss.

"Do you think you know where he's headed?"

Glazier nodded as the elevator doors slid open. "He was last spotted outside Glenwood Springs. I don't know what happened to him in Vail, but I think he's headed for Aspen—I think he's going after Don Seaton!"

49

————◦✳◦————

MICHAEL DROVE PAST the Aspen-Pitkin County Airport, past the boutiques and taverns lining the mountain town's quaint snow-covered streets. After crawling sedately through town to avoid any chance of getting stopped, he drove another ten minutes along winding mountain roads to the Seaton estate. But instead of stopping, he kept going past the driveway until he found a service road a half mile up. Parking the car, he threw on his coat and began bushwhacking through the snowy wilderness.

Don Seaton sat staring into the fireplace, his gaze lost somewhere between the fire and the stones. He slumped in the leather chair, a half-empty glass of Scotch in his hand. Raising the glass again, he downed the contents and went on watching the wood shrivel into black pellets before peeling away from the logs and falling into gray ash below the grate. Another log popped, spitting embers up the chimney. Impulsively, he hurled the tumbler into the fire, shattering it.

With restrained anger, he got up, pulled a bottle of Glenury Royal off the bookcase, and poured two fingers into a fresh glass. He approached the window of his study, took a drink, and looked out at the snow circling the front drive of the mansion. Less than an hour had passed since the Denver homicide detective telephoned to inform him that Lucas had been killed. "His neck was snapped," the detective had told him. "There's an investigation under way. Your son Lance was questioned earlier. We're following up on some leads and will call you if anything develops."

Seaton would wait till morning to visit the coroner's office in Vail—a snowstorm was moving through the central mountains, making travel impossible for the next twelve hours. He didn't mind the forced delay. Even though he had stopped loving his sons the day his wife died, he needed a night to beg her forgiveness for his failure as a father before he could face the reality of his son's corpse.

Michael reached the edge of the clearing behind the estate. The wide courtyard that he remembered from the party a month ago was now silent as a tomb. At the far left, light escaped through the small windows of the back kitchen. The door was again slightly ajar, and he recalled Lance explaining how the cook couldn't stand the unventilated heat of the mansion's old kitchen without cracking at least one window or door.

He scanned the backyard once more. Nothing moved—he was alone. But something was unusual—some lingering tension, some sense of commotion within the mansion. Too many lights were on, the house too active at this late hour . . . News of Lucas's death must have beaten him to the estate.

He sprinted toward the mansion, his boots crunching through the crusted snow. Hidden spotlights suddenly illuminated the area, but they caught his image for only an instant before he reached the mansion and leaned against the dark wall. Inching along in the shadows, he peered around the kitchen door. A plump man was sprinkling something into a steaming pot. The man's back was to the outside, making it easy to slip into the kitchen and turn up a narrow staircase leading to the servants' passageway. He was halfway up the stairs when the backyard spotlights turned off.

Inside the darkened servants' passageway, he could hear sounds all around him. The mansion was filled with activity. He slipped past a door with light seeping from underneath, then another, and reached the end of the narrow hallway. He was about to turn around in the darkness and find a way to the main hallway when he heard the distinct sound of glass breaking. He leaned his ear against the end wall and listened to the faint clank of two glasses hitting, as if someone were toasting or pouring a drink. Kneeling on the wood floor, he felt a slight recess under the panel and realized that he was in front of a hidden doorway to one of the main rooms. Carefully, he returned his ear to the wood and listened to the sounds inside the room.

The Siberian husky ran through the trees behind the mansion, with Marcus walking after it. It snuffled along beneath the trees, pausing, sniffing, then leaping through the snowbanks.

Marcus had used the dog as an excuse to get some fresh air. He had been with Seaton when the phone call came from the Denver detective. Despite the snowstorm that was crawling west through the mountains, he had insisted he could push the Hummer through the roads to Vail if necessary. But his boss had declined the offer and retreated to his study.

Walking through the snowy woods, Marcus hadn't taken long to conclude that Lucas's death meant nothing to him. The only thing that concerned him was Mr. Seaton's safety. But one thought had bothered him: Lance and Lucas were always together. How could Lucas have died alone? The investigators claimed that Lance had given them a statement about Lucas's death before leaving the police station in Vail. Since then, Marcus had tried in vain to phone Lance, and no one else had heard from him in almost two hours. Lance seemed to have vanished, which made Marcus very nervous.

As Seaton's head of security and as his personal bodyguard, Marcus was constantly turning every situation over in his mind, searching for the hidden threat. When the twins had increasingly concealed their business activities from their father, it was Marcus who convinced Seaton to pay for a thorough background check on the twins' lives during their college years: obtaining confidential school records, interviewing old acquaintances and professors under false pretenses, and even discovering certain buried campus police reports. His findings had revealed enough concerns that he began having the twins watched occasionally.

He would never forget the look on his boss's face when he had presented him with the files from the investigators and advised the billionaire that his own sons now posed a potential security threat.

Marcus came to a sudden stop in the trees, instantly on full alert. He stared at the tracks in the snow: size eleven or twelve hiking boots—one man, running. Still deep, even with the wind pushing fresh powder along the forest floor—the tracks were fresh. He looked back in the direction the tracks came from: disappearing into the woods that stretched away from the estate, perfectly in line with the direction of the service road a half mile behind the property. Of more immediate concern, however, was where the tracks were headed: directly toward the mansion. He looked just in time to catch the faint glow of the backyard motion lights a hundred yards away, the instant before they turned off. He bolted toward the mansion, unholstering his gun as he ran.

50

WITH HIS EAR against the doorway, Michael again heard the crash and tinkle of breaking glass, then a murmuring voice, which he recognized as Don Seaton's.

"I couldn't do it without you," he heard Seaton say. "I never really tried. I failed you. Forgive me."

Michael was almost certain Mr. Seaton was alone, and the old man's mumbling seemed to carry a note of inconsolable sadness. Suddenly he saw a strange reflection off the wall in front of him. Was the door opening? He leaned back from it, watching the narrow slat of light at the bottom, waiting for it to grow, but it didn't change. No, he realized, the light was coming from behind him. Just then he heard a sound in the passageway and turned to see a small flashlight beam shine brightly in his eyes. He tried to stand up, but before he had gotten to his feet, a heavy blow to his chest sent him flying backward. His body broke through the hidden doorway and came crashing into Seaton's study.

Seaton whirled clumsily around from the window. "What the hell!" he yelled as Michael fell into the room, rolling over one shoulder and springing to his feet. His attacker jumped through the doorway and knocked him to the floor with a blow to the solar plexus. The pain all but paralyzed him, and he curled into a defensive ball like an injured animal.

"Marcus . . . !" Seaton yelled, looking to his bodyguard for an immediate explanation.

"He snuck onto the property and then entered the mansion through the servants' passageway in the kitchen," the bodyguard replied.

"Who is he?" Seaton demanded.

Marcus stepped toward Michael and kicked him in the midsection, then reached down and took his wallet. "Name's Michael Chapman," the bodyguard said, flipping through the contents. "Hey, he works for Cooley and White!" He held up a business card.

Groaning, Michael sat up, and Marcus leveled a gun at his face. "Stay down," he said. "What are you doing here?"

Michael looked first at the gun, then at the man. He was about to answer when he noticed something unusual: a twitch at the corner of the left eye. A few seconds later, it twitched again.

"It was *you!*" Michael exclaimed.

"What?"

"It was you. You're the man that visited Dr. Speer the week before I did—the man asking questions about how Kurt Matthews died."

"I'm going to ask you once more: what are you doing here?" Marcus growled.

"Mr. Seaton," Michael said, ignoring Marcus, "I'm a federal agent for the U.S Treasury Department. I'm working undercover at Cooley and White as part of a prototype operation created by a Senate oversight committee three years ago. I was the senior auditor on the X-Tronic engagement this year. When Kurt Matthews was killed, I was placed on the engagement. I've discovered a fraudulent conspiracy between certain high-level

THE ASPEN ACCOUNT 273

employees from both X-Tronic and Cooley and White. I believe the conspirators planned to inflate profits illegally for personal gain from stock options and an aggressive bonus system, as well as for career security in case the Cygnus takeover was successful. Kurt Matthews was murdered because he discovered the fraud. And your sons are involved."

Marcus held the gun steady but glanced toward Seaton for instructions.

"Wait," Seaton said. "We've met before, haven't we?"

Michael nodded, fighting nausea from the blows to the midsection. "In a break room at X-Tronic. We both arrived to work early one day. That was more than a month ago."

"Would you like a drink?" Seaton asked.

The man's composure surprised Michael. It seemed almost as if he had *expected* to hear such things about his company and his sons.

"Now that you mention it, I could use a drink, sir," he replied.

Seaton splashed some of the Glenury-Royal into the last two unbroken glasses and gave him one. Michael took a drink to help ease the pain in his ribs. He glanced at Marcus, who did not have a drink.

"Oh, don't worry about Marcus," Seaton said. "He doesn't drink. Now, I believe you want to tell me the details of your investigation at X-Tronic."

Michael still could not find even a hint of surprise on the billionaire's face. "You knew something was wrong at the company?" he asked.

"Please," Seaton insisted. "First tell me everything you know."

Michael nodded and then proceeded to tell everything that had happened since he was first assigned to the X-Tronic engagement. He told of his discovery of the revenue overstatements from the illegal recording of software contracts.

He then described his growing suspicions surrounding Kurt's death, and how everything tied in with the pending acquisition talks with Cygnus.

But it wasn't until he began detailing the individual roles of the key managers and officers involved in the conspiracy that he felt a scrutinizing glare from Marcus. Although Seaton was focused on the details of Michael's findings, Marcus seemed suspicious that he was holding something back. And he was. Because considering all that he was about to ask of X-Tronic's billionaire CEO, he did not know how he could possibly tell the man that he had been the cause of Lucas's death.

51

D ON SEATON APPEARED exhausted as he slouched down
in the leather chair by the fireside. Michael had never
imagined how the billionaire might look without the glowing
confidence that had exuded from his photos and media
interviews during the past twenty-five years. Now he saw the
exhaustion in the man's face, as if he was suddenly on the very
brink of death.

"Should I call someone?" Marcus asked, also noticing
Seaton's pallor. Indeed, the bodyguard seemed more concerned
about the billionaire's health than the man himself was.

"Because of the merger talks," Don began, "we have a
shareholders' meeting in Denver this Thursday. I can't keep this
news of the fraud from the public." He stood looking into the
fire. "This will destroy X-Tronic," he continued. "It will become
the next Enron or WorldCom or Rockwood Corporation. And
everything I've spent the past thirty years building will be
destroyed." He took another drink of Scotch.

"It doesn't have to be that way," Michael said.

"What other possibility is there?"

Michael swirled the liquor in his glass, stalling a moment before answering the question. He was terrified at what he was about to ask of Mr. Seaton. But everything he knew about the man told him he just might go along with it. He merely prayed he hadn't miscalculated. Finally he said, "How much does X-Tronic mean to you, Mr. Seaton?"

Seaton turned to face him. "It's my company! I built it! It's *everything I am!*"

"No abstractions, please. I'm asking a very specific question. How much are you willing to pay to save X-Tronic and the people who work there and have their lives invested in it?"

Seaton looked at him in surprise. "My heart lies with my company. My wealth is only a cloak that I have been given to wear."

"Then use your wealth to save the company," Michael said. "Do what no one would do for Enron. Do what no one else *could* do . . . Mr. Seaton," he continued, "if you want to save X-Tronic from financial collapse, you need to use the shareholders' meeting next week to tell the world about the discovered fraud within the company. They need to hear it from you first."

Seaton looked at the floor and frowned. "It will still create a panic." He shook his head, causing the orange firelight to slide back and forth across his face. "People will be on their cell phones, selling their shares immediately after the words leave my mouth. It will flood the market with rumors and drop the stock price to the floor. Our credit rating will be downgraded to junk status and will threaten to force X-Tronic into bankruptcy before the end of the day."

Michael glanced over to Marcus, walking toward the splintered doorway. The bodyguard didn't seem to be listening, but Michael knew better. In a steady voice, Michael said to Seaton, "You could contact the SEC commissioner and the chairman of the New York Stock Exchange this weekend. Insist that on the day of the shareholders' meeting they suspend trading of X-Tronic shares for twenty-four hours. This would buy you some time, give you a chance to calm the investors. Demand that they give you their undivided attention during the meeting."

"I don't think the Exchange would allow such a move," Seaton said, staring into the fire. He seemed unwilling to look at Michael when thinking through a problem. "But even if we were able to suspend trading temporarily, what could I possible say to the shareholders that would prevent a panic?"

"There is nothing that will prevent some form of a major financial slide in the market price—especially with all the hype around the better-than-expected earnings release and the analysts' speculations that the merger will occur. By suspending X-Tronic's trading, you're going to allay the onslaught of people selling before the crisis can be explained to investors. Our only argument here is that suspending trade will give people time to evaluate the true impact the fraud may have on future earnings at the company. It's no different from issuing a major press release after trading closes on Friday, giving investors the weekend to analyze the stock value before the markets open Monday morning."

"Then why don't we move the shareholders' meeting a few days to the following weekend?" Don asked.

"We can't change the meeting or there will be speculation that something's happened at X-Tronic."

The windows shook from a strong gust of wind. The winter storm was approaching, and Michael wondered just how much of the Rocky Mountain region had been shut down.

Seaton stood up from the chair and moved slowly away from the fireplace, as if the storm were calling him. "My son's funeral is Tuesday—Jesus, I shouldn't even be having the shareholders' meeting next week at all! I should cancel it altogether . . ." His voice faded to little more than a whisper. "I don't know what to do anymore."

Michael stood up, too. "Look, Mr. Seaton, the shareholders' meeting has to happen Thursday as planned. And you need to make the announcement then. The difficult decision for you is going to be how you want to respond once trading begins the next day."

"What are you suggesting?" Seaton asked, turning to meet Michael's eyes for the first time in several minutes. He seemed to have made a decision to move on to the next phase of whatever Michael was proposing.

Michael walked toward the heavy mahogany desk. "You need to liquidate as many of your other investments as possible and be prepared to put all your eggs in one basket."

"A basket that's about to break!" Seaton reminded him.

"Yes," Michael replied seriously, more than willing to admit the risks involved. "You need to have the funds set aside so that you can start buying as many shares of X-Tronic as you can once trading begins the day after the shareholders' meeting, when the price begins to drop after the public learns of the fraud."

Seaton listened carefully, pondering Michael's strategy. "You want me to buy large volumes of the shares to prevent the price from falling."

"No. I want you to let the price fall. The market will need to see a large drop in the company's share price because of the news. What I want you to do is help the company weather the storm. If you start buying the shares in low volumes when it begins to drop, then increase the volume of shares you purchase as the price continues to drop, it will show Wall Street that not everyone in the world is trying to dump the stock. In theory, it's no different from a massive corporate buyback of common stock. It will show some hope, some future, for the company."

Without moving his head, Michael looked up and left, as he always did when performing advanced calculations in his head. He continued. "The price closed today at a hundred and one dollars a share. I would think that it could drop to ten dollars in one day—after your announcement—and then continue to drop to less than a dollar a share over the next few days. If it goes below a dollar, there's a very good chance it will be delisted from the New York Stock Exchange, which would further encourage the board to declare bankruptcy. But if you purchase shares slowly during the decline, it will slow the collapse of the price. Then, when the price hits thirty-five a share, you buy everything that's offered below that price until you run out of money." His eyes came level and locked back on to Seaton. "You're a very wealthy man, Mr. Seaton, and I know that this will probably be the biggest risk—financially, anyway—that you've ever taken in your life, but you're the only one with the funds *and* the desire to save this company. If the price holds at thirty-five a share, there is a real hope that you can smash out market concerns and begin to turn X-Tronic around."

Seaton's face saddened as he listened to Michael's words. He inched around his desk during the explanation and poured himself another Scotch. Then he walked to the window and looked at his dark reflection.

"How could my sons do something like this to my company?" The billionaire turned to look at him, revealing the deep, rheumy eyes of an old man finally broken by the years. The look Michael saw on his face was the summation of a lifetime of betrayals and broken dreams, as everything that Seaton had in his life—his family and his business—seemed to be vanishing before his eyes.

"I wasn't much of a father to them, but I always made sure they had every advantage they could in life: the best education, world travel, experiences that I could only dream of when I was their age. I gave them *everything*. I was consumed in my work when they were boys. Too busy building my empire. When their mother died, I thought the best thing would be to send them to prep school out east."

He took another drink of his Scotch and turned to look deeper into his reflection, as if discerning something in himself he had never seen before. "Perhaps I hated them a little after their mother died. They had her eyes. They only reminded me of her, of how much I had lost." His eyes fell away from his reflection and held steady on the melting ice cubes in his glass. "And now look what I've turned them into. I gave them independence in their childhoods, hoping that it would make them into strong men, but they only grew to hate me. Oh, but they loved each other. I heard stories that even in college they were inseparable. Twins are often like that, I've been told."

"The truth is," Seaton continued with a sudden coldness, "once I began to suspect they had betrayed me and my company, I lost any love that I may still have been reserving for them." He looked Michael in the eyes. "It nearly broke me when I heard Luke had died, because I knew it would have destroyed my wife if she were still alive. But I don't consider either of them my sons anymore."

Unable to look upon the sorrow in the old man's face, Michael let his eyes stray past him, to the bookcase behind the mahogany desk. There was a long silence between the two men; Seaton seemed to believe the conversation over, but Michael knew there was something left that he needed to say.

"Mr. Seaton, I was with your son when he died . . . I caused his death." He stared at the bookcase while listening to the father's reaction behind him. He heard nothing but the old man's breath and the crackle of the fire. Michael closed his eyes and waited.

"Why?" Don asked with a weak voice.

"Because he was trying to kill me. Your sons knew I had discovered the fraud. And they knew I suspected them of murdering Kurt Matthews."

"My God," Seaton said in a weary voice, and his hand fell to the windowsill to help him keep his balance.

Michael watched him. His words had hit hard, but he could not see any into the depths of the man's soul. At that moment, a powerful gust shook the window, and heavy, sleeting snow pattered against the glass. Both Michael and Marcus were jolted by the violence of the storm outside. But Seaton stood motionless even though he was closest to the window, as if he had somehow been anticipating this storm for years.

52

———⊶⊷✳⊶⊷———

GLAZIER LOOKED OUT the window of the government Learjet, first at the turbulent storm clouds below, then at the dark reaches of space strewn with the winter constellations above. The heavens seemed so peaceful and cold.

"Agent Glazier," a voice broke through an overhead speaker in the small cabin. It was the pilot. "We have a small problem with Denver. The weather's getting pretty fierce down there, so DIA still has all outgoing flights grounded and is turning away all approaching flights outside a fifty-mile radius. They recommended that we turn toward Sioux City or Wichita."

Glazier jumped up from his seat and moved toward the cockpit. "Captain, we're not turning back and we're not going north. Keep this heading. I need to make it to Aspen tonight!"

"*Aspen?* That's completely out of the question. The storm system is pulverizing the Rocky Mountains and everything for a hundred miles east. Didn't you hear me? It's hell down there right now. They've basically shut down Denver's airport. Most of Interstate Seventy west of the Colorado-Kansas line is closed.

Aspen'll be hit within the hour. There's no way we can get through it. I suggest we go up to Sioux City and wait it out."

"Look, Captain, I've got an undercover agent I need to reach in Aspen as soon as possible. If you can't get me there tonight, then at least land in Denver so I have the best chance of reaching Aspen the minute a small window opens in the weather. My agent's life could depend on it."

"It's not recommended, sir. The crosswinds are cutting in at over a hundred miles per hour, ice is all over the area, and visibility's almost nothing."

"Captain, please! I used to fly cargo navigation planes for the military. I understand the risks, but I have every confidence that you can still manage to put us down in this stuff."

The pilot said nothing as he considered what Glazier was asking him to do. "It might be possible to land in Denver. Air traffic is down, so we'll probably have a good look at the area without having to worry about other flights. I'll radio Denver and tell them to be prepared. I'll let them know we're on a federal investigation and that it's urgent we land in Denver. They can't turn us away. Take a seat in the back and get into emergency landing position. I don't know how rough this is going to get."

"I'll stay up front with you," Glazier said, strapping himself into the empty seat next to the pilot. "There might be something I can do to help."

Both men tightened their harnesses as the jet descended from the peaceful stratosphere into the roiling chaos of the storm. The pilot radioed the tower at DIA and informed the controllers of his intentions. Almost immediately the entire cockpit began to shake. Red lights began flashing on the console as they penetrated deeper into the storm. Glazier watched in suspense as the pilot moved through his instruments, hitting various buttons, adjusting the stick, trimming their descent, and barking situational reports back to the tower.

The wind shears knocked them about so hard, it felt as if the jet had completely broken apart and was now cartwheeling to the earth. Then Glazier saw the beacon lights in the distance, barely visible through the flying snow. *Dear God,* he thought, realizing the hell they still must pass through before reaching the runway.

An alarm began beeping from the console, and Glazier realized that this had quickly turned into another of the half-dozen moments in his life when he truly felt as though he was walking on the edge of death. He looked at the pilot's face, drawing some comfort from the man's disciplined, steady concentration. But then he saw something new in the pilot's expression: a distinct look of concern. Glazier turned to look back out the windshield and was horrified by what he saw—or, more accurately, didn't see: the beacon lights had vanished. It was as if the storm had just tightened its grip around their falling jet.

53

THE BLACK GMC Yukon cut through the smooth, white expanse of mountain highway, defiant against the blizzard. Its tires occasionally spun and drifted, kicking plumes of snow in front of the covered government plates. The snowstorm had dumped so heavily through the night that half the roads in the high country had been closed.

"Every highway within sixty miles of Glenwood Springs has roadblocks searching for his description," Deputy Marshal Jarrod Beasley said excitedly to the driver, his youthful enthusiasm betraying his inexperience. "There's a team of officers waiting for our arrival at the police stations."

"Still no choppers," said the older African-American man in the backseat. Anthony Noble's strong face showed no concern over the encroaching storm. "All search efforts are still taking place on the ground. Weather's supposed to let up this evening. Then we can bring in the birds."

"He won't get far, Jason," Beasley said with unjustified cockiness. "We've got him pinned down in the mountains. He can't keep moving; all he can do is hide—but we'll find him."

Jason Kano held the wheel with the relaxed confidence of a professional driver. "What do we know about the officer Chapman overpowered?" he asked, sliding the Yukon through another turn.

"Good record," Beasley replied. "One of the best officers in the county, so they say."

Kano drifted back into his own thoughts. He was considering every angle, every motive. "And the officer wasn't hurt?" he finally asked.

"A few bruises, that's it. Chapman never even fired the gun."

"How did he knock the officer unconscious?"

"No one knows. There was no bruise on his head or anything—maybe a carotid hold."

"This Chapman guy is interesting," Kano said. "An accountant that can handle a good officer this easily and vanish without a trace . . . There's something not right here. If he didn't discharge the gun, then he didn't even panic. He's a cool customer."

"The cop said Chapman claimed to be an undercover federal agent," Beasley added.

"Trying to throw the man off balance," Noble said. "Pretty smart, really."

Kano was silent. He had tracked down and captured over a hundred fugitives in the past five years. After so many cases, he could immediately understand and classify 90 percent of his targets based solely on the factual background of their situation before the start of the manhunt. But the other ten percent were the wild cards, dangerously unpredictable. And the more Kano concentrated on the facts surrounding Michael Chapman's alleged murder of Lucas Seaton, the more complicated the situation seemed. Whoever this Chapman was, Kano was the one man hunting for him who would not be foolish enough to underestimate him—not until the hunt was over.

*   *   *

Michael squinted, dazzled by the morning light as he walked into the glassed-in patio were Mr. Seaton sat. Snow was pressed up two feet high outside the window, giving the room a partly submerged feel.

Seaton was sipping an espresso when he looked up to see Michael. "Dumped pretty good last night," he said. "Somehow Marcus still thinks he can move the Hummer through this. Well, who am I to argue? I trust the man with my life." He paused. "Please sit down, Michael."

Michael sat down at the small table as Seaton spoke into a small intercom box near the table. "Hopkins, please bring Mr. Chapman an espresso." Clicking off, he said, "Michael, there's something I want to ask you . . . something that bothered me a little when I was thinking about your plan."

"Yes, of course. What's your question?"

"Well," Seaton said thoughtfully, "I guess I can't figure out why it's so important for you to save my company. It just seems that you're taking such a grave personal risk."

Michael knew the reason. He had felt it burning in him ever since realizing that the fraud was large enough to destroy the company. But how could he explain to Seaton the complex feelings so tied up with his own family history?

"My great-great-grandfather started a steel mill in Elk County in central Pennsylvania in the 1890s," he said. This seemed to surprise Seaton. "The steel industry was booming. Over the years, it became a solid business, and by the time my great-grandfather took over during the 1920s, an entire community had grown around my family's business, with nearly four hundred workers at the mill and close to two thousand people living in our town, Bethel."

"That's wonderful," Seaton said.

Michael felt a little glow of pride at his ancestor's accomplishment. "Years later, the great depression hit the community hard, like it did everywhere, but my great-grandfather was more willing than most businessmen of the time to make personal sacrifices. He made every effort to avoid layoffs even during those years when the company was losing money. It's said my great-grandfather kept Bethel alive when many similar communities were turning into ghost towns."

"Sounds like he was a good man," Seaton said with admiration.

"Mm-hm. When World War Two pulled the economy out of the toilet, he diversified the business into iron to help with the war effort. Things were good again for another ten years. But then the unthinkable happened."

Marcus interrupted the conversation by entering the room and walking straight to Seaton. "Excuse me, sir. I have important news. I've received word that Glenwood Springs has been set up as the new headquarters for the search effort for Michael. I've also heard that a U.S. marshal has been dispatched there to take over the manhunt. Sir, they have checkpoints everywhere. Michael will never make it through if he travels the roads."

"I need to get to Denver tonight to start preparing my findings for the shareholders' meeting," Michael said.

"You'll never make it through if you travel the roads," Marcus replied.

Concern showed in Seaton's face. "He can take the jet this evening when the weather clears a bit."

"Is it safe to wait that long?" Michael asked.

"The airport's still closed for the weather, so you don't have a choice," Seaton replied. "But don't worry. They suspect you in my son's death, so this is the last place they'll think you could be hiding."

"Sir, what about Reynard?" Marcus said.

"Reynard?" Michael asked.

"My butler: Reynard Hopkins. He was very close to the twins when they were younger. He did as much to raise them as anyone when they lived here. He's not exactly one to wear his emotions on his sleeve, but I know Luke's death must be hitting him hard. Nothing's been made public about you. It might be best if he didn't know you were involved."

"You don't trust him?" Michael asked.

"That's not it. I do trust him, but that doesn't mean I know how he'd react to something like this."

Just then Hopkins appeared, with Michael's espresso on a silver tray. The three men already in the room ceased their conversation as Hopkins set the tray on the table between Michael and Seaton, and when he turned to leave the room, Marcus left with him.

"Don't worry, Michael," Seaton said once they were alone again. "We'll get you out of here. Now, please, you were telling me about your family's business. What happened?"

Michael looked down at the colorful Navaho rug beneath them, knowing he wouldn't be able to hold his head up during the rest of the story. "Well, eventually my great-grandfather stepped down and my grandfather took over the business in the 1950s. But my grandfather wasn't as savvy as his father or his grandfather. And he certainly didn't understand the accounting and financial procedures necessary for a business that size."

He took a long breath and exhaled. "Then one day his chief accountant didn't show up for work. He didn't show up the next day, either. Then the bank called. That's when my grandfather discovered that the man he had put in charge of watching over the company's finances had embezzled a fortune without my grandfather suspecting a thing."

Seaton shifted in his chair, and Michael thought he heard a muffled grunt.

"Then my grandfather learned that the company was in debt. Most of the family wealth was tied up in the business, and now the worst imaginable scenario had happened. After seventy years of operations, the family business was destroyed in the space of a few years. And down with it went the community. My grandfather was a third-generation owner of Chapman Steel, and now he had to live with the fact that he had let the business that his grandfather and father had built be destroyed. Gone was the family business that he had hoped to pass down to his son, my father, who was about ten at the time."

"Dear God," Seaton said.

Michael glanced up to see the billionaire looking at him with sad eyes, and it occurred to him that the man may understand better than anyone what his grandfather had experienced, because Seaton, too, had witnessed his company grow and now saw its potential doom by the crimes of others.

"Obviously, everything changed after the bankruptcy," Michael said, his eyes retreating back to the safety of the rug. "The family had little money left, and my grandfather could no longer hold his head up."

"What did he *do*?" Seaton asked with a note of concern, as if he feared the story might end in a suicide.

"He moved my grandmother and my father to Kansas, where they would try to build a new life. But my father told me my grandfather could never completely bury the past, and during the last years of his life, when I was old enough to understand something of what had happened, there were times when I thought I spied him glancing with a deep sadness into the tragedy that happened on his watch."

"That's horrible," Seaton said, almost whispering.

"I believe it was because of my grandfather's mistakes that my father got so interested in accounting, as if he was trying to prove something—as if he was somehow making amends for the town that had died because of his family's inability to protect it."

Seaton looked at Michael as if he had just witnessed something profound. "And so now," he said, "you—like your father—feel some responsibility to make amends for your grandfather's mistakes?"

"I don't know," Michael said. "Yes, I suppose so."

"But it *isn't* your responsibility," Seaton said, as if still trying to comprehend.

Michael saw in his mind's eye the image of his grandfather, sitting in a rocking chair on the front porch of his house and staring blankly into the dark night. "Mr. Seaton, I have to do everything I can to prevent your company from being destroyed by this fraud."

Michael realized he had kept these thoughts locked away in his mind for too long as he was unraveling the fraud at X-Tronic, and now he felt some relief after finally telling the story aloud to someone else. Outside the huge window behind Seaton, the snow fell as if it had never stopped, and the wind picked up, swaying the evergreens into each other like drunken sailors walking arm in arm. The second wave of the storm was coming fast.

54

THE YUKON PULLED into Glenwood Springs, barreling through snowdrifts that the storm had built in the streets during the night, jostling its three passengers. At last, the truck lurched to a stop, sliding sideways into a parking lot where a half-dozen mountain rescue jeeps already waited.

The three men jumped out of the Yukon and headed toward the rustic sheriff's office. Beasley looked sporty in his cashmere jacket; Noble, trying to hide his annoyance with the cold, was bundled in a heavy ski parka; and Kano betrayed his city roots by wearing a black trench coat that fell past his knees.

Inside the building, a disarrayed group of officers tried frantically to manage the biggest manhunt any of them had ever seen.

"Captain Muller?" Kano asked.

"Sheriff Muller," announced a stout man with a trace of Native American ancestry in his weathered features, emerging from the center of the group.

"Sorry, Sheriff. I'm Jason Kano with the U.S. Marshal's

Office of Colorado. We understand you've begun a local search for one of our fugitives."

Muller gave a gruff chuckle, but then his face locked into the serious expression of a man clearly in charge of his turf. "He's not a fugitive—he's a suspect in a murder investigation and therefore doesn't fall under your jurisdiction. This is our county, our suspect, and our search."

"There's a federal warrant out for Chapman's arrest," Kano replied. "The moment your officer pulled a gun on Chapman and had him on the ground, he was legally considered to be in custody." He glanced around the room: concrete walls with paint that looked decades old, two file cabinets scratched up and jammed in a corner, gray paint peeling from the baseboards like a snake shedding its skin. He spoke clearly to make sure everyone understood that his authority superseded everyone else's here. "When Chapman overpowered the officer, he technically became an escaped fugitive, even though he hasn't been sentenced for a crime. The investigation is suspended until Chapman is reapprehended. As a federal fugitive whose last known whereabouts were in Colorado, the hunt for him falls under the direct jurisdiction of the U.S. Marshal's Office of Colorado. That's why I've been dispatched to take control of your search and to lead the coordination efforts from this point forward. I appreciate the full cooperation of you and your men. You need to bring me up to speed on everything that's happened here in the past twelve hours."

Looking blindsided by Kano's rapid and concise explanation of his authority over the manhunt, the sheriff seemed to accept that the marshal was now in charge. Nodding to acknowledge the newcomer's seniority, the sheriff led Kano into a makeshift operations room. On the wall was a large map of Colorado with red and blue pushpins scattered at various locations.

The sheriff pointed a thick finger at the map. "Blues are towns or campgrounds we believe Chapman may be trying to hide in. Reds are checkpoints we've set up along highways or roads."

Kano memorized the map at a glance. "You think he's either still in the area or heading for Grand Junction," he determined from the placement of pins.

"That's exactly right," the sheriff said, a little awed by the marshal's instant grasp of the situation. "We know he's suspected of the murder in Vail, so he was obviously heading west through the mountains. We think that his original plan was to go through Grand Junction—maybe all the way to Las Vegas or L.A.—but he may have been forced to stop over in one of these locations because of the storm."

"Why west?" Kano said, standing in front of the map. "Why not go back to Denver? That's where he lived."

The sheriff clomped over to the small wood table with three metal folding chairs pushed unevenly into it. Sitting on the table, he propped a foot on one of the chairs and stared at Kano with renewed confidence. He seemed back in his comfort zone. "Before Officer Rodale tried to arrest him, Chapman said he was going to Grand Junction," the sheriff said matter-of-factly.

"And you believe that?" Kano's eyes had drifted above the map to a water stain in the ceiling.

"He obviously panicked after he killed the man in Vail— wanted to get as far away from Denver and Vail as possible. Going west is the best way. He may have figured the storm would make it hard for law enforcement units to respond in the mountain region, which could buy him time—maybe an extra day."

Kano looked over his shoulder at the sheriff. "We don't know for sure that he killed the man in Vail. And he didn't seem to panic when your officer pulled a gun on him." He grinned a little, as if he was starting to find the whole thing fun. "No, there's something else going on here. Did you check to see if he has any family in the area?"

Frustrated, the sheriff glanced back at the open door leading into the main room, where the other officers had fallen into a general chatter, oblivious to the conversation in the next room. "We're still waiting on the FBI database for his file request. Having some sort of glitch with the file—trouble accessing his information. Could be the storm. Resource priority may have changed. Most of the state is shut down right now, and I'm not sure how many channels the request had to go through."

Kano looked back at the map, his long leather coat swaying slightly as he moved. "You know, Sheriff, when I was a kid, my church used to have these huge Easter egg hunts once a year. They would tell us how many eggs had been hidden in this little park across from the church. And as all the other kids used to cluster together in certain areas, I would always go as far away from the others as possible. I was always alone on my hunts." He clasped his hands behind his back. "You see, there would be too many kids concentrated in one area, while they left entire sections unsearched. This increased my chances of finding more eggs than anybody else. And while they always fought over the few eggs that had been hidden in the most obvious spots, I would find lots more in the most unusual places."

Kano turned back to Beasley, standing in the doorway. "Let's not waste our time with this," he said. "If Chapman was in one of these places, we would have found him by now. Focus all our efforts on the areas that no one's thought of looking at yet. Start by examining his phone bills over the past few months. I want a list of all the places he's had incoming or outgoing calls that are between Vail and Las Vegas. I don't think he's trying to run from anything. He seems too calculating to just be doing something random and desperate. I think he's moving towards someone or someplace that he knows."

*   *   *

Kano was seated in a wooden chair next to a window. The blizzard outside was moving slowly through the mountains, and it seemed that the marshals were currently in the center of it. He heard a knock at the door.

"We have three locations," Beasley said, coming into the room. "The first is the home of a Dr. Melvin Speer, who lives just outside Breckenridge. The second is a camping lodge between here and Grand Junction. The third is the home of a Don Seaton, who lives in Aspen."

"Seaton?"

"Uh-huh. Father of the victim."

"When was that call dated?"

"About a month ago."

"All right. We'll focus our efforts on those three areas until we hear something. It's been sixteen hours since our last known sighting of Chapman. Sheriff Muller will provide us with two additional unmarked vehicles. Have Anthony visit Dr. Speer, you investigate the camping lodge, and I'll pay a visit to Don Seaton in Aspen. Contact local law enforcement in each area and have them provide armed backup in case we find Chapman at one of these sites. Make the calls now; we leave in five minutes."

As the others scattered from the room, Kano grabbed his coat and moved outside to the snowy parking lot. It was cold and windy. Overcast clouds floated low over the area, slicing the peaks off the white mountains surrounding the town. The sky was even darker in the east, warning him of the returning storm. Between the snowstorm and law enforcement, Colorado was in complete lockdown. Wherever Mr. Chapman was hiding, he would be stuck there, and it was only a matter of time before Kano found him.

Anthony and Beasley joined him outside, where they stood in silence, heads down, peering at the snowy ground. He slapped Beasley on the shoulder and nodded at Anthony, and the three men climbed into separate four-wheel-drive vehicles. At the highway intersection they split up: Anthony toward Breckenridge, Beasley toward Grand Junction, and Kano toward Aspen.

55

———————◦◦❋◦◦———————

MICHAEL EXPLORED THE mansion like a child in a
museum. Seaton and Marcus had left for Vail early this
morning to claim Lucas's body. There had been a temporary
break in the storm, but more bad weather had started an hour
ago.

On the second level of the mansion, the walls were decorated
with historic artifacts and cultural souvenirs: the first model of a
Westchester clock sat next to a "Zulu egg" from the New
Orleans Mardi Gras; a Manet oil hung across from a Warhol.

"Can I help you, sir?"

Michael turned, surprised to see that Hopkins, impeccably
turned out in black livery, had sneaked up behind him.

"Here to give me a tour of the place, are you Mr. Hopkins?"

"If you desperately require one, sir," he replied.

"Tell me, Mr. Hopkins, how long have you been with Mr.
Seaton?"

"Twenty-five years, sir." He spoke the answer as if reading a
poem.

A slight smile emerged on Michael's face. He envied the intimate understanding that Hopkins must have of Don Seaton's complicated life. "So you knew him before his wife's death," Michael mused aloud. "What was he like then?"

"I couldn't say, sir."

Michael tilted his head. "Oh, come on, Hopkins, you can tell me more than that. This place seems so lifeless, so forgotten. And Mr. Seaton spends half his life locked up in this estate these days." Michael turned to the bookcase and ran a finger along the bindings. "I remember reading about him when I was in college. He traveled the world on extreme adventures before my generation even conceived of the idea. He was the idol of everyone from entrepreneurs to alpinists. He was the one man everyone in America envied—energetic, rich, smart, a beautiful wife, twin sons . . ."

Michael withdrew his hand from the books and looked around at the lifeless artifacts in the room. "His wife's death changed everything, didn't it? This place turned from Camelot to a ghost town. Now this place has no joy or life. It's cold and dark, isolated up here in the snowy mountains, away from the world. It has nothing but memories."

"Mrs. Seaton's death was a loss to us all," Hopkins said, maintaining his stiff demeanor. "If you insist on comparing the past with Camelot, sir, then you should recognize what happens when the queen is taken from the kingdom. You are right: in many ways it turned our bright world dark. And now we're facing another tragedy with the loss of Lucas—one of the princes of this little kingdom, if you will. Mr. Seaton is a strong man, and he has dealt with the devastating events of his life as best he can. Sometimes, sir, we find ourselves at a point in life where all we have to hold on to *are* memories."

Michael noticed a family portrait on the wall: Seaton and his wife sitting on a white bench, with Lance and Lucas standing behind them. The boys looked about ten, but the defining features of their faces were already set. It must have been among the last pictures of all four together. Seaton looked much younger, full of the energy Michael remembered from early biographies. Michael saw something of his own life reflected in the oppressive sadness of the mansion, saw his joy and energy being steadily drained away by the mounting tragedies.

"Mr. Hopkins, sir," a younger servant announced, entering the room, "there is a visitor at the front door who wishes to speak with Mr. Seaton. His name is Jason Kano, and he's a federal marshal from Denver."

"I'll be right down," Hopkins said. After the servant left, Hopkins turned back to Michael. "Do you know anything about this?"

Michael took a moment too long to reply. "I think Mr. Seaton would want you to get rid of the marshal as quickly as you can."

Hopkins held Michael's gaze for a second, then turned and left the room.

Jason Kano waited patiently in the receiving hall of the Seaton mansion. He heard footsteps approaching. A servant, much older than the one who had greeted him, came toward him.

"Mr. Kano, I'm Reynard Hopkins, Mr. Seaton's butler."

"So, then, Mr. Seaton's not here," the marshal replied. "Any chance he's in Aspen Village? I'd like to ask him a few questions, if possible."

Surprised that Kano had so quickly deduced Seaton's absence, Hopkins made a mental note that the marshal had a talent for perceiving and assimilating small details.

"You are correct in your assumption, sir. Mr. Seaton is not currently present at the estate. Unfortunately, he is not in Aspen, either. Perhaps I may be of some assistance."

"Perhaps," Kano said, looking around the room. "I'm investigating the murder of his son Lucas. I apologize;

'investigating' is not the correct word. I'm leading the manhunt for our lead suspect in Lucas's death."

"You have a suspect?" Hopkins asked, unable to hide his intrigue.

"Yes. Someone Lucas knew through an accounting firm contracted by X-Tronic—a man by the name of Michael Chapman. His vehicle was spotted an hour north of here last night, and we're expanding our search parameters to include Aspen."

A slight gasp escaped Hopkins's lips. Kano turned when he seemed to sense something wrong, but he caught only the end of the butler's reaction. "Is something wrong?" he asked.

"Did you say Michael Chapman, sir?"

"You know him?" Kano asked. "Has he attempted to contact Mr. Seaton or anyone else in the household? Mr. Hopkins, please think carefully. This is very important. He's a fugitive, and he's considered armed and extremely dangerous."

"Mr. Chapman . . . yes, of course I know him," Hopkins said. "I met him when he came here."

"He's *here*?"

"He *was* here, sir. Last month, for a party that Lance and Lucas held."

"Last month? And you haven't seen him since?"

"I'm afraid not, sir," Hopkins replied.

The marshal nodded, as if to say he had nothing further to discuss. "Well, sorry for the intrusion. I need to return to Glenwood Springs. If you don't mind, could you give me Mr. Seaton's cell phone number? I'd like to ask him a few questions. Anything he could tell us about Michael Chapman would be useful."

"Of course, sir," Hopkins said. "I'll have someone get you the information on your way out. Good day, sir, and good luck with your search. What happened to Lucas was a tragedy, and justice must be served."

Hopkins nodded at the man, turned, and left the receiving hall. As soon as he was out of the marshal's sight, he quickened his pace until he found the underbutler, and instructed him to give the marshal Seaton's contact information. And then, with all the speed that stiff decorum would allow, Hopkins strode down the well-appointed hallways toward the security room at the mansion's far end.

56

HOPKINS WATCHED THE video monitor from the security room, panning through different video feeds until he saw Jason Kano leaving the premises. Then he flipped to the upstairs hall monitors and saw Michael walk into Seaton's study.

Closing the door to the security room, the butler pressed the speaker button on the gray Avaya phone beside the monitors. The speed dial's tone trilled a few seconds before Seaton answered.

"I'm sorry to trouble you, sir, but I have a rather urgent matter to discuss."

"Go ahead, Hopkins," Seaton replied.

"Sir, we have just received a visit from a U.S. Marshal Jason Kano. He claims to be heading a statewide manhunt for Mr. Chapman. He wants him in connection to Lucas's death. Mr. Kano said that Chapman is the lead suspect in the investigation of the accident."

"What did you tell him?" Seaton asked.

"I told him that I met Mr. Chapman at the twins' party a month ago and hadn't seen him since."

"Thank God, Hopkins," he said, his relieved sigh audible over the line. "Listen, this is a trifle hard to explain, so I need you to trust me. Lance and Lucas have been trying to undermine my efforts to fight the proposed merger between X-Tronic and Cygnus. They wanted the merger to go through so they could hide accounting frauds they have been instigating at X-Tronic. I believe they are trying to take control of X-Tronic's operations after the merger, and they are determined enough that I even believe they were responsible for the death of an external auditor a few months ago. Michael also discovered the fraud, and when the boys found out, they tried to kill him. Lucas died during the attempt on Michael's life. I know this sounds crazy, but I need you to do everything you can to protect Michael Chapman from the police. I've arranged for him to take my jet back to Denver so he can work on some important items for me. The pilot's been instructed to do whatever is necessary to get Michael to Denver tonight. Do you understand? Hopkins, I need your help on this not just as an employee, but as a gentleman and a friend."

"I quite understand," Hopkins replied, trying to blot out images of the twins playing in the woods behind the mansion as children, trying not to think of all the times he had taken care of them.

Seaton continued, "Whatever happens, it is imperative that Michael leave for Denver on my jet this evening. He may need your help getting past the authorities. I don't know how they managed to link me to his whereabouts, but you must assume that they have the estate under surveillance. I'm counting on you, Hopkins. You must make sure Michael gets away."

"I understand, sir," Hopkins said. Seaton ended the call, and he turned to look back at the monitors, watching Michael move through the hallways. *So you killed a prince of Camelot,* he thought to himself. *And now even the king has gone mad!*

*   *   *

Michael had just finished outlining part of the presentation that Seaton would need for the X-Tronic shareholders' meeting. He disconnected the thumb drive from the computer and slipped it into his pocket. Then he placed an emergency call to the First United Bank after-hours line to schedule a meeting Sunday to retrieve the X-Tronic documents in his safety deposit drawer.

As he finished the call, he noticed Hopkins standing in the doorway. "Is the marshal gone?" Michael asked.

"Yes."

"What did he want?"

"You," Hopkins replied.

Michael frowned. "Did he say why?"

"Yes." A long silence followed.

Michael didn't know how much Hopkins knew, so he decided to ignore the subject unless the butler pressed it. But Hopkins hadn't sold him out. If the marshal had received the least intimation that he was here, local law enforcement would have stormed the mansion and he would already be in custody.

"Mr. Seaton needs me to travel to Denver tonight," Michael said, a little louder than he meant to. It made him nervous that Hopkins lingered in the doorway without actually entering the room. "I am to leave for the airport in an hour to catch his jet."

"Yes, sir, I'm aware of your schedule. I spoke with Mr. Seaton a moment ago. He wants me to make sure no one interferes with your making that flight. Sir, I recommend that you leave through the back of the estate. I'm told that you are already familiar with the landscape, so I will have a car waiting for you on the other side of the property wall. I will send a decoy vehicle out the front drive since they will surely be watching."

"I have a rented Volvo just outside the back of the property," Michael said.

"Not anymore. Mr. Graham moved it into the garage early this morning."

"Marcus did? How? I still have the keys."

"He is a very talented man," Hopkins said evenly. "Don't worry, we will have someone leave a new vehicle for you—something better suited for these weather conditions should you have need of additional performance . . . and you might. Trust me, the marshal is having the estate watched."

Michael pondered Hopkins's words. "How do you know?" he asked, still lost in thought.

"We have cameras around the property—quite well concealed. He has three vehicles out front and two in the rear of the estate, on the road leading to the pass. But they left an opening. They don't have anyone on the service road through the Parks and Wildlife land on the other side of the hill. It passes down by the creek bank and leads directly to the airport highway. You'll be using an off-limits government road to avoid the government," Hopkins said, giving the closest approximation of a smile that Michael had yet seen from him.

"A government road? Sounds like a good place for a trap," Michael pointed out. "No offense, but am I sure I can trust you?"

"Mr. Seaton trusts you, I trust Mr. Seaton, and now it appears that you must trust me—it seems to be the only way you're going to make it back to Denver tonight."

Michael smiled as he looked at Hopkins in a new light. Perhaps this was not the reserved butler he had taken him for. "Hopkins, I think you and I would get along well if we had a chance to grow on each other."

"If you think so, sir."

"Thank you," Michael said. Hopkins nodded before leaving the room, and Michael was grateful that he had not been obliged to explain Lucas's death to him.

He turned out the lights in the study and moved through the shadows toward the window. Through the sliver between the curtains, he tried to look past the falling snow into the dark, cold wilderness beyond. His training gave him confidence enough to keep his cool and focus on the situation the way a good chess player would, thinking five or more moves ahead instead of just one or two. But this man Kano had training, too, and was good enough to track him here. That worried him.

He stepped away from the curtains and stood in the center of Seaton's dark den. Things had gone much further than he ever intended, and he would have to push them further yet if he wanted to follow this through to the end.

57

⸺⊶⁕⊷⸺

MICHAEL LEFT THE mansion through the kitchen, the same way he had entered last night. He stood in the dark for a few minutes, allowing his eyes to adjust to the faint light in the backyard. Pressing the dim LED on his watch, he read "8:24:38"—only twenty-two more seconds before he would run. By now Hopkins would be sitting in the '63 Rolls-Royce Phantom, waiting for the precise moment. The backyard security lights had been disarmed. Everything was ready. He crouched like a sprinter in the blocks, resting a hand against the cold door, and got ready to run faster than he ever had in his life.

Jason Kano stood next to three Aspen police jeeps on the snowy road hidden from the mansion's front gate. Vapor from his breath rose into the night as he panned the binoculars across the terrain. The front entrance to the mansion was partly visible between the trees.

"What makes you think he's in there, Marshal?" asked a young Aspen police officer who stood next to him.

"Can't say if he's in there or not, but that butler was sure hiding something."

"How do you know?"

"His eyes widened slightly during the conversation," Kano responded. "That's his tell. He had been very reserved at first, but his eyes widened when I asked about Chapman and mentioned he was a murder suspect. It was only for a second; then his eyes returned to normal when he answered the question. That's when I knew he was holding something back."

Suddenly the front lights of the mansion blazed on, and a silver Rolls-Royce pulled out of the five-car garage. "This is it!" Kano announced into his radio to the other patrol cars in the area. "Watch the lead man and concentrate on the target! Hit 'em hard, boys! Go, go, go!"

Michael exploded from the back of the mansion as the front lights blazed from the other side of the estate like an exploding star. He tripped and fell in the deep snow as he entered the woods, then pushed himself up to continue his hell-for-leather sprint. Slipping wildly in the snow, he scrambled through the woods, which darkened around him as he got beyond the range of the house lights.

Sprinting around a hummock of aspens, he vaulted a thick stone wall and fell into a deep snowdrift on the other side. And there, glowing like a beacon, not forty yards away, he saw the parking lights of a Range Rover. The keys were in the ignition. There was no trace of whoever had brought the vehicle. He started the engine and within seconds was rolling quietly along the snow-covered road, toward the airport.

Kano waited impatiently for news from the checkpoint officers at the bottom of the hill. He wanted his men out of sight of the mansion when they stopped the Rolls, but the minutes it was taking for the patrol jeep to intercept it felt like an eternity.

"Marshal Kano?" a voice finally broke through the radio. "We've searched the vehicle. Our man's not here. Over."

"Who's in the car? Over."

"Two men who claim to be the butler and the master chef. Their IDs check out. They say they're heading into town for some supplies."

Kano shook his head in frustration. "Let 'em go," he said, swearing under his breath. Then a thought occurred to him, as he flashed back to the privileged lifestyle of his childhood. His father had been one of the top heart surgeons in the San Francisco Bay area, and young Jason had attended plenty of black-tie parties. Even as a child, his gift for identifying individual behaviors had been well developed. He turned to the young officer standing next to him.

"Butlers and cooks don't get along."

"What . . . ?"

"Conflicting orders, constantly stepping on each other's toes. I've never met a butler and a cook that got along. They're not going out to get supplies, not together . . . not on a night like this!"

"I don't follow."

Kano closed his eyes to finish his thought. "The blast lights at the front of the mansion came on before they left, but they were already in the car. They didn't need the lights to move from the house to the garage. They wanted to get our attention. They wanted us to see them. They needed the cook so we'd see two people in the car! They wanted us to focus on the Rolls! Is there another road from the mansion? Something besides the mountain pass road behind the estate? Something smaller . . . a service road—*anything*."

The officer didn't know.

Kano ran toward his jeep. "Chapman's out!" he yelled into the radio. "Chapman's out of the mansion. Block off all roads around the estate, shut down the highway, and lock down all activity at the airport. He's on the move, trying to slip out. Close off every possible route from the area. He'll have nowhere to go."

58

M ICHAEL SAW THE police checkpoint outside the Aspen/Pitkin County Airport at the last moment. A car was idling in front of him, its driver speaking to the lone officer. He couldn't escape. He waited until the officer had let the other car go and waved him over. He inched the Range Rover forward and stopped a few feet short of the checkpoint, forcing the officer to walk towards him. He lowered the window as the man raised a flashlight and aimed it inside the vehicle.

"Sorry to bother you this evening, but we're having a little activity in the area at the moment. We're checking everyone's identity as they enter the airport. All departing flights have been grounded indefinitely."

"Really?" Michael said, trying to act surprised.

"Sir, could I please see some identification?" the officer asked.

"Yep, just a sec." Michael slid his hand into his pocket and tapped nervously on the mace canister Hopkins had given him before he left the Seaton estate. "What's all the hubbub?" he asked.

"We're looking for a fugitive we believe is in the area."

"Just one?" he said with a disarming smile.

"Just one. Identification, please."

Michael looked into the officer's eyes, desperately searching for a way out. He could tell that the man was getting suspicious—his fumbling hesitation was too obvious.

"Sir, could I ask you to step out of the car?"

Michael tightened his grip on the canister in his pocket. Looking at the officer, he nodded reassuringly, then whipped the mace from his pocket and sprayed him in the face.

The officer yelled, dropping the flashlight and raising both hands to his burning eyes and throat. He stumbled backward into a snowdrift off the road. Michael jumped from the car and moved toward the man to grab the shoulder radio, but he stopped dead in his tracks when he saw the man reaching for his gun. The blinded officer managed to draw his gun and was waving it wildly in the air. Michael took a step back toward the car. At the sound of the crunching snow, the officer fired two shots that flew past him and pierced the steel doors of the Range Rover. Michael dived into the vehicle as two more shots rang out and the passenger window exploded. Stomping on the accelerator, he sent the Rover lurching forward through the snow. Five more shots cracked behind him as the vehicle raced toward the airport.

Jason Kano was driving the big Yukon away from the estate when the call came over the radio: "Officer down! All patrols, we have a ten thirty-three at the Aspen airport. The officer down on the scene sighted the fugitive, Michael Chapman, fleeing in a black Range Rover. I repeat: we have a ten thirty-three at the Aspen airport. Officer down. All patrols respond to the location. Over."

Kano pushed the floor emergency break with his left foot, forcing the vehicle into a 180-degree slide on the snowy road before popping the release and accelerating in the direction of the airport. *What the hell are you doing, Chapman?* Kano thought to himself. *You're drawing too much attention. You'll never get out now.* His eyes flipped up to check his rearview mirror. *I thought you were smarter than that.*

Within five minutes, the Yukon had caught up with six patrol jeeps, their blue and red strobes flashing as they weaved through the outskirts of Aspen.

Michael flipped off his lights and turned toward the single runway that ran the length of the airport. The Rover's tires churned through the snow, and it plowed into the chain-link fence. The fence gave, and the big SUV rolled over it, bouncing violently over the uneven ground. Reaching the runway, Michael turned onto it, racing with his lights out toward the far end of the airport. As green airport lights flashed through the snow flurries, he was too focused on making it to the hangar to notice the flickering train of blue and red lights rolling up out of the distance behind him, toward the terminal.

He parked in back of the third hangar. Inside he found Seaton's pilot, Captain Steiner, walking around the corporate jet. He shook Steiner's hand and then fidgeted while the man continued to walk around the jet, finishing the preflight check. The pilot seemed to examine every rivet and hinge pin. Finally he turned to Michael and gave a brisk nod. "Ready to go," he said.

Michael jogged toward the platform stairway. "I want you to turn off all the lights to the hangar and the jet. Do it before you open the door."

"I can't do that," Steiner protested. "It's against FAA regulations, not to mention bloody dangerous."

"And you can't radio the tower for clearance," Michael said. "This will have to be a blind takeoff. Because of the angle of the airport's location between the mountains, I'm told the runway has only one direction for landings and one for takeoffs, so you don't need the tower's radar for takeoff."

"Wait a second! What you're asking is ridiculous—I can't do it."

Michael had assumed he would encounter some problems with the pilot. "Read this, please," he said, handing Steiner an envelope that Seaton had given him this morning before leaving for Vail.

The pilot opened the envelope and read the short handwritten note. Then, folding it in half and tucking it into his pocket, he exhaled slowly. "I'll lose my license for this," he said, "maybe even go to jail."

"You won't go to jail," Michael promised him.

The captain nodded reluctantly. "So what exactly do you want me to do?"

"I want you to get me out of Aspen. We need to get this jet off the ground in the next very few minutes—before the police discover that Mr. Seaton has a jet here. Once they find out about this jet, they'll surround the hangar to prevent us from taking off. There isn't much time."

"It may already be too late," Captain Steiner said, looking through the cracked hangar doors at an approaching police jeep.

"Damn it!" Michael growled. "Start up the jet and get ready to taxi out of the hangar. Leave the fuselage door open so I can get into the cabin. I'll stay here to open the hangar doors and make sure no one from the jeep comes over here. I'll let you know when we need to take off."

But the moment he finished speaking, all the runway lights went out, casting the open stretch in front of the hangar in darkness. At the same time, two medium-size maintenance trucks lumbered onto the field and parked in the middle of the runway. After stopping, the drivers jumped out of the vehicles and ran back through the snow toward the terminal.

"Dear God!" Captain Steiner exclaimed. "Now it's impossible. I can't take off with those trucks parked in our path."

Michael looked into the sky and saw a small light approaching the airport four thousand feet above. "There's a plane up there," he said.

"Yes," the pilot confirmed, looking at the blurred light faintly visible through the thinning clouds above. "And they're landing. No one's taken off from this airport in over twenty-four hours. That's someone else up there, coming into Aspen. They're landing here for sure."

"If they're landing here, then the tower will be forced to turn the runway lights back on and move the trucks," Michael said, a note of hope creeping into his voice.

"Yes, but they'll only move them for a minute or two, just as the plane is landing. They'll want to keep the airport as locked down as possible because of you."

"But we will have a small window, right?"

"A *very* small window. I'll have the jet ready. The moment the runway lights come on and the trucks start to move, we could throw the intake jets to full power. There might just be enough time to accelerate onto the runway and take off before the other plane lands. The timing's critical. If we don't get off the ground in time, the other plane'll hit us from behind as it's coming in."

"We can't put the other plane in danger," Michael said. "Will it work? I need to know if it'll work."

"It'll work," Captain Steiner said. "From its airspeed, the other plane looks small. If it doesn't look like we'll make it, they'll have maneuverability during their descent. They won't be in danger. The biggest danger is that we'll be exposing ourselves if we can't take off in time."

"Okay," Michael said. "We don't have much time. That plane will be landing in less than five minutes, and the police could be here any second. Get the jet ready. I'll open the hangar doors and keep an eye on the jeep that's coming at us. The moment the lights come on, I'll jump into the jet and let you know that we're ready to take off."

As Captain Steiner jogged back toward the jet, Michael crouched just inside the hangar doors, watching the blurry halos of the approaching jeep's headlights in the falling snow. From his waistband, he pulled the gun he had taken from the police officer yesterday, and held it low to the ground. Arming himself against law enforcement—how had things come to this awful pass? Forcing himself to breathe deeply and evenly, he counted the seconds, waiting for Captain Steiner to ready the jet, waiting for the incoming flight to circle to its final descent. The patrol jeep was going to arrive at the hangar before he could escape. He prayed that he would have the strength—and the luck—to do what was necessary to escape.

59

—◦❈◦—

T HE YUKON SCREECHED to a stop ten feet from the glass
doors to the terminal. Jumping out into the packed snow of
the parking lot, Kano ran toward a bewildered-looking security
guard, who had run outside to meet the wailing sirens.

"Jason Kano, U.S. Marshal's Office. What's the situation?"
he asked urgently.

"No sight of your man, sir. We've double-checked all
surveillance footage running for the past twenty minutes.
Nothing!"

"Have all your men reported in? The fugitive has already
taken out two officers since all this started."

"Yes, all my men are accounted for. How are the two officers
doing?"

Kano looked away from the guard and waved his men to
spread out along the entrances. "Both are fine. Chapman seems
to have the ability to subdue armed men without severely
injuring them."

"Except for that rich guy he killed," the guard added.

Kano shot him an annoyed look. "He's considered armed and extremely dangerous. I don't want anyone trying to take him down alone. If someone spots him, they are to report to me immediately. I'm the only one that will coordinate Chapman's apprehension. Understand?"

Kano followed the security officer into the terminal. An intercom interrupted the chaos with another apology for the continued flight delays, falsely blaming the weather to prevent civilian panic. Inside the small terminal, the people in line sat on the floor, leaning against walls, or used their carry-on luggage as uncomfortable pillows. Babies cried, and the air was stale.

"Lot of people," Kano said.

"All flights for the past twenty-four hours were canceled due to the blizzard. Most of these passengers have been waiting here since yesterday. They were hoping to get out this evening, but just when the weather was looking better, we got word to lock everything down because of Chapman."

Kano looked at the weary faces of the trapped travelers. "Have those guys start making as many pizzas as they can," he said, pointing to the pizza stand in the small food court. "Then start passing out the food to everyone."

"Who's gonna pay for that?" the security officer asked.

"Don Seaton harbored a fugitive; that's what caused this problem. Send him the bill—he can afford it."

The security officer laughed before giving the order to one of his men.

Kano turned his focus back to finding Chapman. "You've passed out his picture to your men?" he asked.

"Yes. You know, if I may say so, I don't think there's much chance that he's even here. All departing flights have been canceled, and no one's seen him anywhere on the premises. After he had trouble at the outside checkpoint, he probably hightailed it. I mean, why would he even be here? He would have known that the moment the downed officer reported the encounter, we'd react by halting all takeoffs. If he's as smart as you say, he'd leave the airport and try to find another way out of the area."

"No," said Kano. "He knew there was no other way out. The airport was his only chance. There must be a reason he'd still come here." He looked around the terminal at the weary travelers. His eyes paused on a businessman leaning into the relative privacy of a pay phone to talk on his cell. The man wore a tan overcoat over an expensive suit.

"A lot of millionaires live in Aspen, right?"

"Quite a lot, I'd say."

"How many own private jets?" Kano asked, turning toward the officer.

"Jesus! You think Chapman has access to a personal jet?"

"Find out if Don Seaton has a plane here!"

The man spoke into his radio, waited a few seconds, and said to Kano, "No. Nothing."

"You're telling me that one of the richest men in the United States doesn't own a jet?" Kano looked down at the tiled floor; then his eyes shot back up at the security officer. "Wait . . . X-Tronic! See if there's anything listed under X-Tronic."

The security officer relayed the question into his radio. Listening, he nodded to the marshal. "Yeah. X-Tronic has a jet registered in hangar twenty-six—that would be on the far side, close to the runway."

"This is U.S. Marshal Kano," Kano announced into his police radio. "I need two units to meet me outside the terminal. The fugitive is believed to be inside a hangar and trying to use a private jet to escape. Form a perimeter around all hangars and wait for my arrival. Go! Go! Go!"

60

———•❈•———

"**O**KAY!" MICHAEL SHOUTED toward the cockpit as he climbed into the jet. "Okay, Captain! Let's get the hell out of here!"

Captain Steiner looked back at the fuselage from the cockpit. "We're ready to go! The runway lights just came on and the trucks are starting to move out of our path! We can make it if we hit it right now!"

"The deputy in the jeep started to get out after I opened the hangar door, so I had to fire some shots near his jeep. He won't come any closer, but you can expect the police to be here in force soon. I'm ready! Let's get out of here!"

The pilot stood up to close the cockpit door. "Shut the airstair door; then take a seat and buckle up," he said. "It's gonna be bumpy, but we'll make it." Then he disappeared behind the cockpit door.

Michael turned to the outside door, still open with its stairs reaching down to the cold concrete of the hangar. He pressed the button and watched the steps slowly rise and fold into the fuselage. He prayed there would be enough time to get the jet off the ground before the incoming plane landed.

Jason Kano raced out a side door of the airport terminal and was met by a squadron of Aspen Volvo patrol jeeps bouncing across the uneven snow. As he burst out into the cold air, the runway lights blazed back on. "What the . . . ! Will someone please tell me why the runway lights are on?" Kano barked into his radio. "I gave specific instructions that all runway lights remain off!"

"Marshal Kano," a voice broke over the radio. "We have a situation here in the tower. There is an unscheduled incoming flight with government clearance on final approach. They are descending and landing here in Aspen. We have been forced to turn on the runway lights and have removed the trucks blocking the runways to accommodate their landing."

"No, no, damn it!" Kano shouted into the radio. "We think we know where the fugitive is located on the airport premises. Put those trucks back on the runway. Have the plane circle for twenty minutes before letting it land. We could have Chapman in custody in five minutes! Just have it circle the airport until I give the okay for it to land."

"That's a negative, Marshal. The plane has government clearance and is demanding to land immediately. The weather's getting worse, and this may be their best chance. They're already in their final descent. They'll be down in less than two minutes."

Kano pulled the radio away from his ear and waved the front jeep to a stop. Just as he slid into the passenger seat, the police radio crackled. "This is Deputy Lincoln. I'm on patrol on the south end of the runway and just had a visual on Chapman. He opened the door to a hangar and got inside a jet. It's starting to taxi out towards the takeoff strip. I repeat, Chapman is on a jet that just left a hangar on the south end of the runway."

"Lincoln! You're sure it was Chapman?" Kano asked into the radio.

"Yes, sir! I tried to stop him from getting on the jet, but he fired shots at me."

"How close is he to taking off?"

"The jet is about to turn onto the main runway!"

"Take us there now!" Kano said to the driver.

The jeep took off toward the runway with three other patrol jeeps in tow. The snow, being blown in hazy circles along the dark ground, blurred the surface as if it were a moving body of water. Kano could see other police units approaching from the side. Then, at the far end of the airport, he saw the jet turning onto the runway for takeoff.

"Hurry!" Kano yelled. "It's already on the runway . . . He's about to take off!"

Already the jet had moved onto the runway and was picking up speed, roaring past the green lights outlining the snowy runway. Kano's jeep, followed by three others, bounced violently across the uneven no-man's land between the taxiway and the runway. In the sky south of the airport, a low-flying jet descended toward the runway, its growing halos of light gleaming through the blustering snow.

Fishtailing wildly, Kano's jeep hurtled onto the runway just behind Seaton's jet, followed by the tight pack of patrol jeeps, but eventually the aircraft picked up speed and pulled away from them. Snow kicked up from the intake jets and was thrown back at the jeeps as the front wheel of the jet lifted off the ground.

"Pull back!" Kano said into the radio once he realized they couldn't prevent the takeoff. "We can't stop him! Pull back!" He turned to look at the growing spotlight in the sky behind them. "Stop the pursuit! Pull off the runway *immediately*! The other jet's nearly on the ground! It's coming in! Get off the runway *now*!"

The jeeps darted off the runway like quail running for cover, just as the incoming jet drifted over the front of the runway and touched down. One of the jeeps had flipped onto its side in the mad dash, but all were clear of the jet's path. Kano slammed his fist on the dashboard in frustration as the Seaton jet became airborne. The front lights of the jet vanished into the clouds, with only a faint red light blinking incessantly back at them, as if his escaping quarry were laughing at him.

Kano turned to the deputy at the wheel. "Get me back to the terminal. I need to contact the Air Force and have them ground Chapman's jet."

"Can you use military resources to help capture a fugitive?"

Kano glared at the security officer. "I don't have the authorization to use fighter jets to capture a fugitive for murder. But this has escalated."

"How?"

"Chapman just became a fugitive who has illegally taken off in a private jet and appears to be heading toward Denver. We don't know what he's capable of. It's not unreasonable to be concerned about a possible terrorist intention. That's within Homeland Security's warning protocol."

"You think he's a terrorist now?"

"I think Chapman has escalated this situation enough to justify taking actions appropriate for the national security protocol. I need to contact the Air Force. I'm not taking any more chances with him. We have to find a way to put that jet on the ground."

The police vehicles had almost arrived back at the terminal when another deputy's voice came over the radio. "Marshal Kano, we've made contact with the second jet. There is something you should know, sir. There is a man here who wants to speak with you. His name is Troy Glazier, and he appears to be an agent from the U.S Treasury Department. He says he needs to speak with you immediately about Michael Chapman!"

A *Treasury agent*? Was it possible Chapman had been telling the truth to the officer in Glenwood Springs? Chapman was accused of killing Lucas Seaton, so Kano still had a responsibility to capture him. But at least he could now get some answers about Chapman's background. As the police vehicle bounced through a snow drift with the airport's terminal shinning a hundred halos through the fast falling snow, Kano saw a large man in an overcoat at the base of the jet's airstair waving his arms frantically.

61

———————··❋··———————

"**G**OD DAMN IT!" Jerry Diamond screamed into the phone. "Those fucking little brats have done it again!"

"Slow down," John Falcon replied, holding the cell phone close to his ear while closing the door to his home office. "Just relax for a moment. Who's done what?"

"The twins. They tried to kill Michael Chapman. Haven't you been watching the news?"

"What are you talking about? The news said they tried to kill him?"

"No," Diamond replied. "The news is saying Lucas Seaton died skiing in Vail yesterday afternoon. Lance reported to the police that Michael Chapman pushed Lucas over a cliff during an argument. The details are fuzzy, but there's currently an arrest warrant out for Michael."

"Michael killed Lucas?" Falcon asked. He was still having trouble sorting out Diamond's frantic words.

"Hell, nobody knows for sure what happened up there. But you and I both know the kind of history the twins have, so I don't think it's a stretch to assume they tried to kill him. I can't believe they'd try to repeat the same mistake they made with Kurt Matthews."

Suddenly Falcon felt terribly vulnerable in this conversation. Something didn't seem right. Diamond was restating, in clear detail, too many things they both knew perfectly well. It was the last comment in particular, making specific reference to Kurt, that triggered the alarm bells. Was Diamond trying to get him to admit something over the open phone? Could Diamond be *recording* the call?

Falcon wasn't sure if he was just being overly suspicious or if his instincts were correct, but he wasn't taking any chances. He still hadn't said anything incriminating. "What are you talking about?" he said. "Kurt died alone in a skiing accident, and I know nothing about the twins' 'past,' as you call it. It's horrible that Lucas died yesterday, and if Michael had any involvement in it, I hope he's brought to justice."

"What?" The word was drawn out, signaling uncertainty, even confusion.

"Jerry," Falcon interjected before the man could say another word, "it's the weekend. Let's schedule a meeting Monday morning. Let's discuss any public news related to Michael, the twins, or X-Tronic that we need to consider. There is nothing we can do until we get more information about what happened; then we can determine how this will affect our work."

"Are you sure that's how you want to handle this?" Diamond asked.

"Yes, I'm sure. Thanks, Jerry." Falcon snapped his cell phone shut and walked to the double doors of his home office. He reached for the handle, then stepped back after seeing that his hand was shaking. He made a fist, pressed it against his lips, and held it there while he took a few slow breaths through his nose. Closing his eyes, he focused on the emergency scenario he had played out in his mind as a precaution during the past few years. Now the time had come, and he knew exactly what he must do.

Opening the door, he left his home office and walked briskly through the opulent home, tucked away in a gated community outside Denver. He entered the main dining room, where his wife, Karen, was coaching their two daughters in the fine points of making tuna casserole. Rounding the counter, he leaned over and whispered something in his wife's ear. She dropped the measuring cup and looked at him in fear. Leaving the children, she followed him into the next room.

"No," she said after closing the door behind them. "No, no, *no!*"

"We don't have a choice, sweetheart. We have to be prepared."

"No. I won't do it. The girls and I are staying right here. You'll find a way out of it. You always do."

"It's not that easy this time. This time it's not going to go away; it's only going to escalate. This could be our last chance to get out . . . We don't have a choice."

Her eyes teared as she covered her mouth in a vain attempt to keep her composure.

"Karen," he said, putting a hand on her shoulder.

"Don't!" she snapped. "Don't touch me." She moved away from him and reached for the door before turning back to look at him. "You are so stupid, you know that? So *stupid.* We had a *life* here." Then she turned and fled the room.

Falcon looked down at the immaculate white carpet, at the antique hutch and expensive furnishings that surrounded their lives. His wife was right. It would not be easy to leave their life in Denver behind, but they had no choice.

He left the room to return to his study. As he walked through their home, he could hear his wife leading the girls upstairs to pack. She would leave with them in the morning, and after wrapping up a few necessary things, he would join them.

As he entered his study, he flipped open his cell phone and dialed his account manager at the Imperial Bank in London.

Looking at his watch, he noted that it was just after five on a Sunday morning in England. Someone picked up on the third ring.

"Donovan here," a man said in a British accent.

"Donovan, it's John Falcon in Denver. Sorry to ring you at this hour, but I need you to transfer some funds for me."

"Yes, Mr. Falcon, just one moment, if you will—just logging into your file."

Falcon knew that Donovan had access to all banking files for Imperial from his home and that he offered twenty-four hour banking services, which was one of the reasons Falcon was so willing to pay the high premium for Imperial's services.

"Right, then, I have your information up. What would you like me to do?"

"How much do I have in all funds that can be liquidated within forty-eight hours?" Falcon asked.

"Just over forty-two million U.S. dollars."

"I want you to transfer all funds according to my profile strategy number three."

"Number three, sir? You're quite certain?"

"Yes, Donovan, I'm certain. Please execute all trades as soon as possible. Use the Tokyo exchanges if you have to, since their trading will commence fourteen hours before the New York exchanges reopen. After everything's liquidated, transfer them into the alternative accounts we set up a few years ago. Shake it around if you have to. I want it impossible for anyone to follow the money trail of my transfers. You understand?"

"Consider it done, Mr. Falcon. I'll have someone confirm to you after the transactions are complete." There was a short pause. "Anything else I may do to be of service?"

"Nothing else for now."

"Good luck, Mr. Falcon."

He looked out his study window at the piled snow on the street outside his drive. Then he looked at his watch. Forty-eight hours. He needed to wait for just the right moment to make his move. Timing was everything. He still had a chance.

62

———————·:❉:·———————

TWO F16Cs took off from Buckley Air Force Base at the Colorado Air National Guard in Aurora, having received an urgent command from Homeland Security in Colorado Springs to intercept a private jet en route from Aspen to Denver. They were to escort it to Peterson Air Force Base in Colorado Springs, where the occupants would be held until representatives from the U.S Marshal's Office and the Colorado attorney general's office arrived at the base. The Homeland Security director was currently speaking on the phone with the White House to determine the rules of engagement should the private jet refuse to deviate from its current course to Denver.

The fighters cut across the sky at 1,300 miles per hour in parallel formation. Dark shadows of mountain peaks shot past beneath them. As they outran the calm weather of the Front Range and closed in on the retreating remnants of the snowstorm, they tipped their noses to the heavens and climbed above the storm system. In less than fifteen minutes they had traveled halfway across the state of Colorado and could now see the subject aircraft on their radar.

Spreading out to both sides of the oncoming jet's path, they held their formation until the jet's beacon lights were in sight on the horizon. Both fighter craft slowed to 500 miles per hour so they would be visible to the pilot of the approaching aircraft. As the jet grew closer, the fighter pilots pulled away at the last moment, screaming past the jet with calculated precision that left no doubt about who controlled the situation.

After passing the private jet, the two fighters turned around in a crossing pattern and came up on it from behind. One of the pilots made radio contact, stating that the private jet was being placed under military detainment and would be escorted to Peterson Air Force Base in Colorado Springs. If the pilot did not comply, it would be shot out of the sky. Without any hesitation, the private craft gradually banked right, following the lead of the front fighter. The pilot of the second fighter radioed back to Homeland Security, reporting that Chapman had been intercepted and that the military police should be expecting them at the security landing strip in less than an hour.

"If Lucas Seaton was part of Chapman's investigation, then why would Chapman kill him?" Kano asked Troy Glazier in a small back office at the Aspen airport.

"He wouldn't," Glazier said, backhanding the air in front of his face, as if batting away the question. "This all has to be a mistake."

"Then why would he run?" Kano said, with an edge to his voice. He was obviously still upset about Michael's escape. "And why would he assault the officer in Glenwood Springs and then flee the scene as a fugitive."

The half-dozen other men in the room were growing uneasy at the escalating argument. Glazier's voice rose to match Kano's. "You have to understand how smart he is. I assure you, whatever it is, he has a very good reason for what he's doing."

"You can ask him yourself," Kano replied. "I just got word that Seaton's jet has been forced to land at Peterson Air Force Base. The military police have set up a teleconference in an interrogation room, and they'll patch us in as soon as Chapman's situated."

"I understand your situation, Marshal, but I'm asking you to give us some leeway here." Glazier felt his frustration building. He and Michael had worked too hard just to let some uncooperative marshal stall their investigation. "If Michael wasn't willing to give himself up, it was because there's something he needs to do first. He knows that given time, I can resolve this situation for him. We're in the middle of an investigation. I urge you to listen to what he has to say and to consider releasing him on bail. You can always conclude your investigation in a few weeks after we've finished our fraud case against X-Tronic."

"Accounting frauds don't concern me as much as murders do—I'm not about to authorize his release."

"Damn it!" Glazier yelled. "You're not hearing me. We've been working undercover for over two years to—"

"No. You're the one who's not listening," said Kano. "He's a fugitive wanted for murder. I'm not releasing him; that's final!"

Glazier glared at Kano, trying to control his seething anger. He thought of every possible favor that he could call in. He even considered the Treasury Secretary's influence over the Homeland Security Department. But even then it would take at least twenty-four hours to work through the red tape of the convoluted legal process that allowed one cabinet department to take precedence over another.

"Sir, we have a phone call for you," a deputy announced, handing a phone to Kano.

"This is Marshal Kano," he announced into the phone. His face muscles hardened as he listened to a voice on the other end of the line. "What! How is that possible? Keep questioning him! I want to know everything!"

Kano slammed down the phone and looked at Glazier. "That was Captain Gavin at the Air Force base. Chapman wasn't on the plane. They found the pilot and an Aspen sheriff's officer, Deputy Spencer Lincoln."

"Lincoln?" Glazier gurgled, dribbling coffee down his chin.

"Yes," Kano said. "The same deputy that called in and claimed to have seen Chapman taxiing onto the runway in the jet. Chapman must not have ever gotten on it, or he jumped out before it left the hangar. Christ! It was a decoy. The man that informed us of Seaton's jet on the radio must have been Chapman, pretending to be Lincoln. Damn it! We had every officer trying to prevent the jet from taking off. Chapman could have stolen Deputy Lincoln's clothes and police vehicle, and he would have had no problem slipping out through our checkpoints in a policeman's disguise after we already thought he escaped in the jet."

Furious, Kano yelled for a search to continue within a two-hundred-fifty-mile radius of Aspen. He had the feeling that they would never get as close to catching Michael again. As the room galvanized into action, Glazier had to turn his face away from Kano to hide his grin.

The all-wheel-drive police SUV had no trouble keeping traction on the snow-covered mountain roads. Michael had gone through five checkpoints coordinated by the U.S. Marshal's Service. He was still wearing Deputy Lincoln's uniform and had managed to roll through each police barricade with no more than a wave, while the highway patrol troopers gave every other car a meticulous check.

He hadn't planned to use the deputy's identity to escape, but when the man got out of the jeep and slowly approached the hangar through the blowing snow, he knew he had no choice but to stop him. Waiting until the deputy was peeking into the hangar, Michael had lunged out from the shadows and put him in a choke hold, rendering him unconscious in seconds. He had dragged the deputy into the hangar while Captain Steiner was busy going through the preflight checks in the cockpit. He removed the deputy's uniform before dragging him onto Seaton's jet and handcuffing him to the bed frame in the bedroom at the back of the fuselage. After shutting the bedroom door, he told Captain Steiner it was time to leave, without ever hinting to him that the deputy was aboard. Once the pilot closed the cockpit door moments before taxiing onto the runway, Michael pushed the button and watched as the airstair slowly folded up into the side of the jet. But just as it began the closing process, he took a running jump out of the jet, over the side of the staircase, to land hard but unhurt on the concrete floor of the hangar. He ran to the office behind the jet, threw on the deputy's uniform, and then circled outside, in the snow, to the idling police jeep. After assuming Deputy Lincoln's identity on the radio, he reported in a winded voice to Marshal Kano and started the false chase of the escaping X-Tronic jet. And then, just as every police vehicle was chasing the jet down the runway, he calmly drove through the airport's checkpoint—just a uniformed officer in a patrol jeep.

He had assumed that the jet would either be intercepted in flight or be traced by radar and apprehended once it landed. Almost three hours had elapsed since he left Aspen. He figured that Kano would soon find out he was not on the jet.

Hitting the last downhill stretch of I-70 toward the Denver skyline, he felt good to be home. He was still a fugitive at large, though, so he must take precautions. He needed to get to the Brown Palace Hotel, where Don Seaton had reserved the presidential suite. He would have the most lavish hideout in town. The X-Tronic shareholders' meeting was in four days, and he would need every minute to work on the presentation and

press release if he hoped to help Don Seaton expose the
conspirators without destroying the company. However, it would
be dangerous to drive the Aspen Police Department SUV all
around downtown Denver. Before he reached the city, he needed
to make a phone call.

63

———— :i✻i: ————

IN HIS ROOM at the downtown Hyatt, Lance Seaton laid his cell phone beside a silver laptop on the desk. The computer's liquid-crystal screen displayed four minimized windows. Two were secure links to offshore bank accounts, one was a user connection to a freight transport company in Los Angeles, and the last was a member sync-up with a GPS satellite service. He poured a second drink of Grey Goose vodka into a heavy tumbler with a sparkling Hyatt logo cut into the glass. Taking a sip, he felt the pleasant burn in his throat, which conjured memories of his brother and him drinking together atop of Aspen Mountain during a full moon party years earlier. Then his happy recollections turned to fury at the thought of Michael Chapman.

He had more than enough money stashed away to start a new life anywhere in the world he wanted. With the conspiracy at X-Tronic on the verge of exposure, he had no doubt that future indictments would eventually expose the murder of Kurt Matthews. But while he played through scenarios of a new life in hiding in Switzerland or New Zealand or Panama or Malaysia, he knew he couldn't leave Colorado before avenging his brother's death. The two calls he had just finished would help him conclude this final bit of business Stateside before he left the country forever.

*   *   *

Michael knelt as he watched another pair of headlights circle the parking lot. *Come on, be her!* he thought. He waited for the headlights to flash, but when they didn't, he ducked his head below the window and cursed. He was crouched in the driver's seat of the SUV, parked in one of the large ski shuttle lots between the Front Range and Denver, where people left their cars before carpooling into the mountains. He had thought about calling Alaska for help but hadn't wanted to involve her in his problems. Besides, it was Sarah who had helped put him on the path to discovering the fraud, and she understood the risks involved in helping him.

His eyes caught a new shifting pattern of highlights sliding along the ceiling of the SUV. He hadn't even had time to lift his head before he saw their rapid flashing. He opened the door and ran up to the red jeep.

"Go!" he said.

Sarah zoomed out of the lot, and as they turned onto the entrance ramp and merged onto I-70, they saw a Denver police cruiser with flashing lights race down the exit ramp across the highway, toward the parking lot.

"Is that for you?" she asked.

"Christ, of course—the SUV must have LoJack! Damn that was close!"

"What the hell's going on Michael!"

"They think I killed Lucas Seaton," he said.

"You're involved in that!" she said excitedly. "I knew it. I tried to call your cell when I saw on the news that he died, but your phone was off."

"I pulled the SIM card out after Vail," he said.

"What happened?"

It was time to tell her everything. As they raced along the highway toward the lights of Denver, he told her about Glazier and about being recruited as a federal agent for the Treasury Department. He told how twelve members of his cadet class had pulled different assignments throughout the country, focusing on the public accounting firms where fraud seemed likeliest. "Seattle, San Francisco, L.A., New York, Dallas, Chicago, Phoenix, Boston, Miami, Cleveland, Philadelphia, and Denver," he rattled off to show he was not alone.

"So you knew something illegal was going on at X-Tronic *before* my brother's death?" she said.

"No. I didn't even know if anything illegal was going on with any of the firm's clients. After the flood of financial scandals years ago, the Treasury Department decided to experiment with a shadow operation, sending agents under deep cover inside the high-risk areas of the financial world: essentially, the largest international accounting firms."

Another police cruiser, coming the other direction on the highway, flew past them with lights flashing. He leaned back in the seat, feeling suddenly exhausted.

"Hell, no one ever expected to actually stumble onto the next big fraud. These things are almost impossible to recognize from the outside—Treasury was only fishing. Prototype government agencies are routinely set up to experiment with new types of investigative procedures for all kinds of federal crimes in other sectors, so someone in Washington decided it was time to try something bold in the financial world. No one ever expected it to work this well. At most, we thought we'd get a clearer picture of the level of fraud prevention that firms were actually doing." He paused, looking at her, gauging her reaction. "I didn't even *begin* to suspect fraud at X-Tronic until after Kurt's death, and I hadn't found the right place to start looking until you e-mailed me about his notes. You brought 'em with you, right?"

"You said you needed them. They're in the back."

"Great! I also need some documents I have stored in a bank downtown. I'll be working nonstop in the Brown Palace, making the presentation that outlines the fraud, and it's too dangerous for me to move around Denver in the daylight. I can contact the bank and clear it for you to pick up the documentation Monday morning."

"Whatever you need," she said, "just as long as we bring Kurt's killers to justice."

"Bet on it."

The lights from downtown spread out in front of them. The snow had been cleared from the main highways and streets, but here in town he could see sand trucks with flashing yellow lights plowing through snow-covered neighborhoods that looked in deep-winter hibernation. The city seemed strangely quiet considering that in just a few days it would have the attention of the entire financial world.

64

——⊶◈⊷——

B Y MONDAY AFTERNOON, Michael had been working in the penthouse of the Brown Palace Hotel for thirty-six hours straight. He had compiled half his findings into a summary report for Don Seaton to present at the annual shareholders' meeting. Exhausted from the relentless work, he needed a break. He grabbed the phone and dialed a number.

"Glazier," the familiar voice answered.

"It's Chapman."

"Chapman! I've been waiting for you to call. Everyone on my team is impressed you were able to slip past the authorities in Aspen."

"I shouldn't have to be slipping past anyone," Michael said, annoyed. "I'm a federal agent. Why hadn't you cleared my name?"

"It's in the works. Another forty-eight hours and everything'll be resolved."

"That's cutting it close, Glazier. Contact my mother just in case the news has reached Kansas. Explain *everything* to her.

And tell her not to worry, that I'll call as soon as I can. Now, did you get my e-mail?"

"Yeah, I saw it. What the hell kind of message was that, anyway?"

"Did you do what I asked?"

There was a pause. "Yeah. Despite having no viable evidence, I pulled some strings. Put my career on the line, too, I'd like to remind you."

"Good."

"What the hell's going on?"

Michael had worked with his case officer long enough to know that it was best to answer in short, clear sentences without a lot of hemming and hawing. "The twins tried to kill me when I went skiing with them on Friday. Lucas and I fell over a cliff. He broke his neck during the fall. It wasn't murder. I managed to ski away from Lance and then drove to Aspen to find Don Seaton."

"And that's why you asked me to have Treasury contact the Secret Service—so they could work with domestic banks and Interpol to freeze Lance's assets?"

Michael had been so distracted by the frantic work he was doing for Seaton, he had hardly had time to think about anything else, but he more than anyone knew the importance of tracking down Lance as soon as possible. "I think he's on the run. When he and his brother couldn't kill me, he must have figured the conspiracy would unravel. The only problem is, we don't know a complete list of his bank accounts. Even though you probably froze everything that's on record, he may still have some offshore accounts he can access."

"We're doing what we can. I have some people running a trace through his financial transactions with the banks we know of, in hopes of finding a trail to any offshore accounts." Glazier paused. "Why did you visit Don Seaton?"

Michael sensed the tension in his case officer's voice. Even before he told him the truth, he could tell that Glazier didn't approve of his taking the initiative to involve others outside the Treasury.

"We were wrong about Don Seaton—he's not part of the conspiracy. He's as much a victim in all this as anyone."

"Christ, Michael! It's not our job to prioritize the victims. We're supposed to just turn our findings over to the SEC. We don't get involved with the resolutions, for good reasons. That's up to other agencies. And we sure as hell don't confront the founder of the corporation under investigation."

Michael tensed for the argument he had been anticipating for days. "Glazier, we can still save this company!"

"Save it for what!" Glazier shot back. "For Seaton and his billions? For the software engineers and accountants that were happily nestled into their cubicles for so many years and will find new jobs within months? For the rich stockholders who gamble with their riches and cry foul anytime they actually lose money? We work for the federal government, Michael; we're here to safeguard the system, and when the system fails, then those failures need to die a very painful and public death. It's a deterrent for future failures. It's what keeps the machine of capitalism well oiled. I'm sorry, but it's the only way things can change. Don't you know anything about history?"

"I know enough history to know that governments can fail the system and the people!"

"So you want to overthrow the government now, is that it? Think you're working for the wrong side? What good will it do to save a failing company that eventually resorted to fraud? What good will it do?"

Michael raised his palm to push back against the pressure in his forehead. "You remember how it all fell apart for Enron?" he said in a quiet, weary voice. "Ken Lay authorized the draw on the remaining amount of Enron's line of credit while still pretending there was nothing wrong with their financial position. Their credit rating was soon downgraded, Dynegy backed out of the merger talks, and a month later Enron filed for bankruptcy, making the stock virtually worthless. You always hear the stories of the people that lost their entire life savings because of the fall of Enron. The top executives ran the fraud. The workers of Enron had nothing to do with it, yet many of them lost everything. And when that happens it can affect families and sometimes even entire communities. You talk about protecting the system, but the system failed *them*. If anyone needs to be protected, it's X-Tronic. Don't kill it just to make an example. Destroy the conspirators, not the corporation."

"Michael, we've done all we can. You've uncovered the fraud. We know that Kurt was murdered by the twins. And we're putting an end to the conspiracy at X-Tronic, which is going to save tens of thousands of people hundreds of millions of dollars in the future. Could you imagine how many *more* people would have lost their asses if news of the fraud had come out after the merger with Cygnus? Jesus, do you even realize how much you've saved the financial world by what you've uncovered?"

Michael understood the good that they had done, but they could do more. And at this moment, he didn't especially care what Glazier thought. He had done the right thing by breaking from his case officer to contact Seaton. But now Glazier could help Seaton and him do what was right.

"We can still save X-Tronic," Michael repeated, ignoring Glazier's comments. "Please, just hear me out. I've worked everything out. Don Seaton has billions of dollars he's willing to risk to keep X-Tronic alive. He's tried discussing it with Arnold Pym of the SEC, but Pym isn't going along with our plan. I need your help. You've got influence within the department. I need you to convince Shevalin to back Seaton's proposal. Shevalin could convince Pym to freeze trading on X-Tronic in order to give us a chance to thoroughly explain things at the shareholders' meeting. It could give people time to consider the information, give securities analysts time to digest the impact—*anything* to avoid a mass panic in the marketplace."

"Shevalin? You want me to sell this idea to the *secretary of the treasury*? You really want this to go all the way to the White House cabinet?"

The question startled Michael. He had been so focused on the local effects of the accounting fraud, it never occurred to him that the White House would want to have a look at his work. But that was now the level the game had to be played at. "Glazier, *please*," he said. "This is the right thing to do for the employees and other stakeholders of X-Tronic. We owe it to them to do everything we can to salvage the situation."

"Look," Glazier said, "I don't like this idea at all. It's not for us to play wizard with the marketplace. Sound economic theory bets on X-Tronic to collapse. That's the free market; that's how corporate evolution is supposed to work. But I have some people here, so I'll run the idea by them. If we decide it's something we're willing to back, then I'll propose it to Shevalin's office. But no promises."

"Just remember what's at stake," Michael said.

"I am. Are you?"

Michael sensed the tension in Glazier's voice, and he knew better than to push him any further. "Let me know what you decide. I have to get back to my work."

"What are you working on?"

"I'm preparing the presentation Don Seaton's giving to the shareholders in three days."

"Christ, Michael, you're already working for the Treasury Department and Cooley and White! Now you're working for Don Seaton, too?"

"I don't have a choice," he replied, ending the call. He turned back to the stacks of files strewn across the fine carpeting of the penthouse's main room. His last thought, as he began walking through the loose ends of missing contracts, was that all his efforts might come to nothing.

65

MICHAEL NEEDED TO do something to get his mind off the building storm. Grabbing the hotel phone from the white marble countertop, he dialed the one person who could distract him from all his cares. He needed a break, even if it was nothing more than a short phone conversation.

"Hello," Alaska answered.

"Darling, I've fallen, and I need you to pick me up," he said playfully.

"Michael . . . ?"

"Yes. Chapman, too, in case you've forgotten." He was already feeling better.

"Oh, God, Michael. I'm sorry, but I can't talk to you right now."

"What? Why's that?"

"I just . . . can't."

"What's wrong?" he asked.

"I just don't want to talk right now, okay?"

"Hey, wait. Come on, what is this?"

"Michael, look—oh, fuck!—I need a break, *all right*? I just don't want to see you anymore. I just don't care anymore. *Okay*? Things are happening in my life—things I need to get control of. I don't know what you think we had together, but I shouldn't have led you on." She paused, waiting for his response. "I'm really sorry."

"Something tells me this isn't a joke," he said, shaken.

"Good-bye, Michael." The phone went dead.

He felt as if a door had been slammed in his face. Her words hadn't made any sense. It was as if he had just now spoken to a different woman from the one he had met at the nightclub. What had happened to that sweet girl he took snowmobiling? A thought entered his mind that made him gulp. A resource he could use. He printed a document from his computer and cut and pasted a name before scanning it into his electronic files. A number he could dial to obtain answers . . . He grabbed the phone again and dialed the number he had committed to memory long ago, after graduating from the academy in Alabama.

"Agency operator," a voice answered. "Authorization code, please?"

"Special Agent Michael Chapman—authorization code US748AUG7 Alpha Sigma."

"Confirmed," the voice replied. "Direction?"

"Network records processing. Telephone. Civilian."

"Restricted! Court authorization?"

"Signed warrant—the Honorable Susanna Clarke—U.S. Tenth District Court. Fax number?" Michael spoke the lie with confidence. After penning the number the operator gave him, he slid over to the fax and sent through the forged warrant. Taking advantage of a system that relied too heavily on integrity, trusting pieces of paper with illegible scribbles of ink signatures as a basis for important decisions, it had not taken him long to turn a copy of the warrant for Lance Seaton's phone records into a federal document that offered him immediate access to Alaska's phone records.

Waiting while the operator worked on the other end of the line, he held the cordless phone to his ear and paced around the room. It wasn't the first time he had taken advantage of the agency for personal reasons. Besides, after the success of the X-Tronic case, his career in the Treasury Department would be untouchable. He was on the verge of exposing one of the most complicated corporate fraud scandals in the history of the United States, but at this moment all he wanted was to know if Alaska was seeing another man. He wanted to see if she had called anyone after their last conversation.

"Sir? Right, I've accessed the files through Telenet's system for the number you've indicated. How would you like me to transcribe them for you?"

"I don't need a transcription this evening. I need to know of all incoming and outgoing calls after five o'clock Mountain Time."

"This evening, sir?" He detected the trace of uncertainty in the operator's tone.

"Quickly, please."

He could hear the soft click of computer keys in the background.

"Only two calls, sir: one incoming at 19:04 local time, one outgoing at 19:14."

"What can you tell me about the outgoing call?"

"303-641-8932. Hold on, please." More typing. "No listing in our directory. Cell phone. The number has been canceled recently, so the call was relayed to an auto response message. Hold on." More typing. "No, no luck, sir. Can't find a user name. Business phone—corporate account, used for pooling. Generic contact name on the account, no way to trace to individual."

"The number was disconnected? Who did it belong to? It has to be traced to someone."

"Not this type of account. Addressed to some sort of corporate sales department. No specific person attached."

"Name of the company?" he asked, grasping for any clue about the person Alaska had tried to call.

"X-Tronic, sir," the operator spoke dully. "Like the software company."

Dumbstruck, he stepped back from the fax machine, his mind racing to catch up with the operator's words. How could Alaska be tied to X-Tronic? He had met her at the nightclub around the same time he had been placed on the engagement. She had come on to him so strong, practically seducing him. And she was also from Aspen—had she known the twins growing up? She had been at their party. Had she been involved with them the entire time?

"Sir?" the operator said, interrupting Michael's thoughts. "I just noticed something strange . . ." A brief pause. "Are you aware that the 19:04 incoming call was from the same number that you're currently using? Did you call the suspect listed in the warrant?"

"Thank you," Michael replied, hanging up.

He leaned against the table, feeling as if the ground had moved from under him. The night had been too long. After a moment he opened his eyes and promised himself he would not shed a single tear—not for her. Then he went to the closet, grabbed his jacket, and—against his better judgment—left the Presidential Suite.

Michael had the cabbie stop a block from Alaska's apartment building. He got out, the rim of his baby blue Nuggets cap tipped over his eyes, the collar of his leather jacket upturned against the cold wind. Alaska's building was in the middle of the block. As he approached it, the glass door in front swung open, and there she stood.

Alaska stepped out into the night, her black scarf waving behind her in the breeze. She was twenty yards from him. Veering off the sidewalk, he slipped into the tall shadows along the building and watched as she moved toward him.

"Alaska," he said just as she walked past.

She spun her head around so quickly, her long, black hair swung up and wrapped around her face. Pulling the hair aside with one hand, she fixed her dark eyes on his faint outline in the shadows. Her eyes widened as he stepped out into the light with the rim of his cap still hiding the top half of his face.

"Michael?" she asked, still uncertain who it was.

"Alaska," he repeated.

"Michael . . . Jesus! I said it was over. Just leave me alone. It was good for a while. Please! Let's just leave it at—"

"X-Tronic?" he said, silencing her with a single word. His arms hung low, with open palms toward her, as if pleading for an explanation.

She stepped back suddenly, frightened as if the mere word had the power to harm her. She looked up at him with a guarded mysteriousness just as she had at the Church that night when they first met. "Michael, you don't understand. My father—"

"Don't," he said, trying to hold back his rage. "I don't want to know why. I just want to know *when* they first got to you."

She was silent for a few seconds, as if looking back in time for the answer. "Before we ever met," she replied.

"You had me marked in the club that night. You already knew I was on the X-Tronic audit. Lance and Lucas hired you to spy on my personal activities. You helped them make sure I wasn't discovering too many of X-Tronic's little secrets."

"I don't know anything about the company. They just wanted me to inform them about your personal life at first."

"So we never had a single real moment together," he said, anger burning in his eyes, just behind the tears.

"I don't know, Michael," she said, her head still lowered, unable to look at him. "It felt real."

"Where's Lance?"

She shook her head. "He only gave me a number to call if you contacted me. It's not even a phone he's using anymore. He must have disconnected it without telling me anything."

"No, he wouldn't have told you," he said, trying to register her answer. "Lance would be smart enough to know not to trust *you*." And he turned and walked away without giving her a chance to reply.

As he moved along the cold street, only fifteen blocks away from his own apartment building in Capitol Hill, he realized that Denver was too small a city for him ever to forget about her. He could barely control his anger. With any luck, he would never see Alaska again.

66

————◦❋◦————

O N THURSDAY MORNING, valets at the Downtown Hilton jockeyed the cars of business journalists, securities analysts, and X-Tronic shareholders. The lobby was full of overnight guests mingling loudly with new arrivals. As they introduced themselves to one another, debates quickly sparked up over the possibilities of the new X-Tronic-Cygnus Corporation. The excitement over the merger vote had caught enough interest from Wall Street that seven of the largest brokerage houses had sent small teams of analysts to monitor the shareholders' meeting.

As nine o'clock approached, the lobby crowd thinned, migrating up the elevators to the Mount Evans Ballroom on the fiftieth floor. The walls of windows stretching from floor to ceiling, with their panoramic view of downtown and the mountains beyond, gave one the sensation of floating above the city.

Set apart from the ranks of chairs, well-spaced microphones, and digital feed systems for the securities analysts, a long table for the board of directors sat on the elevated stage at the front of the room. At the center of the table, Don Seaton sat masked in a false smile, waiting uncomfortably for the meeting to begin. Tensions were already mounting in the room, as shareholders learned that the SEC had just halted all trading of X-Tronic shares on the New York Stock Exchange. Most assumed it was a hedge against immediate volatility during the merger vote, but some interpreted it as a sure sign of danger.

Michael stood hidden from the guests in the wings behind the stage. He watched Don Seaton waiting to begin the meeting. Then he turned his eyes to the fifth row, where John Falcon and Jerry Diamond sat together. He had never seen these two conspirators in one place before. Lance Seaton would have made it a full house, but he was still nowhere to be found.

Don Seaton seemed to be waiting until the tide of conversation in the ballroom rose higher, before he calmly leaned forward and spoke into the microphone, just seven minutes after the meeting was scheduled to begin. "Ladies and gentlemen, fellow shareholders, please take your seats so that we may begin today's meeting."

Seaton took a few seconds to shuffle one last time through the notes Michael had prepared for him. Then he took a deep breath, his smile faded, and all signs of confidence left his face. "Fellow shareholders," he said, "I have a lot to discuss with you today. Our meeting this morning will be instrumental in forging a new corporation, a new X-Tronic. It is my hope that this new corporation will be faithful to the core values and beliefs on which I founded this company more than thirty years ago— values and beliefs that have not been much in evidence at X-Tronic in recent years. Values and beliefs that have, unfortunately, been lost under the company's current management."

A quiet murmur ran through the room as the shareholders tried to decipher Seaton's words. His concerns were something no one in the room seemed to expect.

"Ladies and gentlemen," he continued, "I regret to inform you that there will be no vote on a merger between X-Tronic and Cygnus." The murmur exploded into an outraged roar. In the blink of an eye, everything had changed.

Michael watched as Seaton raised a hand in a vain effort to calm the uproar. "I know that most of you have reviewed the ten-K filing. You've seen strong performance by X-Tronic during the past year. I also know that many of you have just discovered that all trading of the company's shares have been temporarily suspended by the SEC and the New York Stock Exchange only a few minutes ago. In a moment, I will explain why this has happened. I know that many of you have traveled far to be here today. Let me assure you that today is going to be no ordinary shareholders' meeting." His eyes scanned the room until they found the table of securities analysts at one side of the room. "Today we will make history."

Michael watched as Don turned to make eye contact with him. Once the billionaire had given him the slow nod, Michael raised his left hand to his mouth and spoke quietly into the small send-receiver embedded in a black wristband. "This is Chapman. We're ready. Send 'em in."

Within seconds, the rear doors burst open as a small team of federal agents, accompanied by two uniformed police officers, quickly made their way down the center aisle. A loud grumbling spread through the room, then turned to shocked silence, as the shareholders watched events unfold. The agents reached Jerry Diamond. He sat bolt upright, his big shaved head staring forward, looking like a jacklit deer, then began laughing hysterically at the agents as they read him his rights. It wasn't until he lunged toward Seaton in a burst of rage that the officers subdued him and hauled him from the room. Falcon ignored this activity completely, staring forward as if in a trance.

The room had fallen utterly silent as the agents escorted Diamond out. Falcon remained, still untouchable. As Michael watched him, looking for any trace of a reaction, he found himself almost admiring the man's iron self-control.

Once the agents left the room, the spell broke, and the shareholders erupted into chaotic chatter. Seaton tapped on the microphone until the noise again subsided.

"Fellow shareholders, you have just witnessed the arrest of one of the men currently being charged with securities fraud in a wide-ranging conspiracy to manipulate X-Tronic's financial results." The room exploded with shouts of dismay. Seaton continued to speak, raising his voice, determined to say his piece. "The conspirators enriched themselves through a scheme involving bonuses, the granting of stock options, and career positioning at the potential merger with Cygnus. They engaged in activities that knowingly and fraudulently misrepresented X-Tronic's financial condition and performance."

The securities analysts were on their cell phones, frantically relaying the information to their investment firms in New York. The news would reach Wall Street immediately, eventually gliding across bottom tickers on the news channels, followed by immediate article postings on the ever-fluid online issues of the Western world's financial news sources, and eventually in a wave of abrupt announcements on news channels across the country.

Someone yelled out an unrecognizable question that was lost in the commotion. Seaton seemed to struggle as he tried to regain control of the meeting. A dozen shareholders had already left the room, fumbling with the small buttons on their cell phones. A small scuffle broke out in the far corner of the room.

Noticing Seaton looking over at him, Michael realized that the old man needed help, so he pushed through the curtain and marched directly onto the stage. He grabbed the microphone and faced the room. "Everyone, listen—please!" he said in a tone that commanded attention. "My name is Michael Chapman, and I am a federal agent with the U.S. Department of the Treasury. I am the principal investigator into the alleged conspirators' fraud. Unless you want to lose every nickel you have invested in X-Tronic shares, I suggest you listen to the plan that Mr. Seaton and I have outlined to keep the corporation from filing bankruptcy." The room fell silent—he had their attention. As he waited to continue, his gaze fell downward and he made direct eye contact with John Falcon for the first time in over a week. The man glared stonily back at him.

As the room quieted, he stood aside and let Seaton take over. Recalling his impassioned conversations with Glazier, he could understand how his case officer might lose hope, might forget those moments of illumination, back in college, when economic and financial theories resonated with supreme clarity in his mind. But Michael could still remember. And as he watched the crowd wait in horrified anticipation of Seaton's final words, he found himself remembering the things his father had taught him from an early age about business and finance. He thought about how proud his father would be of him if he could see this. Watching Seaton try to calm the people, he thought now of his grandfather and the burden of pain he had carried for the last forty years of his life. He wondered what his grandfather would think if he could see him standing on this stage before panicked shareholders, trying to help a company through a crisis. And he felt, in a strange mix of emotions, that he was finally living up to the covenant that his family had failed to keep to their community in Elk County two generations ago.

Seaton had concluded the presentation. The shareholders were leaving the room, each struggling with the weight of the decisions to be made. There was nothing more to be said; it was now just a matter of waiting for the opening bell on the floor of the New York Stock Exchange tomorrow morning, and the few short hours when the fate of X-Tronic would be decided.

67

———❋———

JOHN FALCON STEPPED out of his silver Jaguar XKR
coupe on the isolated airstrip and stared at the single-engine
Cessna 206H Stationair bathed in the headlights. Inside the small
hangar, a gangly man jumped up off a threadbare couch patched
with duct tape. "Z'at her?" the man asked, practically drooling at
the Jaguar. "Lord Almighty, you sure weren't lying, Mr.
Falcon—damn if she ain't a beauty!"

"I want to leave it in the hangar until you return," Falcon
said. "I don't want it discovered while we're gone—I don't want
any surprises. The title's in the glove box, signed over, so she's
yours once you get back."

"I can appreciate that, Mr. Falcon. Anything you say."

"Move the plane out. I'd like to leave as soon as possible."

With an eager nod, the man pulled the plane out of the
hangar and started his preflight check.

Getting back in the Jaguar, Falcon heard "Clear!" and then
the sound of the engine starting. After stashing the car inside the
hangar, Falcon slung his travel bag over his shoulder and walked
back to the plane.

"Now, you *know* I can't fly all the way into Canada," the pilot said.

Falcon reached over and dropped the Jag keys in his lap. "Just get me as close as you can. I have people who can get me across the border and eventually out of North America. People will come looking for you once you register the car in your name. You've done nothing illegal, so tell them anything you want. As far as you know, I'm nothing more than an eccentric, paranoid businessman who gave you an offer you would have been a fool to refuse."

The pilot throttled up the engine, and the plane vibrated as a roar came from the propeller. As they began rolling down the runway, Falcon tried not to think of the life he was being forced to abandon. For the moment, he needed to focus only on escaping and surviving, on helping his family start anew. But as the plane lifted off the runway and climbed into the night sky, his mind colored with fantasies of revenge against the young man who had ruined his life.

*   *   *

"Is Stuttgart already here?" Michael asked Marcus as he walked into Seaton's Denver estate. He had seen the red Porsche near the entrance.

"Beat you by fifteen minutes."

"The eager little prick," Michael said, grinning. "He never liked my plan from the beginning. You know why he made sure to arrive before me?"

"Let's see," Marcus deadpanned. "To get a better seat?"

Michael laughed. "To try one last time to talk Mr. Seaton out of buying back X-Tronic's shares. He's here for the money, Marcus. He's here to try to save his biggest client from putting all his wealth on the line."

Michael moved through the enormous house, went down a wide staircase, and rapped lightly on the double doors of the game room.

Seaton smiled. "Michael! Good, you're here with plenty of time. Trading begins in twenty minutes."

Michael was pleased to hear no wavering in the old man's voice. He looked over at Stuttgart. The financial advisor had the look of someone who had fought and lost the battle. Now he would have to stand by and watch his client risk everything. Michael knew that no matter what happened, both Stuttgart and Seaton were going to lose a lot of money this morning. Indeed, there was no way to gain financially. The only victory would be to keep X-Tronic's stock from tumbling so low it became virtually worthless or was delisted on the NYSE. To survive the fraud scandal, the company would have to face serious challenges. But of all the things X-Tronic must do to survive the fallout of the fraud scandal, the first crucial battle would be Seaton's attempt, this morning, to keep the stock from tanking.

"I can't believe we're going to watch the trading from this game room," Joseph Stuttgart said.

"Can you think of a bigger game than this one?" Michael replied.

Cracking a brief smile, Seaton pressed a button beneath the arm of his chair. The windows that stretched across the eastern wall, with their spectacular view of the rising sun behind Denver's skyline, slowly began to tint until they lost all translucence. A wall opened in the corner of the room, revealing a wet bar stocked with juices, an espresso machine, and alcohol. A projector in the ceiling fired up, displaying on the wall screen the early ramblings of a securities analyst in a pin-striped suit, mouthing muted words as green ticker symbols flowed below her in an endless stream of data. To the side of the projector screen, a second panel opened and lowered a custom-made Bloomberg display. A myriad of financial information and market data was displayed for X-Tronic's stock.

"Five minutes till showtime," Seaton announced. The clock on the display showed 09:25:08 EST. They could see "X-Tronic" listed in bold letters below the anchorwoman.

"This is going to be the talk of the day across all the networks," Joseph squeaked. "What are you hoping the floor price will be?"

"Twenty-five dollars?" Seaton asked, glancing at Michael.

"Twenty-five a share," Michael confirmed.

Seaton walked to the center of the room, where a spider phone rested on a flat podium. The speakers on the phone came to life as he dialed a number.

"Fiduciary Wave Investors—this is Grant DeLarma speaking."

"Grant, it's Don. Are we ready to do this?"

"Good morning, Mr. Seaton. Yes, we're ready. Everyone has been conferenced into the call."

"How many?"

"We've got seven traders in total."

"Good. Start by buying a million shares at ninety-seven dollars. We'll see how long that holds."

Michael looked up at the display. It was one minute before the opening bell on the New York Stock Exchange. One minute before the fast-paced frenzy of the market began to ravage X-Tronic's last stock price, quoted at the end of trading two days earlier at a hundred and two dollars per share.

The displayed changed to 09:30:00 EST. Muting the phone with a remote switch, Seaton turned to Michael and Joseph. "I want both of your advice as we go through this."

The two men nodded.

Suddenly, the price on the display began to drop: *one hundred, ninety-eight, ninety-two, eighty-six.*

"My God!" Stuttgart exclaimed. "Our bids didn't even slow it down!"

Seaton unmuted the phone. "Grant! Buy three million at eighty dollars!" Then he muted it again before turning back to Michael. "Still think we can control this?"

"We always knew it would drop fast at the beginning."

Eighty-three, eighty-one, eighty, seventy-seven, sixty-eight.

Stuttgart, unable to keep still, paced the room. "Bastards! All the other investors are dropping the stock like it's a disease. I told you they wouldn't listen to your speech at the shareholders' meeting. No one cares about the bloody company; they just want to protect their portfolios."

"Grant! Seven million at sixty dollars!" Seaton said while fiddling with the remote.

The price dropped immediately to sixty per share and held for almost two minutes before continuing to drop.

"It's still going down pretty fast," Seaton said. Michael had no answer.

"Don, please—this is insane!" Joseph pleaded. "You can't just throw away everything you've built up over the last thirty years!"

"Joseph! I'm trying to *save* what I've built over the past thirty years! Now, either help me analyze these prices or go!"

Fifty-four, forty-seven, forty-three . . .

"Mr. Seaton," Michael broke in, "buy fourteen million at thirty-seven dollars."

Seaton nodded and gave the bid to Grant, who immediately relayed it to his team. The price dropped to thirty-seven . . . then thirty. All three men stared in suspense at the display as the number held at thirty dollars per share. For six minutes there was virtually no change in the price. Seaton broke a slight smile until he looked back and saw Michael slowly shake his head. He turned back to watch the display, realizing they were not out of danger. Then, eight minutes after the price had seemed to stabilize, it dropped to twenty-nine dollars per share . . . then twenty-eight.

"Christ! It's going all the way to the bottom!" Stuttgart cried out.

"Michael?" Seaton asked.

Michael gave a little sigh. "Can you buy fifty million at twenty-six?"

"You fucking bastard!" Joseph yelled. "Where do you get these numbers from? Don, you can't listen to this guy anymore—he's going to destroy you!"

"That taps me out, Michael. Are you sure?" Seaton asked. Michael nodded. The old man took a deep breath, ran his hand down his face, and relayed the bid to a baffled Grant DeLarma.

Twenty-seven, twenty-six . . . Then it held. Five minutes went by as they watched and waited. Then another five minutes. Still it held at twenty-six.

"It'll never hold," Stuttgart said.

"It'll hold," Michael insisted.

Fifteen more minutes passed with no significant change. Then the price dropped to twenty-five.

Seaton slugged the couch in frustration. Stuttgart murmured a steady stream of profanity. Seaton looked at Michael with a lost expression. "I've done everything I can," he confessed helplessly.

Michael lowered his gaze. He could not bear to make eye contact with either man. Once again he had overstepped his bounds. He had imposed himself on the personal lives of others, and they had suffered from trusting him. "If we had just gotten support from the other shareholders," he spoke as an afterthought.

Joseph shook his head bitterly. "Why would they? They have nothing invested in the company other than capital. And their capital is liquid. What made you think that they would be willing to risk anything?"

Michael shook his head. "I'm sorry, Don. I truly thought the drop in market cap could be stopped."

To Michael's surprise, Seaton managed a faint smile. "I loved my company as much as anything. We did the right thing in trying. You have to believe that. I'm not sorry about the money I've lost. We did everything we could. That's something to be proud of, Michael. At my age, self-respect is worth more than money."

He looked at the old man in awe. Besides his father, he had never met a more honorable man in his life. In that moment, he realized that it hadn't been greed that made Seaton a billionaire—it had been the man's vision and passion. And now that same passion and absence of greed would cost the man most of his net worth.

"Hey!" Stuttgart yelled as he jabbed a finger at the screen.

Michael and Seaton turned to look at the Bloomberg data. The price had dropped to ten dollars. "How long has it been around that price?"

Seaton flipped through the panel to get a breakdown of the historic data for the past hour. "Nine minutes!" he answered. "You think it's stabilizing?"

"I don't know," Michael replied. "But something else must have happened, because we sure haven't placed any more orders."

They unmuted the news channel screen and listened to the anchorwoman run through the events of the past hour. She highlighted how X-Tronic's founder, Don Seaton, had been purchasing enormous quantities of shares of X-Tronic and now owned more than 65 percent of its common stock. She explained how a number of additional investors had become attracted to the stock after it had dropped to a fifteen-year low. There appeared to be a growing attraction to the stock through a number of different parallels: Mr. Seaton's loyal dedication to the company was encouraging some investors to reevaluate the honesty of the company's presentation outlining all available information related to the fraud, and as a result, X-Tronic was winning back a certain degree of trust. Investors were reevaluating the company's prospects, and they were encouraged by Seaton's aggressive purchasing of shares. Additional analysts were quoted as saying that if X-Tronic was able to get through the fraud proceedings without further damage and managed to turn around, in two to three years it could potentially climb to its previous value. There seemed to be a sense on the Street that X-Tronic's stock price had taken the beating it deserved, but that now the company was slightly undervalued. One analyst praised Seaton's foresight in purchasing vast amounts of the stock to prevent a detrimental panic that likely would have dropped the price to the floor, freezing trades permanently until the NYSE delisted the shares.

All three men watched the price and financial news the rest of the day. The panic seemed to have left the market. Seaton had lunch brought in as the three played games of Spanish billiards while keeping one eye on the screen. At the end of the day, the price had risen from its low of ten dollars to thirteen by the closing bell. Don Seaton had lost nearly eighty percent of his net worth—over seven billion dollars—in one day's trading, but he had saved X-Tronic from collapse.

68

————:✳:————

A S LUNCH HOUR interrupted the rhythm of work at
Cooley and White, troops of accountants poured from the
building for a midday pillaging of the nearby luncheonettes. The
office grew quiet within minutes, and Michael soon found
himself alone, sidling past the morning's aftermath, careful not
to brush against a tower of documents that rose precariously
from his desk like a house of cards. Would he miss this? he
wondered. Would he miss the thrill of living a secret life? The
question haunted him, for although he had long yearned for
freedom from his tormenting situation, he now realized that he
might occasionally find himself missing the life of a senior
auditor at one of the world's top international accounting firms.

It had been two days since trading began for X-Tronic shares.
In that time, he had been given notice that his last day at Cooley
and White would be today. Even though he had earned his
position at the firm through a fraudulent identity, he wasn't being
fired; indeed, the firm was in enough legal trouble from the X-
Tronic case that it was in no position to battle the federal
government over an ambiguous precedent for undercover agents.

In the end, Cooley and White had given him two days to wrap up his affairs and any pending documentation for client engagements before his mutually agreed-upon departure from the firm. Ironically, his entire employment here had been a fraud, and he was not surprised they were forcing him out so soon after his true identity was revealed. And now the time had come for him to go.

He took a deep breath as he stepped onto the elevator for the last time. *Going down, please—thirty-seven floors to the next chapter of my life.* The car was packed. Hypnotized passengers stared at the video monitor's advertisement blurbs, while Bloomberg took center stage with a breakdown of the market watch as the U.S. economy lurched forward in another fine day of trading. No bad news, most stocks happy, every investor counting down the hours to the day's end. Michael was the only one not entranced by the media. He studied the tops of his shoes as a lost traveler might ponder a map. At last the chrome-plated doors slid open to a gleaming sea of black marble.

Out the doors and in the sunshine, he found himself moving through the outside square as fast as possible. No more strolling; he had momentum now. Contented urbanites grazed in the courtyard between the MCI and Bank of America buildings—the common ground between corporate giants. What a lovely day. How could the city stay so warm in the winter? Thin air, some said, as if that alone explained everything unique in the Mile High City.

He had survived the winter of his life.

*   *   *

On Monday morning, after a long phone conversation with Glazier over the weekend, Michael walked into the Denver District Office of the Kansas City Federal Reserve Bank. True to its image, the office had a cold, gray interior, watched over by three security guards in white uniforms. A stone staircase ran from the corridor up to a second-floor mezzanine, which held a collection of artifacts worthy of any museum of economics, telling the history of the Federal Reserve and the impact its policies ultimately had on the U.S. economy.

"Your office is just down the hall," said the midlevel economist who met him on the mezzanine and walked him through security.

Michael was feeling depressed. The phone call from Glazier had mapped out what his responsibilities—or lack thereof—for the Treasury Department would be for the next six months. Since he had chosen to expose himself as an undercover agent at the shareholders' meeting, the department was limiting his responsibilities until all the indictments and legal proceedings involving X-Tronic had begun. So he had left the high-adrenaline world of corporate finance for a dull government bureaucracy.

They arrived at an open door to an office strewn with boxes.

"What's this?" Michael asked.

"It's your office."

"What are those boxes?"

"Ah! You've been assigned to help with the Treasury's Payment Application Modernization. Since we transferred our savings bond operations to Minneapolis and Pittsburgh last year, the Fed governors have assigned our branch with new initiatives. The Treasury is understaffed in this department, so you've been assigned to help out."

"This isn't what I do," Michael protested. "I'm not a banker. I'm an investigative agent in the Financial Crimes Division."

"That's who you *were*, Mr. Chapman. You've been reassigned to this project until further notice. I'm not privy to any more information than that." The economist looked around the room and nodded for show. "IT should stop by soon to set up your log-ins on our network. Also, Mr. Glazier said he would be stopping by this morning before his flight back to Washington. Until then, just make yourself at home."

Half an hour later, an IT guy with an astonishingly large belly and a crisp beard gave Michael's computer all the network access necessary to carry on the fight against inefficient payment applications. With all the department's documentation available for exploration on the shared drive, the ex-agent and newbie banker, demoted by his superiors for pursuing their cause and achieving results beyond their control, found solitude in the World Wide Web and the countless articles examining the aftereffects of X-Tronic's fraud:

Bank of Cincinnati cancels line of credit with X-Tronic in post-fraud fallout.

Merrill Lynch downgrades X-Tronic common stock to "underperform." Credit rating drops to BBB.

Civil actions filed against X-Tronic by Boston Investor Group. More lawsuits likely to follow.

Links to accounting fraud in Cooley and White may extend as high as engagement partner John Falcon in the firm's Denver office. A call to Mr. Falcon's office was not returned.

Treasury Department close to fraud allegation charges against Don Seaton, someone close to the issue said. Wall Street teeters on rumors, but stock price holds strong against speculations.

Michael breezed through the articles. X-Tronic was a sinking ship, taking on water at an overwhelming rate, financial institutions were all but abandoning the software giant, and now Don Seaton was coming under fire.

"Knock, knock," Glazier said from the doorway.

Michael looked up from his computer. "Glazier, what the hell am I doing on a banking project for Treasury?" he fumed. "You have fifty agents working around the clock on X-Tronic's accounting files, yet you dump me in this dead-end office."

Glazier gave him a consoling grin. "Things are complicated, Michael. Your phase of this operation is over. Some of the top boys in Washington have stepped in to delegate on this one. It's bigger than Enron and WorldCom because we still haven't determined how high up the fraud goes. It's clear to us now that the twins weren't running the show."

"Then Falcon was."

"No, we don't think he could mastermind things from Cooley and White. His resources were too limited. At this point we're working under the theory that Don Seaton masterminded the conspiracy to regain control of X-Tronic. This is consistent with all the evidence we have. It's been interesting to see the fallout effects of the fraud announcement. And we're beginning to see a connection between the fraud and the fact that Seaton has now been able to repurchase enough shares of X-Tronic to have a majority ownership again. We are not, however, pressing any charges against him at this time. More conclusive evidence is expected after we finish negotiations with the attorneys for Jerry Diamond."

"You're going to cut a deal with that hyena!"

"We're going to do whatever is necessary to take down the top person responsible for the fraud."

Shocked at what he was hearing, Michael shot to his feet. His chair rolled backward, hitting the wall. "But you know you can't trust that scoundrel—he'd sell his own children to plea-bargain a deal. And you can't seriously think Don has anything to do with this."

"Oh, 'Don,' is it? Jesus, Michael, you're on a first-name basis with this guy? Don't you see how clouded your judgment has become? The SEC noticed some suspicious trading activities in X-Tronic's shares a few days before the fraud was announced at the shareholders' meeting. We think Seaton was involved."

"What suspicious trading? What are you talking about? It doesn't make sense that Don was involved," Michael protested.

"There's an angle here that you're not seeing. Think! How could Seaton profit from this?" Glazier asked.

"He couldn't. The stock value could only go down after the announcement. He lost nearly seven billion dollars saving the company from bankruptcy after the announcement."

"Not necessarily. Someone very wealthy shorted three hundred million dollars' worth of X-Tronic shock two days before the fraud announcement. In shorting the shares, they had committed buyers to the market price at the time of the short, before the announcement. When the price dropped, they called the shorts, selling the shares and profiting from the difference. Whoever pushed the shorted stock derivatives on the open market made almost three billion dollars. Whoever it was is obviously wealthy and well connected. The transaction was hidden through dozens of offshore venture funds that are privately owned. I have people from the Treasury and the SEC investigating the transaction for insider trading. We haven't turned up much yet, but we will."

"I can't believe it," Michael said. Leaning low over the desk with arms spread, he craned his neck up at Glazier. "I can't believe Don would be capable of that."

"He fooled all of us, Michael. He's even made it look like his top executives committed the fraud behind his back. They've been at odds with Seaton for years, trying to get him to sell the business to a larger competitor. He must have known he was losing control of his company. Even the board of directors was against him. This way he could get rid of these executives without the board's approval and regain a majority control of the company without losing much money." He pointed a beefy finger at Michael. "You told me how calmly he reacted to his son's death. What kind of father reacts that way? He didn't care. As far as he was concerned, you did him a favor. Maybe it was even part of his plan. His sons are probably the only ones that could successfully implicate him in the fraud in front of a judge. That's why we must find Lance," he said, making a fist in front of his face. "He may be the only one that can really give us enough evidence to prosecute his father."

"You think Don will try to kill his only remaining son?" Michael asked.

"That's exactly what he'll try to do. For all we know, Lance may already be dead."

"Look," Glazier continued, "I'm sorry we have to separate you from the remaining investigation. We just need to be careful where we place you because of your public exposure from the case. Plan on being here in Denver for six months. Let things calm down. Then we'll move you into a departmental role in D.C."

Glazier left, and Michael turned back to the pile of cardboard boxes. He had a meeting with the project manager in twenty minutes, but he couldn't concentrate on anything other than the new suspicions against Don Seaton. Was Glazier right? Had he really let his long-held admiration for his business idol set him up to be the unwilling participant in a scheme by Seaton to regain control of X-Tronic? Had the entire drama been nothing more than an internal power struggle for the software company? Had Michael played right into the hands of the true master conspirator behind the X-Tronic fraud? He wrestled with the questions plaguing his mind, knowing all the while that it didn't matter anymore—he had been cut loose. Glazier and his team of investigators were prowling through the ruins of the financial catastrophe, searching for any clues to what had really taken place. And Michael now understood why Glazier had taken him off the investigation: he had made a huge mistake and could no longer be trusted now that Don Seaton was fingered as the master conspirator.

Michael had become so used to his undercover life that he found reality a shock to the system. Was he just supposed to resume a normal career in the Treasury Department after such a fast start as an undercover agent? He now found life as hopeless as it had seemed when he was trapped in his world of lies and subterfuge.

The biggest piece of the puzzle was still missing from the X-Tronic investigation. What was Don Seaton's true involvement in the events leading up to the fraud? But then an idea occurred to him. As he sat in the room full of boxed documents for a boring Federal Reserve project, he realized just how the true mastermind of the conspiracy could have played everyone involved in the fraud in order to benefit secretly from its eventual fallout. Glazier was right: the X-Tronic fraud had always been meant to be exposed at the right moment. The answer to everything was now so clearly illuminated in his mind that he was surprised no one else had figured it out. But there was something even Glazier had missed—one last thing Michael needed to do before he could put the X-Tronic incident behind him. And there was only one man he could contact to help him bring the curtain down on one of the darkest chapters in the history of corporate America—the one man powerful enough to challenge Don Seaton.

69

SARAH MATTHEWS KNELT in front of her brother's tombstone and brushed her hand across his name. Behind her she heard the growl of a car crawling up the hill in low gear. Turning her head, she saw Michael's silver Audi come to a stop next to her Jeep. She returned her gaze to Kurt's epitaph and listened as feet swished through the wet grass toward her.

Michael watched Sarah's back as he approached: her stooped shoulders hidden beneath a cascade of red hair that stood out among the gray tombstones. He knelt down next to her.

"I saw your article in the *Denver Post*. It got picked up by both the AP and the Dow Jones Newswire. You told the story of X-Tronic better than anyone."

She kept her gaze on her brother's tombstone without replying.

"Kurt always said you'd become a great journalist—one of the best investigative journalists of our generation."

"How much do you think he really knew?" she finally asked, still looking ahead.

"Enough to be curious . . . enough to be suspicious."

"But not enough to know for sure?"

"No, not that much. But he was on the path. He would have figured it out."

"What about the day he died? You were in the trees with the twins, just like he was. What would it have been like for him?"

Michael lowered his chin to his chest. It was a question he had often asked himself. "It would have been a surprise," he finally said. "They would have caught him off guard . . . It would have been quick."

Sarah closed her eyes. A cold wind pushed through the cemetery and blew her long hair across her face. She opened her eyes and looked at him for the first time. "I'm running a story in tomorrow's *Post* that reveals suspicions of Don Seaton as the mastermind behind the X-Tronic fraud."

"You should hold the story. You don't want to run it yet."

"Why not?"

"Because it's more complicated than that. There will be a lot of other papers running a similar story tomorrow. The Treasury Department will be leaking it to the press, but I want you to stay away from it."

"Why? Is Don Seaton guilty or not? What's going on, Michael?"

"Give me some time. We'll know everything there is to know about Seaton's involvement soon. I've put something together that will answer all our questions. Give me a little time, and I'll give you an exclusive that will be bigger than you can imagine." He sniffled in the cold air. "All the other papers are just guessing—they have zip in the way of details. I'll give you everything you need. I've spoken with people at the Treasury. We all want you to be the one who breaks the final story when we're ready to release the information to the public. You'll know how to keep things in perspective. You're the only one who will truly understand how to write about everything that's about to happen."

Sarah opened her mouth as if to ask another question, or perhaps to say thank you. But she turned back to Kurt's tombstone without a word. Michael knew she wasn't the kind to hold back a probing question, so he pretended that it was a word of gratitude she had been tempted to offer him.

Knowing the difficult task before him, he looked out at the rolling field of weathered tombstones and found that she had just given him reason to be happy. She finally understood his sacrifice, and must know that he was about to make good on his promise to give Kurt justice.

70

————— ·:✸:· —————

A WEEK AFTER Michael had met Sarah in the cemetery, on one particularly stultifying afternoon at the Denver Fed field office, Michael couldn't imagine continuing on his current course for the next six months of his life. He knew what he had to do. The time was right. He sat up at his desk and composed an e-mail to Fredrick Kavanaugh, president and CEO of Cygnus International—an offer that the Texas tycoon would find hard to refuse.

That evening, he walked under the lights along the Sixteenth Street pedestrian walkway downtown. It was cold out. As Michael strolled past inviting Italian restaurants and stylish boutiques, he kept reciting in his mind the e-mail he had sent to Kavanaugh three hours ago. In it, he had requested that Kavanaugh call Michael's cell when he was prepared to discuss the offer. Stopping near the Pavilion Theaters, he moved away from the crowds out for a bit of nightlife and looked at his watch for the umpteenth time since sending the message. Three hours and ten minutes. Knowing Fredrick Kavanaugh to be the kind of man who moved quickly to resolve problems, he was increasingly nervous that it was taking so long to get a response. Perhaps he had made a mistake in trying to contact Don Seaton's nemesis. Taking a deep breath, he walked the remaining blocks to his apartment.

Entering his apartment, he noticed a foreign smell in the darkness. Reaching to turn on the lights, he was puzzled when the switch failed to illuminate the room. Muttering a curse, he fumbled through the darkness to a reading lamp in the corner, flipped it on, and turned back toward the center of the room. Then he gasped in alarm to find two men standing against the opposite wall.

"That's quite a view you have," said the taller of the two. The man who hadn't spoken was stocky, with a flat nose and ears that had taken considerable abuse in the ring. At first glance, he seemed the muscle for the man who had spoken.

Michael forced a smile. "I was surprised that Mr. Kavanaugh hadn't phoned me yet," he said. "For a moment I was concerned that I hadn't gotten his attention."

"Oh, you got his attention," the gangly one replied.

"So what now?" Michael asked.

"Now you come with us."

Just outside Austin, the limousine pulled into a gated community, then through a second gate to a private driveway, stopping at an estate surrounded by stately cottonwoods and live oaks. Still trying to get his bearings after the two-hour flight, Michael stepped out of the car and was greeted at the front door. The servant led him into a wide hallway inside. "Just up the stairs here to the second level. This door, sir. Go right in. He's waiting."

"Mr. Michael Chapman," Kavanaugh announced from behind the huge mahogany desk. "I've read so much about you over the past few weeks. Glad we could finally meet."

"Mr. Kavanaugh, it's a pleasure," Michael replied to the CEO of Cygnus.

"Scotch?"

"That would be fine, thank you."

The billionaire pointed to a shelf alcove in the corner of the room. "Third bottle from the right," he said. "Glasses are just above."

Pouring the liquor, Michael rehearsed the proposal that would nullify any trust and respect he had ever held for Don Seaton. *Not too much,* he told himself, taking a sip.

"Lovely estate," Michael remarked as he took a seat.

"It's a ranch. We don't have 'estates' in Texas. Now, Mr. Chapman, exactly what the hell do you want? Your e-mail was quite enticing. Can you live up to what you promised me?"

Michael nodded and took a sip of whiskey. "I'm here to give you something you've wanted for a long time. But remember, my terms are very specific. This has to happen exactly as I say, or it doesn't happen at all."

"For Christ's sake, Mr. Chapman, just get to it, will you?"

"I'm here to give you X-Tronic."

A wide grin spread across the wily old tycoon's face. "Continue."

"I have evidence from the Treasury that implicates Don Seaton as the mastermind in X-Tronic's fraud—testimony from two of the accused. As you know, a story was leaked to the press recently that Mr. Seaton would become the subject of an investigation." He paused to let his words sink in.

"Then," he continued, "the story disappeared—no fallout, no follow-up, nothing. Rumor in the Treasury was that Mr. Seaton had executed some emergency legal measures that illegitimized the deposition testimonies. A preruling was permitted in this case because of the costly damage the allegations could do to X-Tronic's share price, which had already diminished significantly."

"So Don Seaton's untouchable," Kavanaugh remarked.

"By the Treasury Department, he is. But not by you."

"Mr. Chapman, I don't know who you think you're talking to, or what ace you think you have up your sleeve, but if there's anything I can't stand, it a cheat and a liar. And you're lookin' a lot like both."

"Mr. Kavanaugh, you have the ability to expose Don Seaton for what he is: a robber and a murderer. Now, that's a lot worse than a cheat and a liar—which I am not, by the way."

"Oh, come on, Mr. Chapman. I know everything about you that's in the press, and a great deal that isn't. You were an undercover agent for the Treasury for two and a half years. That's a long time to live a lie. Lying to everyone in your life for what you thought was the greater good. Horseshit! Look where it's gotten you: a professional betrayer who's now been short-leashed by his masters. How do you like workin' in the payment application section of that *little* bank in Denver? Already missing the glory days, I suppose. What's your fella's name again? Troy Glazier? Oh, he's a piece o' work, all right—runnin' some clandestine operation for those Senate assholes in Washington. I reckon you're a little bit grateful your daddy died too soon to witness the mess you've made of your life."

"You would be wise to leave my father out of this, Mr. Kavanaugh," Michael said. "I came here to talk business."

Looking mildly amused, the man stood up from the desk and walked over to a wooden humidor. Taking a precut cigar from the case, he held a silver lighter to it. "Good for you, son. Nice to see you haven't betrayed *every*one."

"Do you want to hear my proposal or not?"

"Mr. Chapman, don't get sassy with me. We'll talk at the pace I choose."

The notoriously impatient billionaire, who had acquired more empires in the past three years than had all the firebrand generals of Napoleon's armies, was now entertaining himself with such leisurely speech that Michael had no choice but to lob his pitch over the plate and pray that he didn't line-drive it back into his face.

"I need your company to announce a hostile takeover bid for X-Tronic," he blurted.

Kavanaugh began laughing so hard, the cigar dropped from his mouth and bounced to the hardwood floor. He bent down and, with some huffing, retrieved it. Then, his face rosy from mirth and exertion, said, "Just because I wanted X-Tronic a month ago doesn't mean I still want it. Good Lord, son, look at how much has changed since the fraud was exposed. The company's value is a tenth what it was before their little jack-in-the-box show at the shareholders' meeting. All their top executives have either been arrested or jumped ship. One twin's dead; the other has vanished. And now Don Seaton will soon be under fire from every agency the U.S. government can sic on him."

"That's why X-Tronic needs you. It needs your company's umbrella. The market needs to see that there is hope for X-Tronic's survival. New, strong leadership can restore it to legitimate strength."

"Supposin' I was interested—what about Don Seaton?"

"Fuck 'im. He masterminded this whole thing to regain control of his company, but he made one fatal mistake: he failed to realize the volatile, predatory nature of his own sons. When they overreacted and killed Kurt Matthews, they ended up propelling the implications of X-Tronic's fraud to a level that became irredeemable. As much as Mr. Seaton continues to fight the market, he must know he can no longer save the company. If you make a private offering to him before announcing the merger, he'll accept. He owns the majority of X-Tronic's stock again. He can make the deal without any shareholder vote. And he will."

"How do you know?"

382   BRYAN DEVORE

"If he doesn't accept your offer, the company will go bankrupt before the end of the year. If he accepts, he'll make a few hundred million when the value increases after you announce the takeover bid."

Michael paused with his back now facing Kavanaugh. "There is only one thing I ask," he continued.

"I'm listenin'."

"I want you to buy every last share Mr. Seaton has to offer—I want him completely out of X-Tronic."

Kavanaugh grinned as his large, white teeth crunched down on the remains of his cigar. "You really hate him, don't you, son?"

Michael looked as if all the wind had been knocked out of him. He seemed to have drifted a thousand leagues from where he had begun. He had failed his father, his family, his friends—everyone. Was there nothing he could do to make his life good again?

"Why do you hate him?" Kavanaugh probed.

"I've stopped believing in the decency of corporate America because of Mr. Seaton."

"You believed it was *decent*?" Kavanaugh chuckled as if Michael was now the butt of some new joke.

"When I was growing up, my father taught me that it could be. Then I did my graduate thesis on Mr. Seaton and X-Tronic. The things he did while building the company—there was no businessman in America I respected more. And during the X-Tronic investigation, I fell into his plan like all the gullible investors. I looked up to him like . . ."

"A father," Kavanaugh offered.

"Like a mentor," he replied. "But he betrayed both me and the very system I thought we were trying to protect. Because of him, I've lost faith in myself, and I've lost faith in everything that my father taught me about what corporations represent."

"But you still want me to save X-Tronic."

"You must agree there will be no layoffs," Michael said. "I'm requiring that in writing. You can afford that."

"What's stopping me from taking over X-Tonic on my own? I don't quite see how I need your help."

"My evidence can persuade the Justice Department either way I wish. Without me, you'll have no guarantee of avoiding antitrust blocking. But I can offer you testimonial evidence against Mr. Seaton that will ensure that the Justice Department looks very favorably on your takeover bid."

"And in return I suppose you want a golden executive position in my corporation?"

Michael took another drink of Scotch. "No. I'm through with the corporate world, and I'm through with the government, too. I'm returning to Manhattan, Kansas, to be with my family."

"*What?*" Kavanaugh belched. "Michael Chapman, the great federal superagent, is leaving the spotlight to disappear into the furrowed fields of Kansas? With all the publicity you've been getting, I figured you'd move into politics."

"My mother needs my help. She hasn't been doing well since my father's death. It's time for me to go home."

Kavanaugh eyed him suspiciously. Then a wide grin spread across his pudgy face.

"Your deal is acceptable, Mr. Chapman. I'll begin private talks with Mr. Seaton. We'll agree on an initial bid and work from there. I'll have him sign a noncompete contract to ensure that he sells all of his X-Tronic shares and cannot start another software company ever again. Hell, just like you, I'll take personal satisfaction in seeing the old bastard kicked out of the business. You get me through any antitrust problems, and I'll make sure the employees of X-Tronic are well cared for."

"There is one more thing," Michael added.

"Of course there is."

"Lance Seaton. He's responsible for the death of Kurt Matthews. I have reason to believe he's tried to contact you. I want him."

Mr. Kavanaugh leaned forward on the mahogany desk. "You take everything a little too personally, Mr. Chapman. That worries me some."

Michael was silent. He had nothing more to say.

"Aw, hell, all right," Kavanaugh growled. "I don't know anything about Lance's whereabouts or anything else incriminating, but I can give you a cell number that he *might* be using. With all your government contacts, that should be enough to find him."

As Michael took down the number, he could think of nothing else but tracking down Lance. After all the harm he had done, it made Michael burn with rage to think that he may already have fled the country with a stash of money, ready to start a new life in one of the world's many remote paradises.

As he left Kavanaugh's study, he knew that he would never truly enjoy having his own life back as long as Lance was free to enjoy his.

It was raining when Michael left the ranch in the same limousine that had brought him. Halfway to the airport, he asked the driver to pull over. "I'll be all right," he said as he got out of the vehicle. "I just want some time to think. Thanks for your service. I'll call a cab and get to the airport when I'm ready."

He watched the driver pull away. Alone now, he stared across the black river of rain on the asphalt. Like a soldier after a war, he looked back at the arduous path he had survived, realizing with something like astonishment that he was not dead and now had the entire open mystery of his life still before him. Would the shadows of his past haunt him twenty years from now, on another rainy night like this? Would he at last be able to start living the quiet life he was starving for?

Splashing water warned of a car pulling to a stop behind him. Headlights illumined the threads of falling rain, and when he turned to look at the car he was blinded by two blurred halos around the headlights. Nothing else existed. Michael moved toward it, looking for the driver through the dark windows, seeing nothing but the dazzling lights. He had stranded himself on a vacant Texas road, and all he wanted now was to find his way back to Colorado.

The rain slapped his face. The outline of a man was now visible, standing behind the open door, pointing something at him. *Take me back to Colorado,* Michael thought. *Don't leave me here in the Texas rain.*

The silhouette was now touching the car door. The man stepped toward him. "Did you get it?" the voice yelled over the rain.

"Yeah, Glazier, I got it," Michael answered. "It's a cell number we can use to triangulate his location."

"Good job," Glazier said with a slow nod. "Good job. Now let's get your scrawny wet ass out of the rain."

Michael nodded, but he felt too weak to move. He stood motionless in the rain, as if dazzled by the car's headlights. He had been in the storm for too long, and now he had to wonder, how tough would it be to get back to his own life.

71

------------◦❋◦------------

"**D**IAMOND AGREED TO turn State's evidence for the prosecutor," Glazier said as he poured Michael a drink from the small bar compartment between the seats. They were sitting in the government jet as it whispered through the night over the northwest corner of Texas. They would be landing in Denver within the hour.

"How were you able to get to him?"

Glazier smiled. "I wish I could take credit. To be honest, once Diamond found out Falcon had disappeared, he realized he was ending up with the short end of the stick. Since Lucas died and Lance went into hiding, I guess it rankled a little that he would be one of the few conspirators actually doing time. Well, once he started talking, it wasn't hard to make a deal."

"What kind of sentence reduction did you offer him? You can't forget how much harm he did, not to mention any role he may have played in Kurt's murder."

"That's up to the judge and the prosecutor, of course, and the trial won't even begin for another nine months. But I told him the prosecutor would recommend a reduced sentence, from thirty-to-forty years down to fifteen. That would be for both the corporate fraud charges and any involvement in planning Kurt's murder. He made it clear that it was the twins who killed Kurt without anyone's authorization. Everyone just helped them cover it up even after things started getting out of control. He named Falcon as the head conspirator from within Cooley and White, and Kavanaugh as the mastermind who contacted the twins with the proposal to inflate X-Tronic's earnings. That's how the twins were able to justify the merger and help squeeze their father out. He also named a number of other people from X-Tronic's management team that we hadn't identified yet. For God's sake, Michael, this thing's like the Watergate of the corporate world. Everyone's involvement in the corruption goes way further and deeper than anyone could have imagined. The deeper we dig, the more bodies we find. It seems the only one in the picture that's clean is Don Seaton, but I know that doesn't surprise you."

"No," Michael said. "Don's more like the old caesar who found himself in the middle of a power struggle. But he survived, didn't he?"

"Thanks to you, he did," Glazier said. "Anyway, we're wrapping up the indictments on Kavanaugh, but we won't deliver them until we have a chance to look for Lance, just in case they're still in contact. Thanks to the cell number you obtained, we at least have a lead to where he might be. My men are investigating it as we speak."

"And what about me?"

"You?" Glazier asked. "You're done. You've put more into this investigation than anyone could have asked. But now you deserve some time off. Take as long as you want. Visit Europe, for all I care. Come back to the Treasury when you're ready. We'll put you anywhere you want. You should try Washington for a few years. I think you'd like it."

Michael was silent as he turned to the window and looked out at the dark night. The plan had worked. Sticking him in a dead-end job at the Federal Reserve had helped build the false cover that he was disgruntled and ready to make a deal. That had made it possible to lure Kavanaugh out with lies about incriminating Don Seaton. It had been Kavanaugh who shorted the shares of X-Tronic and made three billion in profits from the stock's fall. The Treasury Department and the SEC had worked with Interpol and seventeen investment banks to track the financial trail of the convoluted transactions, but they had enough evidence for a solid case against the Cygnus CEO. Michael had been the only one to figure out that Kavanaugh had planned to use the scheme to finance a takeover of X-Tronic. He had assumed that Lance would contact the man after Lucas's death. Both men would have figured that exposure of the fraud would devastate X-Tronic—if not collapse it altogether—after they failed to silence Michael. He knew that Kavanaugh was their best chance to get a fresh lead on Lance's whereabouts.

But now Michael couldn't believe things were finally coming to an end. It felt like a dream, winging through the night in a government jet as Glazier proposed an unlimited future for him in the high bureaucracy of the Treasury. He stared into the distance, trying to discern where the black bowl of sky met the dark land. Somewhere there between the void of heaven and the shadows of earth lay a home in Kansas where he hoped to return soon.

Michael walked into B-52's. He had spent too many quiet nights in his apartment, and now he was jonesing for a little excitement in his social life. Most of the friends he had kept in touch with from high school and college were now married and scattered about the country. Many had started families during the years he had spent undercover. Now that everything was over, he tried to slough off the depressing awareness of lost years with a promise to himself that he would start making up for them now.

He slid through the crowd to the bar and ordered an amber ale, then, drink in hand, roamed toward the middle of the main room. After spending a minute or two watching an imaginative Japanese animated film on a giant television screen on the far wall, he went upstairs to the second floor, in search of an open table. But when he crossed the dance floor to sit at an empty table, the grin faded. At a table not a dozen steps away, sitting with friends, there *she* was. Without breaking his gaze, he raised his beer and took a long drink. He couldn't believe she was here. Watching Alaska talk and laugh, he wanted to feel only emptiness toward her. He waited impatiently for the effects of the alcohol to distract him. Unable to turn away, he thought back on their mysterious meeting at the Church two months ago. How easily he had become infatuated with her, how easily seduced.

He pulled his eyes away, thinking of the giddy lost days that may have been a fiction all along. She had only been playing a part, being an actress. Alaska was more beautiful and alluring than any woman he had ever known. She was a talented though struggling artist, with a contagious passion that he loved. And her powerful devotion to her father reminded him of his own family's loyal strength during difficult times. She had been the woman he hadn't realized he was searching for, until he had found her. But where had that left him? Had he loved *her,* or only the idea of her? He wasn't sure anymore. Just another lie in his life, though this one hadn't been his choice.

He took another drink of his beer and turned his eyes back toward Alaska, only to find that she was now staring directly at him. He froze when he met her eyes. Their stares lingered, a sad recollection in their eyes. He wanted to forgive her, for them to be together again as if nothing bad had ever happened. But he just couldn't get himself to forget what she had done.

Suddenly realizing he should go, he got up from the table and pushed his way through the crowd without looking back. Outside, he walked down the steps to the sidewalk when he heard his name called out behind him. He cringed. Turning around, he saw Alaska at the top of the stairs.

"Please don't leave," she said.

He just shook his head.

"Look," she said, "I know what I did was wrong, but I didn't know you were trying to form a case against them in some government investigation. I didn't know the twins were involved in those crimes. I just knew you were auditing their company and they wanted to know everything you were looking at. I've read the articles about you in the *Post*. I had no idea this was something so serious."

"That's not the point," Michael said. "Damn it, Alaska, do you have any *idea* what I've been through?" In his voice was a trace of the pain he had tried to suppress. "I think part of me thought I was entitled to have something really good happen in my life because of the work I've done these past few years. Then I met you and I couldn't believe I'd actually found you. My life felt so energized whenever I was with you. I thought about you all the time, even with everything else that was going on. I think I even thought we could have a future together—as stupid as that sounds now."

"Michael . . ."

"And then I find out you did this *thing* . . . that the whole time, you were pretending to be someone else."

"You know that's not true."

"You were living a lie when we were together. And what really creeps me out is how *good* you were at it."

"You were pretty good at living a lie too," Alaska said.

"That's not the same thing, and you know it," he snapped.

"Why?" she snapped back. "Because you were lying to help the government and I was lying to help my father?"

"At least I was working for the good guys. You helped out the twins and that could have cost me everything. Jesus, you aren't even *sorry* about what you did."

"We can't all be as righteous as you, Michael. Some people have real problems, where the only solutions are ugly ones. I *am* sorry. Sorry that I had to do it. And I'm sorry you got hurt."

Michael shook his head in disgust. "Some apology." He turned and took a few steps away from her before stopping to look back one last time. "How's your father doing?"

"He's doing a lot better now," she answered.

He saw her lips tremble. He could tell she was hurting inside, just as he was hurting. He wondered if they could heal each other. As much as he wanted to forgive her and be with her again, his pride just couldn't find a way past her betrayal.

Perhaps they could heal, if only they had more time.

"There are a lot of things I'm sorry about, too, Alaska," he finally said. "I'm glad your father is better now. I really mean that." He tried to think of what else he wanted to say. He felt the pressure of the moment on him, as if the whole world were watching them and time were slipping away. Then the moment passed. Perhaps on another night he could have forgiven her, but not tonight. "Good night, Alaska," he finally said. And turning away, he walked on, down the sidewalk, leaving her standing somewhere behind him in the night. After a few blocks, he took a cab back toward his apartment.

Getting out at his apartment building, he paid the cabbie and paused a moment to look up at his balcony, sixteen floors up. Above, a full moon glowed brightly in the clear skies. But as he gazed upward, his ears picked up footfalls coming toward him. Capitol Hill could be a tough neighborhood for the unwary. He didn't want any trouble, so he moved quickly to the front door of his building. Pulling the key ring from his pocket, he jammed the front door key into the keyhole, but before he could turn the knob, his head was pushed hard against the door's barred window at the same time a fist slammed into his kidney. Collapsing to the brick walkway, he twisted in pain.

"Get up," the man said. A nickel-plated semiautomatic pistol glimmered under the entrance light.

"Who are you?" Michael managed to ask.

"I said up—now!"

He struggled to stand, but the moment he was back on his feet, the stranger grabbed him by the arm and shoved him toward the street.

"On the other side. Black Mustang. Get in the driver's side and slide over to the passenger's seat. Move it!"

He got in the car and slid to the passenger side. The stranger, still pointing the gun at him, got in and closed the door. "Loop these around the inside grab bar and put 'em on," he said, tossing handcuffs onto Michael's lap. With his captive secured, the stranger frisked Michael's pockets and pitched the cell phone out the window. Then he started the Mustang, driving with his right hand on the wheel while his left hand, across his chest, kept the gun trained on Michael.

72

———⊷⟨✳⟩⊷———

"UNCUFF YOURSELF AND slowly get out of the car," the man said to Michael, handing him a small key. Opening the driver's-side door, he stepped into the snow.

Michael removed the handcuffs and slowly got out. As he did so, the stranger rose with him and held the gun on him over the top of the Mustang. The man had taken him up a winding road to a snowy parking area at the top of Lookout Mountain. Besides a brown SUV with tinted windows next to them, there was no one else around.

"Step over there," his abductor said.

Michael felt an odd tingle of anticipation. He felt the fear, too, of course, but it was not the brain-locking, gut-punch-paralyzing kind. For beneath that fear and somehow suffused with it was the awareness that he would deal with whatever he was about to face.

He turned in the direction the man had pointed to: a small opening in the trees, leading out toward a rock outcropping. Beyond it, a sharp drop-off fell twenty feet to a sloping apron of snow, which disappeared into an abyss of dark trees. In a valley beyond the trees, the full moon cast a silvery glow across the open snow. He moved toward the opening and stood vulnerably in the snow, facing away from the two vehicles and out toward a world of moonlight and shadows. Michael's hands hung at his sides with his palms facing back at the stranger.

He heard the door to the SUV open.

"I searched him, Mr. Seaton," the stranger said. "Took his cell phone. Had no gun or other weapon. He's clean."

"Thank you," said a familiar voice. "I can take it from here."

Michael heard the stranger get back in the Mustang and start the engine. Within seconds, it had pulled away and was roaring back down the mountain road.

"Turn around."

Michael turned to find Lance Seaton pointing a pistol at him from beside the SUV. Shaking his head, he stared at the surviving twin. "You probably should have run while you had the chance," Michael said.

"I can be on a beach on the other side of the world anytime I want," Lance replied. "But you should have known I wouldn't leave without saying good-bye."

"You're such a fool. You had *everything*. Why? Why would you want to destroy everything your father built?"

"Don't even pretend to know anything about me!" Lance snarled. "You don't! You think you could ever understand? Huh! You think you know my life? You think Lucas and I were just trying to get back at *Daddy*? You think we were doing this for money or power? There are no answers I can give you that you'll ever understand. You want to know why we did it? I'll tell you: because we enjoyed it. It was a thrill. And that's something that you, in your pathetic little life, could never understand."

"I'll tell you what I do understand," Michael said as he stood tall near the edge of the drop-off. "I understand that your friend with the Mustang will never make it off this mountain. I understand that right now the cops have barricaded every road exiting Lookout Mountain. Federal agents are already making their way up that road. Your friend will soon be in custody. And so will you."

"Bullshit."

Michael moved his hands slowly to the collar of his shirt and pulled out a string necklace revealing a small medallion. "This is a GPS transponder," he said. "We thought you might try to come after me. A security team of federal agents has been living in the apartment across the hall from me for the past two weeks. We thought you might try to hit me there. This was to signal the team if I saw you. They can track its location. I managed to activate the signal the moment I saw we were nearing the top of this mountain road."

"And you want me to believe they're on their way here?"

Michael raised his head as if smelling something in the air. "No, Lance. They're not coming—they're already here." The low *whop-whop* of a rotor grew louder as a helicopter approached with a spotlight beam stretching earthward. "It's over, Lance. Put the gun down."

But the cold glare said otherwise. Lance showed not the slightest sign of panic or despair. Instead, he seemed to revel in the knowledge that the world was crashing down on him. And at that moment, Michael realized that he had no intention of lowering the gun. He was not about to let the man he blamed for his brother's death walk away alive.

Suddenly there was another sound: two car engines roaring up the mountain road. Lance turned his head to see the flashing lights bouncing off trees behind him, the cars not yet in sight. As soon as Lance turned his head, Michael bolted in a desperate sprint toward the outcrop's edge. Lance heard the crunching snow and whipped back around toward his captive. Steadying the gun, he fired several shots. Michael leaped over the ledge, arms and legs flailing away as if he were still running, when he heard the shots. His left arm suddenly felt as if it had been hit with a baseball bat; the next instant, something stabbed him in the back. Then he hit the snowy slope below, and he was sliding. He slid for what felt like an eternity before finally slamming into a snow mound, which kept him from pitchpoling down to the clearing below.

He kicked at the snow, trying to understand the breathtaking pain that seemed to take over his entire body. He could hear Lance's footsteps moving on the ledge above, but the trees blocked his view. He forced himself to sit up, to focus his eyes on the surroundings. It was then that he realized he couldn't move his left arm. A bullet had struck him just above the elbow. The second bullet had hit him in the side. Tears blurred his vision as he tried to stand up.

A crunching sound came from above the ledge, as he looked up in time to see Lance leap from the ledge and fall where Michael had first landed. But he didn't slide down the slope as Michael had—landing feet first, he had postholed waist-deep into the snow. The gun slipped out of his hand and skittered on the crust, stopping just out of his reach.

As Lance fought to get free and snatch the pistol, Michael fought just as desperately to get to his feet before his attacker could get a clean shot. He got his feet under him and pushed against the snow mound, all but delirious from the shrieking pain in his body. He saw Lance's hand grope outward and just miss grabbing the gun. *He's getting close. Stand up. Hurry!* With a yelp of pain, Michael pushed harder with his legs, fighting to find the strength to stand. *Fight it,* he told himself, just as he had countless times as a collegian wrestler trying to grapple his way to another victory on the mat. *Stay focused. Fight the pain.* If there was one thing he had learned from his wrestling days, it was that no matter how tired or weak he felt, a burst of reserve energy, summoned at just the right moment, could make all the difference in winning a match. It was a lesson he had carried with him throughout his life, a personal credo now embedded in his very cells. The harder the struggle, the harder he always fought. With his back against the snow mound and his knees quaking violently, he stood up enough that he could topple over the mound. And just as he had found his stance, he looked back in time to see Lance pull himself far enough out of the snow to grab the gun. Michael turned sideways and leaned toward the abyss below, falling away from the snow mound and over the slope just as two bullets slammed into the snow where he had stood the second before.

He slid farther down the slope until it leveled out in a clearing. The pain had now receded as a worrisome numbness took its place. Blinking the tears away, he fought to his feet again and plunge-stepped across the open clearing a hundred feet below the first drop-off. He looked back briefly to search for the flashing lights of the police cars, but he had fallen and slid too far from the road. He was alone and could not expect them to find him in time to help.

As he moved through the open snowfield, his right hand pressed his side where the second bullet had gone through, while his paralyzed left arm hung loosely against his body. Knowing that to black out was to die, he concentrated to fight off the darkness collapsing his peripheral vision. He knew that if the darkness came all the way into the center of his vision, he would lose consciousness. A scraping sound behind him let him know that Lance was sliding down the slope in pursuit.

He could hear the low rumbling of the approaching helicopter, still too far in the distance to help him. The stinging cold was attacking his body without mercy. The warmth, along with his blood, was leaving his body. He was too weak to keep pressure on the wound. The bleeding from his side increased, dripping occasional drops of blood into the ground, where they were absorbed by the snow. He took a few more steps before falling to his knees in the center of the clearing. His gaze fell on a patch of snow directly in front of him, then became lost in a sea of sparkling crystals of reflected moonlight. Gravity seemed to be stronger now, pulling him earthward with a force he could no longer fight. Falling back into the snow, he lay unable to move as his eyes stared in wonder at the night sky. All the winter constellations his father had taught him as a boy were now hovering above him in the cosmos. Their familiar images brought back childhood memories of his father and him watching a meteor shower from the roof of their house. *Dad, I'm in real trouble. I don't want to die just yet . . .* He was reminded of the full life he had lived. Orion, Canis Major, and the other familiar shapes had been with him his entire life, and now, strangely, they made him feel that he was not alone as he lay dying in the open field.

Then the silence was broken. Footsteps crunched through the snow, growing louder with each step, stopping when they reached him.

"You look just like Kurt did before he died," Lance said, stepping over him and placing a foot on his chest. Then he raised the gun and fired a shot into Michael's right arm. Screaming as the bullet tore through muscle and nerve, Michael now lay motionless in the snow with two paralyzed arms.

"I hear you used to be a star wrestler in college—wouldn't want to give you a chance to try anything before I finish this." As Lance said this, he sat astride Michael's chest, one knee in the snow on either side of him.

"Your brother . . . was always the weaker . . . of you two, wasn't he?" Michael said between short, panting breaths. *Conserve your energy,* he thought. *Save your strength . . . save it for one final burst.* "How many times . . . did you protect him . . . growing up? But then, you . . . couldn't protect him . . . from me."

With a screech of rage, Lance slammed the gun into Michael's jaw. Michael's head turned sideways as he spat blood and part of a tooth into the snow. Lance hit him again. Without the use of either arm, there was nothing he could do to defend himself.

"Look at me, you motherfucker!" Lance yelled. He grabbed Michael's beaten face and forced him to look at him. "I told you to look at me. I want to see it in your eyes. I want to see the exact moment you fade out and die."

Michael didn't know how much longer he could stay conscious. His only hope was to get Lance to lean back far enough that his legs could reach him. If he wanted to live, he had to get him to sit up straight.

"Look at me," Lance screamed, pulling Michael's face close to his.

At that moment, Michael saw his opportunity. He tightened his chest and spat a mouthful of blood into the leering face. Repulsed, Lance leaned back.

This was the moment—Michael's only chance. His right leg whipped up over Lance's shoulder, heel against his throat, pulling him backward to the ground. In the confusion, Lance dropped the gun. His neck was now between Michael's knees, scissored around his neck, ankles locked. Squeezing with the last of his waning strength, Michael felt light in the head and knew that the strain was making him bleed faster. Lance scrambled desperately, kicking at the snow as his hands tried frantically to overpower the superior strength of the leg muscles choking him. Michael, meanwhile, fought to keep conscious long enough to squeeze the life out of his enemy.

Finally, he felt Lance's body go limp. He continued to squeeze as hard as he could for perhaps two more minutes, knowing that his exertions were surely hastening the blood loss from his own wounds. Finally, he felt himself growing too weak to continue. He tried to open his eyes, but they wouldn't obey. He could feel his life draining away. Everything was silent and dark and cold, and his mind began to drift. He was dying, and he knew it, but he was too weak to care. He could feel it coming now. Darkness, and with it, peace.

Epilogue

———————◦❈◦———————

D ON SEATON WALKED through the beige marble
entrance of the Brown Palace Hotel. Crossing the open
atrium, he glanced up at the stained-glass skylight lofting a
hundred feet above the cocktail lounge in the center of the lobby.
After crossing the atrium, he entered the hotel's historic Old Ship
Tavern, one of the oldest Scotch bars in Denver. He stood at the
far edge of the bar and ordered a Glenury Royal.

After taking a sip, he glanced at his watch. He was ten
minutes early. Unfolding his copy of today's *Denver Post,* he
reread the front-page article updating the world on recent events
at X-Tronic. It was the fifteenth installment in the developing
story that had first appeared three weeks ago. The *Post* had
allowed parts of the story to be picked up by the Associated
Press for national distribution to other papers, and there was
already building hype concerning a Pulitzer Prize for a young
journalist named Sarah Matthews, who had written the articles.

Seaton had first heard of Sarah from Michael before the
shareholders' meeting. He had been told then that she was
involved in investigating the fraud and was the most qualified
person to report the actual events at X-Tronic. When she had

contacted Seaton a few weeks ago, he generously invited her for a series of long, exclusive interviews to discuss all aspects of X-Tronic for her research. And thanks to a previous arrangement that Michael had made after the shareholders' meeting, Sarah had also been provided with numerous contacts at the U.S. Treasury Department to report their involvement in the story.

As Seaton reread the article, he noted how concisely it detailed the events of the past three weeks. It noted how he had lost 80 percent of his net worth doing the buyback that prevented the company's bankruptcy. Many were now calling him the new model for corporate responsibility, and a recent poll in *Forbes* magazine was voting him businessman of the year. The *Post* article went on to detail the challenges still facing the company. Now that both Don Seaton's sons were dead and many top executives were to be charged with various crimes, the future of the company was uncertain. Confidence had been bolstered somewhat by Seaton's announcement that X-Tronic would enter into a leveraged buyout of Cygnus International. Cygnus's stock price had plummeted since the SEC had announced formal charges of fraud and insider trading against its CEO, Fredrick Kavanaugh III. Ironically, X-Tronic now found itself in a position to acquire the very company that had threatened to take it over only a few months ago.

Savoring the rich single malt, Seaton looked ahead at the work it would take for X-Tronic to survive the short-term fallout from the fraud. He knew he couldn't do it alone.

Outside, a man in a long cashmere coat handed his keys to the valet. At the heavy double doors, he carefully grabbed the brass handle before the doorman could react. With a grimace, he strained to open it.

"I'm sorry, sir. Let me get that," said the doorman, rushing over to the man's aid.

"No, please," the man said, motioning him back. "I want to open it." His breathing grew deeper as he strained against the door. After a brief delay, it gave way.

He strode through the lobby, arms hanging stiffly at his side, and entered the Old Ship Tavern to find Don Seaton reading a paper at the bar.

Looking up, Seaton said, "Michael," with a warm smile. "Thank you for meeting me. How are the arms?"

Michael Chapman carefully reached out and shook the billionaire's hand. "Still not a hundred percent, but my doctor says I'll be arm wrestling in a couple of months."

"That's wonderful to hear. Well, should we grab a table by the window?"

Michael followed Seaton to the far side of the bar, where a row of tables and chairs lined a wall with small windows.

"You know," Seaton began, "a lifetime ago I was a professor at MIT. I did a teaching sabbatical in Europe, and one thing I learned traveling through Russia is that it's traditional there to drink while conducting business discussions—lovely custom, don't you think?" He turned to the barman and twitched a finger to indicate the prearranged order. "Then again, Russians drink socially as well."

"Which is this?"

Seaton looked at him, and beneath those hooded eyes Michael could see despair, the kind that could haunt a man after a great tragedy. Michael realized that the Scotch the barman brought for them was for neither business nor pleasure, but forgiveness—to forgive the father for the deeds of the sons. And in return, the father was offering his own forgiveness to Michael for the role Michael had played in the deaths of his sons.

"My sons have caused so much harm," Seaton confessed, "I'm finding it difficult to show my face in public these days."

Michael didn't respond. There was nothing he wanted to say about the twins.

"I want to be level with you," Seaton began. "I know that we've had difficulty because of my sons." He pause a moment as if to reflect on the true weight of his words. "I don't really know the best way to put this, so I'll just say it plain: I was never close to the twins, but I had always hoped they would become the future of my company. I gave them the best education money could buy, and I tried to give them every opportunity to work their way into X-Tronic, with the hope that at least one—if not both—would one day take over the corporation." He looked down at the table, as if, in the grain of its wood, he might discern some clue to where he had gone wrong.

"But they failed me, just as I somehow failed them. Now I am forced to move on. My company is at risk of losing more value than it has earned in the past ten years. And for the first time in my life I cannot see the future in it."

"You still have a good company, with good products," Michael said. "After the Cygnus merger, there's no reason why X-Tronic can't be ahead of its competitors and back on top of the industry in two or three years."

"Yes," Seaton said. "Right now the company's reputation is the most important thing that needs fixing. X-Tronic will be going through difficult times these next few years, and I need strong leaders I can trust to guide it through the challenges it will face. Michael, I want you to be assistant chief financial officer at X-Tronic."

Michael gaped at him in amazement. "Assistant CFO! Don, I've only been out of college for five years. You want to make me an assistant officer in a Fortune one hundred company?"

"Michael, I know your background. You had the second highest score in the country when you took the CPA exam your first time. You're brilliant—a true financial wizard—and your experience in the Treasury shows you have the ethics and leadership this corporation needs. I've contacted an old friend, Peter Gerston, and he agreed to take over as the new CFO for the next two years. He was CFO at Sokie Technologies for ten years before retiring a year ago. He would be your mentor during these first two years. He's a brilliant man and would teach you everything you need to know. At the end of the two years, he would step down and you would become the new CFO of X-Tronic. I'll start your salary at two hundred thousand a year plus potential bonuses of three times that much. You'll also get stock options that could be worth millions if we can successfully turn around the corporation." He paused a second. "How old are you, Michael?"

Michael knew that Seaton already had the answer but wanted to hear it from him. "Thirty-one."

"By thirty-three you'll become one of the youngest CFOs in the history of any Fortune one hundred company. And you will have become a legend in the financial world. You will be the future of X-Tronic. What's more," he continued, "you will also be the face that restores the public's confidence in X-Tronic. You will be responsible for reporting to the media the changes and progress that X-Tronic makes as we begin our restructuring efforts. You will become one of the main presenters at future shareholders' meetings. As the former Treasury agent who exposed the fraud, you would immediately be a trusted voice to the public. You couldn't be more perfect for the job."

Michael didn't need any time to make his decision. "When do you want me to start?"

Seaton raised his glass to Michael's. "Immediately!"

After discussing his future over another drink with Seaton, Michael left the Brown Palace, planning to go straight home. For too long now he had felt trapped by his undercover life. Lying in bed in the hospital had given him ample time to think, and he had told Glazier he would leave the Treasury. Because Falcon was still at large, Glazier had stationed a police officer outside his hospital room. Michael had had a number of visitors, but there was one person he had refused to see. According to the nurse,

Alaska had tried four times to visit him, but Michael had given specific instructions not to let her in.

He drove past the turn to his apartment and kept driving south on Broadway.

True, she had betrayed him, but her repeated attempts to see him in the hospital had made him question things he had been certain about. He still didn't think he could face her, but he wanted to forgive her.

Pulling into the parking lot, he got out of his car and walked toward the red two-story building with the open patio on top. Inside, he found a long room with a bar on one side and a row of high-backed leather-upholstered booths along the other. The only person in the place was the barman at the far end. He nodded at the barman's greeting and walked slowly along, studying each of the paintings that hung above the booths. He stopped near the end and looked longer at each of the last three paintings, which had Alaska's name below them.

"These are great," he said. "You have any others by this artist?"

"I don't, but it sounds like she paints a lot. I can't imagine it would be a problem if you wanted to see more of her work," said the barman, obviously trying to be helpful.

The guy knew her, Michael realized. They had spoken, and he wanted to help her. He, too, had seen a glimpse of her pain.

"I'd like to buy these three," Michael said.

"Great," the man replied. "Look, if you want more, we could get the artist on the phone right now. I know she'd love to show more of her work."

"No. Thank you, though. I'll just take these three."

"Okay. I'll mark them as sold and give her a call. Maybe she can come down here right now to do the transaction."

"I'm afraid I don't have time. I'll pay you cash now, and I trust you to get her the payment. I'll give you an extra fifty for your trouble. Otherwise, I'll just go."

"Oh, sure, man. We can do that. Whatever you want."

"Could you also help me move them out to my car? I had an accident recently, and I don't think I can carry them."

The barman took down the three paintings and carefully leaned them against the side of the bar. "Just let me go get an envelope for the money," he said.

As the barman left the room, Michael sat in one of the booths and looked at the nearest painting. It was a hypnotic image of blue skiers gliding down a white mountain with purple trees against a crimson sky. He was still surprised at how captivating he found her visions. He studied the other two paintings carefully before eventually looking back at the one with the ski slope.

The barman seemed to be taking forever. Suddenly, the snow in the painting lit up as if he were on the actual slopes and the clouds had just parted. He turned toward the front door, which stood open. Framed in the sunlight was a figure that became a young woman as she walked inside. When she saw Michael she stopped and stared, breaking eye contact only long enough to see the three paintings resting against the bar beside him.

"I got a phone call and rushed down," Alaska said. "I didn't know the buyer was you. What are you doing?"

Having no adequate answer, he just stood there.

"I read about you in the *Post*," she said. "I tried to visit you in the hospital."

"I was still healing."

Her eyes gleamed wet. "What are you going to do now?"

"I'm taking a new job out here."

"So you're staying in Denver?"

He nodded. "What about you?"

She gave a little shrug. "I was thinking about moving back to Aspen to be closer to my dad."

He was silent for a moment. Finally, he said, "I've never met your dad, but from what you've told me, I bet he would rather you spent time finding your own life."

"And you think my life's in Denver?" she said. "I have nothing here anymore. Most of my friends are scattered in the wind. The only real family I have is my dad in Aspen. And my painting career is nonexistent."

"I wouldn't say that," he said. "You just sold three."

She grinned. "Only a lunatic would buy three of my paintings when no one else even notices them."

"Well this lunatic just might have a few ideas for helping you market your talent to the people of Denver."

She laughed. "You're still such an accountant. I suppose there's nothing you can't do?"

Michael frowned. "Actually, right now I can't even carry these paintings up to my apartment when I get home."

She seemed to consider this. "You're *really* that helpless?" she said, and gave him an appraising look. "Then I guess—right now, anyway—you need me." She had that same sassy grin as the night they first met in the club.

The grin spread to him. "Yeah, I guess I do."

She carried the paintings out to his car one at a time; then they went back to his apartment. As he drove through the rising neighborhood streets with her sitting beside him, the fading sunset hung over the snowcapped Rockies, its orange glow lighting the bare winter trees that lined the road home.

THE END

About The Author

Bryan Devore was born and raised in Manhattan, Kansas, and received his Bachelor's and Master's in Accountancy from Kansas State University. He is a CPA and lives in Denver, CO. *The Aspen Account* is his first novel. He welcomes comments and feedback, and can be contacted at bryan.devore@gmail.com.

Made in the USA
Lexington, KY
21 December 2016